Competing for Foreign Aid

Competing for Foreign Aid

The Congressional Roots of Bureaucratic Fragmentation

SHANNON P. CARCELLI

OXFORD
UNIVERSITY PRESS

OXFORD
UNIVERSITY PRESS

Oxford University Press is a department of the University of Oxford. It furthers the University's objective of excellence in research, scholarship, and education by publishing worldwide. Oxford is a registered trade mark of Oxford University Press in the UK and in certain other countries.

Published in the United States of America by Oxford University Press
198 Madison Avenue, New York, NY 10016, United States of America.

CIP data is on file at the Library of Congress

ISBN 9780197799253

DOI: 10.1093/9780197799284.001.0001

Printed by Marquis Book Printing, Canada

MIX
Paper | Supporting responsible forestry
FSC® C103567
FSC www.fsc.org

Contents

Acknowledgements

Much like foreign aid, the writing of this book drew from many sources and inspirations. I did not take on this process alone. First, I am lucky to have a loving family helping me manage the ups and downs of this career. Having gone through graduate school themselves and come out alive, Susan and Larry Carcelli were more understanding, and could offer more advice, than any other parents. Their enthusiasm for my academic pursuits made graduate school more exciting, and their ingrained inability to see anything but the best version of me made the bad times easier to shrug off. Lisa Winter has always been a shining example of forward thinking and perseverance. She once told me to "trust my past self," advice I have held with me ever since and that always soothes my scattered brain.

I was lucky to receive support from all corners during my PhD work at UC San Diego. David Lake kept me modest while still encouraging me to pursue my wildest ideas. His capacity to think and support still provides an ideal, although maybe unrealistic, path for all his students. Christina Schneider offered concrete feedback and solutions of the best kind: ideas grounded in so much truth they seemed obvious after she said them. Lawrence Broz first taught me the basics of international political economy, and he kept me on the track of asking interesting, pursuable questions. Sam Kernell reminded me of the reality on the ground in Washington, DC, and helped me to keep American politics in sight. Steph Haggard's suggestions for historical research broadened my understanding of my subject. Lauren Prather's openness and unabashed descriptions of late graduate school gave me a model and helped me with tough decisions. Outside of my dissertation committee, including during my field work in Washington, DC, support from Erik Gartzke, James Fowler, Emilie Hafner-Burton, Chris Deering and James Desveaux proved invaluable. I also benefited from an incredible set of graduate school colleagues, including Michael Davidson, Andres Gannon, Dotan Haim, Andy Janusz, John Kuk, Nazita Lajevardi, David Lindsey, Kelly Matush, Brandon Merrell, Matt Nanes, Debbi Seligsohn, Brian Tsay, Abby Vaughn, and Jack Zhang.

My post-doctoral work was made possible through Princeton University's Niehaus Center for Globalization and Governance. Helen Milner, James Vreeland, and Dan Nielson served as ideal mentors during my time there, as did my cohort of fellows, including Jack Zhang, Haillie Na-Kyung Lee, In Song Kim, Bob Kubinec, Andrey Tomashevskiy, and Lindsay Dolan. This research agenda has also benefitted from a rising community of bureaucracy IR scholars, whose feedback and camaraderie I greatly appreciate.

My current academic home at the University of Maryland could not have provided a better setting for finishing this book. Advice, mentorship, and friendship from Will Reed, Kathleen Cunningham, Todd Allee, David Cunningham, Gaby Lloyd, Fiona Shen-Bayh, Virginia Haufler, Paul Huth and Kris Miler took me to the finish line. UMD also generously supported a conference for this book, attended by Christina Schneider, Dustin Tingley, Jen Tobin, and Sarah Binder. My landing place in Washington, DC, has also afforded me support outside of my own department, and I owe a special thanks to Jordan Tama, Susannah Campbell, Alexander Downes and GWU's ISCS, Dan Honig, Elizabeth Saunders, Margaret Hanson, and Minju Kim.

Finally, Brett Gamb has guided and understood me throughout this process. He walked the dog on those late nights of pre-deadline furor, stabilized the ups and downs of the research process, and encouraged me to follow my dreams across the country. He provided a moral GPS and example of the hard emotional and mental labor it takes to succeed. The last few years would have generated more wreckage without his support, and this book is dedicated to him.

Chapter 1
Introduction

In May of 2014, as casualties were mounting in the United States war in Afghanistan, a Chinook helicopter collided with a communication tower in Kandahar Province, injuring or killing everyone on board.[1] This tower was not built as a Taliban attempt to limit the army's mobility, nor was it a pre-existing Soviet monstrosity. It was the result of poor cooperation and communication within the United States foreign policy bureaucracy.

Back in 2010, two US government agencies had decided to collaborate on a project to bring telecommunication services to southern Afghanistan. The State Department would build six communication towers, and the Defense Department would maintain the towers and use them for secure communications and public diplomacy. By 2012, after costs had doubled, state contractors began to cut corners, building towers that were cheaper to make but expensive to maintain. The Department of Defense, its interests no longer represented, pulled out of the project.

Nevertheless, all six towers were built—millions of dollars wasted on communication towers that would never be put to use. To make matters worse, State Department contractors failed to label the towers to the Defense Department's standards, resulting in the 2014 collision. The two agencies, each following their own self-interest, created a policy deleterious to the war effort. This wartime tragedy is just one of hundreds of examples of waste, duplication, and inefficiency brought on by the complexity and fragmentation of US foreign policy bureaucracy.[2]

At the same time that US bureaucracies were fighting each other in Afghanistan, various US agencies were successfully cooperating to carry out a large aid effort in sub-Saharan Africa. The President's Emergency Plan For AIDS Relief (PEPFAR), an aid program spurred by the George W. Bush administration's concern with global health and headquartered in the State Department, marked a milestone in the AIDS epidemic. A 2008 review

[1] Roth (2014)
[2] For other examples from the United States see Ford (2007), and for more Afghanistan-specific examples, see work by McCloskey et al. (2015) and Whitlock (2019).

Competing for Foreign Aid. Shannon P. Carcelli, Oxford University Press. © Oxford University Press (2025).
DOI: 10.1093/9780197799284.003.0001

of PEPFAR's activities gave it credit for saving 1.2 million lives in its first four years of existence,[3] with continued success from there. This was achievable with a fraction of the Afghanistan budget and was even demonstrated in conflict zones. Although agencies' interests were not always perfectly aligned, they managed to work together to forward US foreign policy.

Why was the government able to collaborate smoothly on PEPFAR but unable to coordinate in Afghanistan—arguably a more important national security goal? The war in Afghanistan was not the only case of bureaucratic conflict in US foreign policy. History provides plenty of examples. For example, in the late 1990s, a small US agency called the Inter-American Foundation incited a foreign and domestic scandal by disregarding the orders of the US Embassy and funding groups guilty of kidnapping American businessmen.[4] Around the same time, the Federal Maritime Commission (FMC), an independent US agency, unilaterally declared sanctions on Japan without consulting the US Trade Representative. The Clinton administration was forced to scramble together an agreement with Japan to appease FMC leaders due to the agency's rogue actions.[5]

When bureaucracies compete instead of collaborating, even intelligence gathering can be problematic. A more cohesive bureaucracy could have gone a long way toward preventing the tragic events of September 11, 2001.[6] Although this event was certainly not *caused* by bureaucratic infighting, the bureaucracy made it more difficult to extract meaningful signals from the abundance of counterterrorism data. Because intelligence agencies were not willing or able to share intelligence quickly and effectively, hijackers were able to enter the United States and even take flying lessons in California.[7] Bureaucratic conflict may also have played a role in intelligence failures leading up to the Cuban Missile Crisis.[8]

Conflict within US bureaucracy touches every area of US foreign policy. Counterterrorism, trade, sanctions, and foreign aid are all controlled and managed by a variety of domestic bureaucratic actors. Sometimes these bureaucracies manage to work smoothly to coordinate goals. But when US foreign policy consists of disparate bureaucratic actors jostling for funding,

[3] Walensky and Kuritzkes (2010)
[4] Lyne et al. (2006)
[5] Epstein and O'Halloran (1999, pp. 155–156)
[6] Zegart (2009)
[7] Zegart (2005, p. 78)
[8] Allison (1969)

policy primacy, and attention, it is difficult to successfully promote the national interest.

The US government is well aware of the importance of bureaucratic cohesion. A search for the term "whole of government" in the Congressional Research Service database provides 206 recent reports, on topics ranging from the COVID-19 crisis[9] to the US defense industrial base[10] to tracking China's global economic activities.[11] Major policy reports of the past decades, such as the State Department's Quadrennial Diplomacy and Development Review, nearly always highlight the need for a whole-of-government approach to foreign policymaking.[12] The struggle with the fragmentation of foreign aid bureaucracy is also not unique to the United States; it is a global issue, with many years' worth of focused reports by the Organization for Economic Cooperation and Development (OECD).[13]

While bureaucratic fragmentation has a long history in US foreign policy, it is not a constant. The bureaucratic infighting endemic in the Afghanistan example was almost nonexistent in PEPFAR's programs. For all the evidence of bureaucratic infighting in foreign policy, one could provide just as many cases of successful bureaucratic collaboration. In short, sometimes agencies manage to work collaboratively, and sometimes they do not. In this book, by explaining variation in bureaucratic fragmentation, I shed light on both the causes and consequences of the phenomenon in US foreign policy.

1.1 Congressional Compromise in Foreign Policy

Rather than being a centralized decision, I argue that foreign policy is the result of an uneasy compromise between domestic fiefdoms, each working with bureaucracies and legislators to craft their own policy agendas. Rather than the president negotiating with allies and adversaries, a plethora of domestic interests work through legislative and executive channels toward their own visions of international relations. These interests may be economic—indeed, as I will show in Chapter 5 of this book, lobbyists play a large role in tearing US foreign policy apart. However, congressional

[9] McInnis (2020)
[10] Peters (2021)
[11] Schwarzenberg (2020)
[12] DOS (2010)
[13] e.g. OECD (2006, 2009)

and bureaucratic interests are driven by many other factors, including identity, ideology, and even family members. Rather than assume that foreign policy supports a specific set of interests and preferences, it is more accurate to say that US foreign policy represents an uneasy, and constantly renegotiated, compromise between various economic, identity-based, and ideological fiefdoms.

Much of this compromise occurs in Congress. I argue that congressional horse-trading has been underappreciated and undertheorized in the study of US foreign policy. Policy ideas do not always span the typical left-right, or isolationist-internationalist, spectrum. Many legislators care not only about *what* foreign policy is carried out but *how* it is carried out.[14] If we are to understand the incoherence common to US foreign policy, then we must first understand the often incoherent dynamics in the foreign policymaking process.

The main mechanism through which congressional negotiations lead to fragmentation, I argue, is so-called vote-buying.[15] By "vote-buying," I refer to the tendency of party and committee leaders to offer side payments to induce rank-and-file legislators to support a foreign policy agenda. In this sense, leaders are continually "buying" the votes of legislators by diverting parts of the policy agenda toward specific projects and special interests. Many of those projects and interests are housed in nontraditional bureaucracies, and when more projects are funded, more bureaucracies become empowered. The very process that creates US foreign policy also creates the conditions for policy fragmentation.

The American political system depends on compromise. In Congress, that compromise is usually guided by party leaders, who craft policy to maximize the number of legislators in their own party who will benefit. Leaders consider their own re-election prospects as well as their party's reputation in developing a coherent legislative agenda.[16] They negotiate with rank-and-file legislators, who decide to support legislation based mostly on re-election concerns.[17] When policies fall into a neat ideological spectrum, then leaders can entice legislators by moving policy toward their districts' ideal points.

[14] Although some of the *how* questions can also be explained through ideology (Fleck and Kilby 2006); as I will show, many of the more parochial policy details cannot.

[15] In congressional politics, "vote-buying" refers to side payments paid to legislators in exchange for supporting a piece of legislation. It is not to be confused with other definitions of vote-buying, in which corrupt officials pay citizens for votes in general elections.

[16] McCubbins and Cox (1993, 2005); Fenno (1973)

[17] Fenno (1973); Mayhew (1974)

However, another way to bring legislators on board is by introducing policy details that are not ideological in nature. These side payments can include elements of traditional pork politics, like district-level projects[18] or campaign donations.[19]

In this book, I suggest a previously unacknowledged form of side payment: the diverting of funding to small agencies and projects—or the creation of entirely new ones—whose agendas and interests benefit a particular legislator or constituency. Offering side payments through the bureaucracy has a few advantages. First, it can be easier for legislators to get their wishes fulfilled while evading critics if they work through bureaucratic backchannels.[20] Second, the US government offers a large variety of bureaucracies with which to partner. This variety, in fact, is only matched by the variety of opinions within Congress. Regardless of a legislator's preferences, there is almost certainly a bureaucracy somewhere in the US government that shares those preferences. This allows for flexibility in building policy without the trouble of directly managing bureaucrats.

If bureaucratic fragmentation is driven by vote-buying, then where does vote-buying come from? The theory in this book focuses on two factors that exacerbate Congress's vote-buying tendencies: low unity and high interest. First, congressional *disunity* makes it more difficult for leadership to pass a foreign policy agenda. The more that members of Congress—especially those in the middle of the political spectrum—disagree on foreign policy, the more hesitant they will be to align into one policy camp. Vote-buying will be higher the more ideologically heterogeneous the center of Congress is. This will necessitate leaders using creative means to enact policies, such as routing funding to members' pet projects, often through unconventional agency sources.

Second, fragmentation is exacerbated by congressional *interest* in a policy. Counterintuitively, the more that Congress cares about a policy area, the more fragmented and incoherent that area will become. This is because rank-and-file legislators are more likely to seek pet projects, and leaders are more determined to forward an agenda, if they are more interested in a policy area. Congressional interest is driven by a combination of international and domestic factors. Some states and topics are more salient to Congress

[18] Alexander et al. (2016)
[19] Jenkins and Monroe (2012)
[20] Ritchie (2018)

than others. This variation, I argue, drives variation in foreign policy fragmentation. Congressional interest and disunity combine to diminish the effectiveness of foreign policy by fragmenting the bureaucracy.

Throughout this book, I measure variation in these two factors—congressional disunity and congressional interest—over time, space, and policy area. The empirics and case studies provide qualitative and quantitative evidence for the theory. As I discuss in this chapter, the empirics focus mainly on foreign aid policy. Foreign aid policy provides a rich source of variation in both disunity and interest. First, Congress varies over time in the unity of parties and legislators. This creates variation in the level of foreign aid fragmentation over time. Second, members of Congress tend to be more interested in some policy areas than others—specifically, interest is higher in some countries and some forms of foreign policy. This leads to variation in time and space that will be considered in later chapters.

1.2 Foreign Aid as Foreign Policy

Although the theory of bureaucratic fragmentation put forward in this book is relevant to many foreign policy areas, the sheer scope of the question requires a more limited purview. The empirical focus of this book, therefore, is on the bureaucratic fragmentation of foreign aid. I choose this for three main reasons. First, foreign aid is an area in which data are both abundant and consistent. In policy areas like trade and international conflict, it can be difficult to objectively measure the relative power or importance of one bureaucracy or another. Bureaucracies in these areas often carry out regulatory roles, and it can be difficult to tell where one bureaucracy's work ends and the next begins. In contrast, foreign aid agencies are mainly tasked with enacting appropriations. An agency's appropriations provide a more precise measure of that agency's relative role in foreign aid.

A second reason that this book focuses on foreign aid policy is due to the versatility and universality of aid as a policy tool. This flexibility makes foreign aid work like a microcosm of all foreign policy, as it involves aspects of military, trade, global cooperation, and international organization policies. The fragmentation of foreign aid describes the fragmentation of all foreign policy. The qualitative chapters in this book highlight the flexibility of foreign aid as a policy tool. Chapter 6 considers the complicated foreign policy decisions involving post-Soviet diplomacy. These policies included aspects of foreign direct investment, trade, environmental agreements, and deterrence policy. In Chapter 7, I consider the fragmentation of reconstruction efforts in Afghanistan. In this case various foreign policy goals, including defense and counternarcotics, played out within the foreign aid realm. Foreign aid policy covers a broad range of policy goals and outcomes; therefore, it serves as a valuable starting point for this research agenda.

Finally, foreign aid provides an ideal fit with much of the previous literature on Congress and foreign policy. Milner and Tingley (2015) note the theoretical differences between geopolitical and economic aid, which fall into separate categories in their model of policy types. Because both types of aid are relevant to my theory, the empirical results are relevant to both groups in the Milner and Tingley typology. Foreign aid is also a particularly Congress-centric policy tool according to most of the literature. Scholars of US foreign policy agree that aid is "the principle vehicle by which [Congress] attempts to influence and make U.S. foreign policy."[21] This is because it "suits the congressional character, always at its most skilled and comfortable with using budgetary decisions as a means of policy control."[22] This suggests that a closer look at Congress's behavior in foreign aid is likely to provide us with a lot of information.

This is not to say that the theory is only relevant to foreign aid. Many other policy areas are vulnerable to bureaucratic and congressional whims in similar ways. First, many areas of foreign policy are similar to foreign aid in their dependence on appropriations. As mentioned previously, many aid programs are actually intended to drive other areas of foreign policy. For example, aid that is delivered through the Department of Commerce can be considered a subset of trade policy, and intelligence cooperation programs are routed through multiple intelligence bureaucracies. Legislators are more likely to exert a variety of policy preferences in areas that provide more distributive benefits;[23] however, this can represent a broader variety of policies than it might seem.

In his 2011 State of the Union address, President Obama famously complained that "there are twelve different agencies that deal with exports... The Interior Department is in charge of salmon while they're in fresh water, but the Commerce Department handles them when they're in saltwater. I

[21] Pastor (1982, p. 253)
[22] Hinckley (1994, p. 102)
[23] Milner and Tingley (2015)

hear it gets even more complicated once they're smoked."[24] Indeed, trade agreements are often overseen by a variety of regulatory agencies, which often compete for the power to determine enforcement. Insofar as these agencies—such as the FDA, Treasury, Commerce, and EPA—align with certain legislators, the theory could easily apply. Extending this theory to regulatory questions is not as far-fetched as it may seem: many of the aspects of foreign aid mentioned in the chapter case studies are regulatory in nature. For example, Chapter 6 describes legislators arguing about the merits of spraying opium fields. This is not a question of appropriations so much as a regulatory issue, and agencies argued not over funding but over policy. It is easy to imagine a similar case in which agencies attempt to persuade lawmakers to side with them over imports and exports of various types of fresh or smoked salmon, leading to a difficulty in designing trade agreements. Military acquisitions is another clear area in which the theory could easily apply.

For the remainder of the book, I will focus on the case of foreign aid fragmentation, and in the conclusion (Chapter 9) I will return to the relevance of these findings to other areas of foreign policy. The building blocks I develop here should help future research to increasingly consider the role of Congress in shaping the bureaucracy in other areas of foreign policy and international relations.

1.3 Core Contributions

The questions in this book demand a new framework for thinking about state behavior in international relations. Much of the thinking on foreign policy treats it as a black box: if foreign policy comes out of the United States, then we can call it US foreign policy. US behavior is assumed to be the result of a decision-making process involving a state leader. Often these decisions are designed to promote the national interest,[25] though they could be the product of presidential whims.[26] Congress might protest and exert its own power, with many of its decisions falling along ideological lines[27] or sometimes driven by economic benefits.[28] If nothing else, foreign policy is at least

[24] Memmott (2011)
[25] Krasner (1978)
[26] Saunders (2011)
[27] Howell and Pevehouse (2007)
[28] Hiscox (2001)

viewed as coherent: the United States behaves as if it has a set of goals—be they economic, security, or ideological—and works to achieve those goals.

This unitary-actor model of foreign policy pervades much of the international relations literature. When scholars do think about domestic institutions, it is often in the context of explaining anomalies. Democratic politics, it is thought, can make leaders more risk-averse in committing to wars,[29] open to liberalization,[30] and favorable toward human rights agreements.[31] What this literature has not shown is the bureaucratic variation in these tendencies. Even within democracies, for example, some bureaucracies are more likely to comply with international agreements than others.[32] An older literature highlights the differences in hawkishness between agencies,[33] which a more recent literature has updated to explain cabinet-level variation.[34]

Rather than assume that foreign policy is crafted by a unitary decision-maker, I argue that many policy outcomes do not reflect the preferences of any particular individual (like the president) or institution (like parties or Congress). Instead, policy outcomes are the result of a collective action problem. Foreign policy options are limited, or even driven, by the make-up of the bureaucracy. And, as I show in this book, this bureaucratic structure is not determined by the national interest either. Some of the decisions that one might be tempted to attribute to a unitary state decision-maker may instead be the product of forces outside anyone's direct control.

In this book, I argue that the unitary-actor framework is best described as an exception, rather than a rule, in crafting foreign policy. Indeed, foreign policy by one bureaucratic institution often contrasts with policy by another institution. The focus on unitary foreign policymaking neglects to explain many anomalies in US foreign aid policy. For example, in 2007 why did the United States spend $245,000 to help India decrease its coal production and $1,000,000 to help India build up its coal production capacity? Why did the United States keep two separate, and quite distinct, databases of foreign aid expenditures until 2022? Why did the United States drive Southern Afghan farmers into the arms of the Taliban in 2005 by spraying their fields with

[29] Reiter and Stam (1998)
[30] Milner and Kubota (2005)
[31] Moravcsik (2000)
[32] Carcelli (2024)
[33] Allison (1969)
[34] Jost (2024)

pesticides after promising to halt the practice in 2004? And why does the United States continue to send aid to sanctioned states even after Congress and the president denounce them?

The foreign aid literature often considers tensions between donors and recipients[35] and between different donor governments.[36] However, the consequences of tensions *within* a donor country's political system, beyond the left-right divide, are often overlooked. This is unfortunate, since this type of tension is common and has clear implications for aid outcomes. I make the case in this book for a greater focus on the conflictual dynamics behind the creation of foreign aid policy.

This perspective also helps to explain some of the more puzzling failures in US foreign policy more generally. Because it often lacks a central authority, the policy coming out of the United States is often a product of internal conflict. Strategic planning becomes difficult when actual policy outcomes are unpredictable to leaders. This can limit substitutability between policy areas that are controlled by different bureaucratic silos. The less centralized the policymaking authority, the less cohesively the various areas of the bureaucracy will be able to work on large-scale goals. Examples of the consequences of domestic clashes in foreign aid arise throughout the book.

This book also provides a framework useful to the American politics literature. Much of the literature on Congress omits policy substance, tending to focus on interactions within Congress itself as the unit of observation.[37] In this book, I move from congressional behavior to the policy outcomes that *result* from this behavior. Although congressional voting is an interesting phenomenon in itself, I use chapters of this book to show how congressional preferences, debates, and votes impact on-the-ground decisions and outcomes all over the world. What happens in Congress can have very broad repercussions.

The literature on congressional bargaining and vote-buying can also benefit from the perspective offered in this book. Much of the vote-buying literature has focused on visible but benign types of side payments, like federal outlays, campaign donations, and trade protection.[38] However, the

[35] Swedlund (2017); Carnegie and Dolan (2020)

[36] Katada (1997); Bobba and Powell (2006); Barthel et al. (2014); Fuchs et al. (2015); Steinwand (2015); Dietrich (2021)

[37] Lapinski (2013) laments the sequestering of congressional studies as a consequence of this tendency.

[38] Evans.(2004); Jenkins and Monroe (2012); Alexander et al. (2016)

effects on US institutions themselves can be more difficult to notice. I show that congressional bargaining can reshape the federal bureaucracy, creating effects that last years, or even decades. These long-term consequences of congressional bargaining are worth considering in more detail, as they are more difficult to undo than shorter-term policies.

Although a growing body of literature on American foreign policy considers Congress as a relevant actor, it tends to treat Congress as single unit. In this book, I highlight the *differences* in power between different members of Congress. Unequal power within Congress is one of the crucial elements of the theory, and little of the literature has considered it. The inherent power of moderate legislators in foreign policy is clear from the empirical chapters in this book. This is a fact that much of the foreign policy literature has failed to account for.

Normatively, the congressional foreign policy literature tends to take a negative view of Congress's lack of involvement in foreign policy,[39] often blaming presidential over-assertiveness for policy failures.[40] However, I suggest the opposite is true as well: Congress's over-involvement in foreign policy leads to bureaucratic infighting and policy failure. In case after case, I find that US foreign policy is ineffective not *despite* but *because of* Congress's interest in foreign policy. This provides a necessary counterpoint to scholars concerned with presidential power and highlights the necessity for further investigation.

Finally, this book has empirical contributions to make. The multi-methods research design provides a model for future work seeking to understand a two-part process. In two strictly quantitative chapters, I control for one aspect of the theory and test the other, allowing me to demonstrate the effects of both aspects of the theory through robust statistical analysis. In three case study chapters, I combine qualitative and quantitative evidence in a single case. I select cases at varying levels of the two major variables, considering the resulting policy outcomes. Each case study uses a combination of data and first- and second-hand accounts to trace the mechanisms of the theory while ruling out alternative explanations. The empirical framework of this book provides varying levels of evidence in each chapter, using data and case studies simultaneously to examine both aspects of the theory.

[39] Hinckley (1994); Howell et al. (2013); Fowler (2015)
[40] Schlesinger (1973); Howell and Pevehouse (2007)

1.4 Organization of the Book

The remainder of the chapters develop the concept and theory and test it empirically in several ways. Each empirical chapter holds at least one of the main explanatory variables constant to determine the role of the other variable. The qualitative chapters provide differing estimates of both variables. Throughout the book, I return to the congressional dynamics leading to the phenomenon of bureaucratic fragmentation, but the case studies also address some of the *consequences* of fragmentation.

Chapter 2 provides background on the topic, the literature, and the history of US foreign aid bureaucracies. It also lays out the congressional policymaking process as it relates to foreign policy and foreign aid. The policymaking process itself tends to be disjointed, with various congressional committees in both chambers taking control of various areas of foreign aid policy. I focus on different parts of the policymaking process in different chapters, but most of the book will consider the appropriations process. I justify this decision and show some initial statistics on US and global foreign aid appropriations.

In Chapter 3, I further develop the vote-buying theory of bureaucratic fragmentation. I begin by explaining the focus on Congress, an underappreciated actor in US foreign policy. I provide a summary of the literature on congressional vote-buying, the consensus of which is clear: moderate legislators, who are most likely to be on the fence about a particular policy, are the most likely targets of side payments. I then expand the theoretical literature to draw longitudinal expectations about the magnitude of vote-buying. This provides the main hypotheses I will test in the book: the "disunity" and "interest" hypotheses. I outline testable hypotheses and lay out the research design for the remaining chapters.

In Chapter 4, I control for congressional interest in order to quantitatively test the disunity hypothesis. I use original data derived from a set of bills that are always highly salient in Congress: US Foreign Operations Appropriations bills. This allows me to estimate the impact of congressional disunity in the resulting fragmentation of those appropriations bills. I find that when congressional moderates are thinly spread ideologically, the fragmentation of foreign aid appropriations increases. Additionally, I find large-scale evidence that moderate legislators—the ones most likely to benefit from the vote-buying that creates fragmentation—are significantly more supportive of fragmented legislation.

In Chapter 5, I choose a low-unity time period and quantitatively test the interest hypothesis, examining whether fragmentation increases when Congress is more interested in an issue area or recipient state. I introduce two novel data sets to proxy for congressional interest by recipient and type of aid, measuring their resulting bureaucratic fragmentation. I find, in line with the vote-buying theory, that fragmentation increases with congressional interest. When members of Congress are more interested in a policy or aid recipient, they demand more pet projects, leading to fragmentation. Congressional interest is correlated with topic- and recipient-level variation in aid fragmentation.

The remainder of the book considers the vote-buying theory through a qualitative and quantitative review of specific cases. These cases vary in their levels of congressional disunity and congressional interest. I test different elements of the theory in different cases. These cases allow me to trace the mechanisms leading from congressional disunity and interest to vote-buying to bureaucratic fragmentation.

The case studies also provide ample evidence that bureaucratic fragmentation diminishes the quality of US foreign policy. When Congress is more interested in a policy, often because that policy is important to the national interest, the resulting increase in fragmentation causes implementation to suffer. The most important policies seem to be the ones that are implemented most poorly. This ineffectiveness comes about *because of*, rather than *despite* congressional interest.

In Chapter 6, I select a case of extremely high congressional interest from a period of high congressional disunity: the early period of nation-building in Afghanistan following 9/11. The vote-buying theory would suggest that congressional disunity and interest should lead to high bureaucratic fragmentation in Afghanistan. I find, as the vote-buying theory predicts, that bureaucratic fragmentation in Afghanistan was both very high and inimical to success. I also provide evidence for the mechanisms leading to both fragmentation and policy failure by tracing congressional hearings, analyzing a data set of legislative amendments, and considering first- and second-hand accounts.

Next, in Chapter 7, I consider a case of high-issue salience and divided-party government. I trace the mechanisms of the theory through a high-profile foreign aid bill that was passed in 1992 as a response to the fall of the Soviet Union. Once again, the vote-buying theory would predict fragmentation to be high in this case. Indeed, the 1992 FREEDOM Support Act

(FSA) was characterized by a great deal of bureaucratic messiness, with little legislated explanation of which agencies were in charge of what. The result was policy incoherence. By considering the details of this legislation, I find that the policy failure behind the 1992 FSA was due to a great number of moderate legislators demanding the inclusion of new programs representing their own pet projects. Many of these programs privileged special interests in these legislators' districts. This suggests that congressional interest does not necessarily supersede the desire of moderate legislators to sell their votes in exchange for pet projects.

In contrast to the first two cases, Chapter 8 analyzes a case of low congressional interest: the implementation of PEPFAR in sub-Saharan Africa. PEPFAR provided a clear policy benefit but few talking points for most politicians to take home to their districts. Therefore, few legislators felt the need to demand pet projects as part of PEPFAR. Additionally, each party was unified in its goals surrounding PEPFAR—most of the congressional amendments and debate fell along ideological lines and had little to do with legislative pet projects. Therefore, the bureaucracy worked surprisingly harmoniously in this case. The lack of congressional interest in PEPFAR resulted in a policy success. Because bureaucrats were not pitted against one another in fights for congressional approval and funding, they managed to cooperate and create one of the most effective aid agendas in US history. This case suggests an interesting new piece to the theory: intra-party alignment may be able to counter some of the negative consequences of congressional disunity.

In Chapter 9, I summarize the findings of the book and consider the policy implications. First, I suggest that the role of Congress be more closely considered in future foreign policy research. Even when Congress has little power over a policy area, it can still often manage to make an impact on policy—if only a negative one. I suggest that one way forward may be to provide alternative ways for congressional leadership to provide side payments. Although congressional earmarks tend to be derided in the policy world, they may be a necessary evil in attempts to combat bureaucratic dysfunction. Alternatively, decreasing bureaucracies' incentives to curry favor with members of Congress, perhaps by limiting or centralizing communications, could provide a path forward. Finally, the role of parties needs more examination: when party leaders have control over their rank-and-file, they can move debates into party blocs rather than individuals demanding their own projects. Future work should more closely consider how parties can overcome the worst instincts of their own legislators.

The conclusions of this book may be relevant to other policy domains and to other states attempting to streamline their foreign policy bureaucracies. The research findings are also relevant to scholars studying bureaucracy and legislatures in various subfields. The phenomenon of bureaucratic fragmentation is not unique to foreign aid, nor is it easy to resolve in practice. An understanding of the phenomenon is simply a first step in the process of improving foreign aid and foreign policy.

Chapter 2
US Foreign Aid and Bureaucratic Fragmentation

Why should we care about the foreign aid bureaucracy? The normative implications of this work depend, in part, on the drivers of bureaucratic structure. If the decision to fragment the bureaucracy is driven by a rational calculation by someone in the government to fulfill a certain goal, we might infer that there are viable reasons for it. However, if it is instead an unintended byproduct of other policy decisions, then the normative implications could be less optimistic. Unfortunately, the foreign policy literature does not currently offer much explanation for the phenomenon of bureaucratic fragmentation. Variation over both space and time suggest that some combination of domestic and international political factors are driving the phenomenon, but the sources of the variation remain unclear.

In this chapter, I define and describe the concept of foreign aid fragmentation and show variation of the phenomenon in US foreign aid. Far from being constant, I show that the foreign aid bureaucracy has expanded and contracted over time since the United States first began delivering foreign aid. The structure of the bureaucracy also varies by the type of aid and by recipient country. This variation, in turn, factors into the effectiveness of aid policy for both strategic and development goals.

2.1 Variation in Bureaucratic Fragmentation

How can we define a "high" level of bureaucratic fragmentation? Throughout the book, I treat bureaucratic fragmentation as a variable. Rather than compare US bureaucracy with some hypothetical "correct" bureaucratic structure, I consider variation over time, place, and subject area. This allows me to determine the factors leading to *relatively* higher or lower levels of bureaucratic fragmentation.

Competing for Foreign Aid. Shannon P. Carcelli, Oxford University Press. © Oxford University Press (2025).
DOI: 10.1093/9780197799284.003.0002

An alternative way to measure fragmentation would be to compare the structure of US bureaucracy with that of other, similar-looking donor countries. For example, Figure 2.1 compares the organizational fragmentation for major aid donors, measured using the Herfindahl–Hirschman index (HHI).[1] As is clear from this figure, the United States is one of the world's most fragmented donors. While the United States only allocates an average of 60% of its foreign aid through its largest aid agency, the US Agency for International Development (USAID), countries like the Netherlands route 95% of their aid through a single bureaucracy. This is despite the fact that the United States spends a relatively low proportion of its national budget on foreign aid.

Instead of digging into this cross-national variation, however, this book compares the United States against itself, tracing the roots of within-country variation in bureaucratic structure.[2] As a major global foreign policy actor, the United States spends billions of dollars every year on its foreign

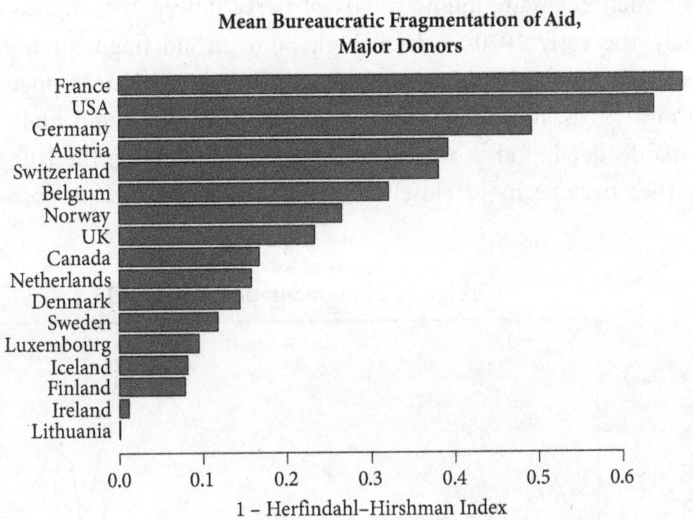

Figure 2.1 Mean bureaucratic foreign aid fragmentation of major OECD donors, 1975–2013, measured using a Herfindahl–Hirschman index (HHI) of the budget share for individual aid bureaucracies within the overall aid budget. Data from AidData (Tierney et al. 2011).

[1] The HHI is calculated by summing the squared budget shares of each foreign aid agency. Subtracting it from one generates the absence of budget concentration, or bureacratic fragmentation.

[2] For an examination of cross-donor variation, see Carcelli (2023).

economic and military budgets. Explaining variation in US foreign policy can be a first step toward generalizing to other states' behavior.

Conventional wisdom might suggest that fragmentation of US bureaucracy is either a constant phenomenon or one that rises consistently over time. This is not what the data show. In fact, there exist significant peaks and valleys over time in the country's bureaucratic structure. Additionally, some policy areas and geographic locations experience higher levels of fragmentation than others. This all suggests that time- and subject-varying characteristics are driving the phenomenon. Understanding these factors is key to deriving normative implications and unlocking policy responses.

Figure 2.2 shows variation over time in overall aid fragmentation. It presents an annual measure of the spread of congressionally mandated appropriations over the many aid-delivering bureaucracies. Fragmentation varies from .41 in 1978 (79% of foreign aid appropriations were channeled through USAID in that year) to .69 in 2006 (only 48% was spent through USAID in that year). Fragmentation exhibits some large-scale trends, which generally follow trends of party power in Congress. Most strikingly, the early 1970s, a local high point in aid fragmentation, was also associated with a nadir in party power. Fragmentation dropped again in the mid-1970s, hitting an all-time low in 1978. Not incidentally, congressional leadership also became more powerful through the late 1970s, and parties became more closely aligned. Aid fragmentation rose again

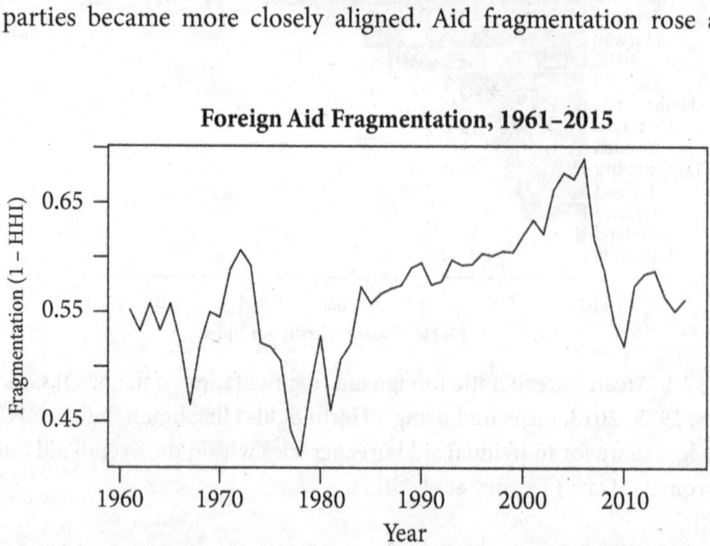

Figure 2.2 Annual bureaucratic fragmentation of the US foreign aid budget, as measured by calculating one minus the Herfindahl-Hirschman Index (HHI).

toward the end of the Carter presidency, peaking in 1980. Reagan's increased focus on military assistance decreased the focus on economic aid for the rest of the 1980s. As mentioned previously, this is far from a stable trend. A theory of bureaucratic fragmentation must explain this over-time variation.

Figure 2.3 demonstrates the same type of variation, this time by recipient country, using USAID-reported foreign aid levels. As is clear in this figure, some recipient states—notably, the former Soviet Union and most of Latin America, receive very fragmented aid from the United States. In other areas, aid from the United States is much more centralized within the bureaucracy. This variation is also poorly explained by the literature.

Finally, bureaucratic fragmentation also varies by foreign aid type. Figure 2.4 shows a snapshot of this variation. Between 2000 and 2019, the United States fragmented its foreign aid to some topic areas while keeping other areas relatively consolidated.

Much of this aid fragmentation is no doubt related to necessity. For example, some issue areas are inherently more complicated than others. It is conceivable that democracy-building might require a more complex bureaucratic infrastructure than building a schoolhouse. However, such a simple explanation does not always pass the sniff test. For example, why should agriculture be so much more complicated than education? What requires so many agencies to be involved in infrastructure projects? And why would any of these requirements change so much over time? The time-, recipient-, and topic-level variation defies any obvious explanation.

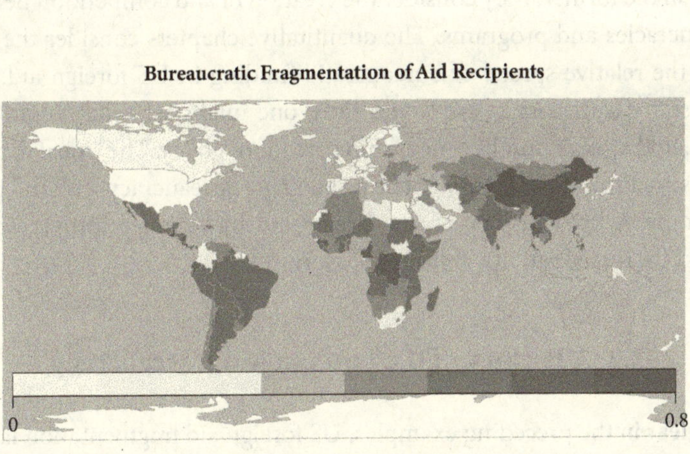

Figure 2.3 Bureaucratic fragmentation of foreign aid within recipient states. Darker red is associated with higher levels of fragmentation.

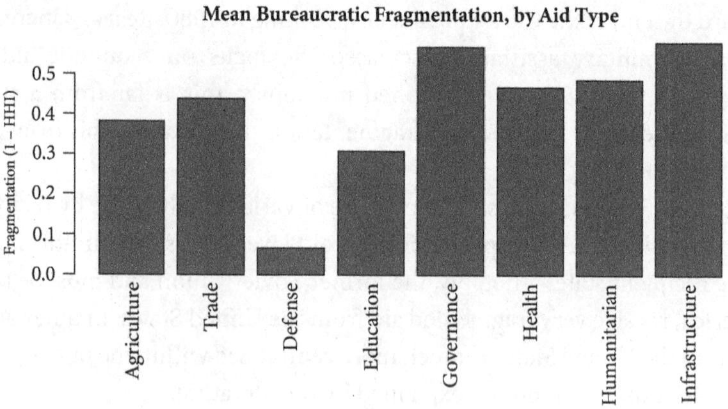

Figure 2.4 Bureaucratic fragmentation among US government agencies' funding for foreign aid projects, by category.

A satisfactory theory of foreign aid fragmentation must take into account variation over time, issue area, and recipient state. The theory developed in this book considers all three types of variation. In later chapters, I leverage these same sources of variation to test a theory of bureaucratic fragmentation in the US foreign aid bureaucracy.

Throughout the book, I define the fragmentation of the foreign aid bureaucracy using two components: (1) a *high number* of competing bureaucracies and programs, and (2) a *thin spread* of authority between those bureaucracies and programs. The case studies in this book tend to focus on the former: they consider the creation of and competition between bureaucracies and programs. The quantitative chapters consider the latter facet: the relative spread of bureaucratic funding in US foreign aid. Both of these measures are relative, and thus, one might ask what ought to be considered a "high number" or a "thin spread" of policy. The "ideal" bureaucratic structure, after all, may not be just a single bureaucracy with full policy autonomy. A brief history of the foreign aid bureaucracy provides more context for this inherently relative measure.

2.2 A History of the Foreign Aid Bureaucracy

As is clear in the preceding examples, US foreign aid fragmentation is quite variable over time. Indeed, history shows that the existence of US foreign aid does not depend on any particular bureaucratic structure. The United States has been participating in some form of foreign aid almost since its inception, but its bureaucracy has evolved over time. Aid programs at the beginning of the Republic were *ad hoc* and often motivated by religious ideals and genuine concern for the poor. Special interests were seldom involved, and foreign aid bureaucracies were initially nonexistent. As early as 1812, with its "Act for Relief of the Citizens of Venezuela," Congress was making its mark on US foreign policy through economic assistance.[3] However, foreign aid bureaucracy as we know it today was not well established at the time.

Historically, the creation of a new foreign aid agency almost always arises from an effort to assuage a dissatisfied constituency. Often, the constituency is economic: many of the earliest foreign aid agencies were driven by business and, especially, exporter, agendas. However, in later years, the dissatisfied constituencies were often ideological in nature. Many foreign aid agencies were created with the purpose of pleasing legislators who were supportive of foreign aid in practice but skeptical about some aspect of its execution. In short, new agency creation has historically been used in an effort to increase the legislative base for foreign aid.

In the earliest days of US foreign aid, patterns of agency creation very closely followed patterns of US exports. Shortly after the Civil War, US corn production increased, and the occasional market glut of corn became a common occurrence. Agricultural producers became interested in increasing demand for their products. This was when policymakers first thought to institutionalize foreign donations of corn in an attempt to increase the market for US exports, while also addressing world hunger.

It is no coincidence that the first US bureaucracy to institutionalize foreign aid was the Department of Agriculture, under Secretary Jeremiah Rusk. Secretary Rusk, a former farmer, congressman, and governor from Wisconsin, was keenly aware of the importance of international markets for American farmers. In the late nineteenth century, Rusk appointed a special agent to investigate foreign corn markets, expressing "...profound regret that there does not exist a foreign demand sufficient to relieve the glut at home."[4] He developed an agricultural exchange program to address this issue.

The Department of Agriculture's monopoly on foreign aid began to change after World War I boosted US banking and manufacturing interests. Banks like J.P. Morgan facilitated billions of dollars' worth of loans

[3] Irwin (2018)
[4] Rusk (1893, p. 49)

to European nations fighting the war.[5] Meanwhile, companies with strong trade ties to the new Soviet Union began demanding that the government support this relationship.[6] This came to a head when the Soviet Union refused to repay its wartime debts, arguing that they had been accrued—and spent—by an illegitimate tsarist regime so were no longer relevant. Infuriated, American bankers demanded that the United States refuse to recognize the Soviet government until the wartime debt was paid back.[7]

It was in this environment that President Roosevelt, having decided to recognize the Soviet Union in November of 1933, created the Export–Import Bank (EXIM) to manage the relationship between the new country and its US creditors. Roosevelt's 1934 executive order was an attempt at compromise between domestic constituencies fighting for and against Soviet recognition. He created an interagency board, which ensured that various interests could be represented in EXIM's financing decisions. The Departments of Commerce, State, and Agriculture shared control with existing New Deal programs.[8] Although EXIM was initially designed to work within the newly formed Soviet Union, the failure of debt negotiations meant that EXIM eventually would focus its efforts in other areas instead.[9]

The Monroe Doctrine, developed a decade later, created a further expansion of US foreign aid. Although not as directly tied to the export market, it was clear at the time that a major reason for rebuilding Europe was the potential market for US products. Business interests beyond farming would continue to lead foreign aid to other areas. The agencies and programs created as part of the plan were highly fragmented and represented the increasingly diverse export profile and foreign policy stances of the post-WWII United States.

The most notable foreign aid agency creation event in US history, the Foreign Assistance Act of 1961, was designed to simplify and streamline the complex set of programs and agendas that came out of the Marshall Plan. At the time, the act was 49 pages long and delegated foreign aid policy mainly to the then newly created USAID. Since then, the foreign aid bureaucracy in the United States has once again expanded. The amended Foreign Assistance Act now contains over 400 pages, with foreign aid policy now

[5] Hall and Sargent (2019, p. 2)
[6] Castle (1933)
[7] Kelley (1933); McIlroy (1933); Packer (1933)
[8] Roosevelt (1934)
[9] EXIM (1935)

delegated to over 100 unique programs in dozens of different agencies. This does not include the several multilateral and regional aid agencies to which the United States contributes. The US foreign aid infrastructure has become more complicated.

Much of the later complexity was driven by dissatisfaction with specifics in the foreign aid agenda. As foreign aid became increasingly militarized during the Nixon years, congressional Democrats began to lose faith in USAID. They demanded a new agency be created for the purpose of demilitarizing aid, taking control away from the president. In the early 1970s, Congress funded the Inter-American Foundation (IAF), an independent agency that diverted funding from USAID.

Crucially, the IAF is statutorily prohibited from working with the American military: it can only create projects in concert with small, grassroots organizations in Latin America. Pacifists in Congress did not just want more funding to go toward the Western Hemisphere—had that been the case, they could simply have created a new program in the State Department, DOD, or USAID. Instead, they cared about *how* Latin American aid was being spent. The new IAF ensured that the aid would serve development instead of military goals.[10] In exchange for legislators' continued support for US foreign aid as a whole, congressional leadership allowed for the creation of this new agency.

The early 1980s coincided with another major agency creation event: the African Development Foundation (ADF). The origins of the ADF are similar to the IAF—not surprising, considering their similar functions and structures. The ADF was the brainchild of Representative William Gray, a Pennsylvania Democrat and member of the Congressional Black Caucus (CBC). Gray was concerned about the current administration (this time, the Reagan administration) increasingly militarizing aid. His solution was to create a new aid program that could not be militarized, this time setting it in Africa, Gray's region of interest. He sponsored legislation proposing the ADF and, with the support of other members of the CBC, threatened to withhold needed support for foreign aid unless the ADF was created.

Representatives of USAID's Africa Bureau testified in Congress in support of the ADF's creation. This is initially surprising, given that they were testifying in favor of a direct competitor for funding. However, it is clear that their support was driven by the fact that the creation of the ADF was necessary in

[10] Ruttan (1996)

order for USAID to receive funding at all that year.[11] Once again, a legislator with strong views about how foreign aid should be spent was able to threaten derailment of a foreign aid bill in exchange for the creation of a new agency that better represented his views. This coincided with an increase in foreign aid fragmentation.

After the increase in the 1980s, fragmentation rose gradually until late in the first decade of the twenty-first century. The next major agency creation took place at this time, under George W. Bush's presidency. Bush pushed a lot of aid funding through his new Millennium Challenge Corporation (MCC), which was designed to correct some of the criticisms common to foreign aid at the time. The creation of the MCC is another example of political compromise. It was clear early on that Bush would be hard-pressed to get enough support from his co-partisans for his strong aid agenda. Creating a new agency was his way of assuring congressional fence-sitters that aid policy would be carried out differently in the future.

Throughout the history of US foreign aid, political actors have used the aid bureaucracy to build legislative coalitions that would not have existed otherwise. When the existing bureaucracy was unable to please all relevant interests, new bureaucracies were created. These new bureaucratic actors arose more out of political necessity than policy improvement. This suggests that their effects might also be more relevant to politics than policy.

2.3 The Costs of Fragmentation

Although the fragmentation of the US foreign aid bureaucracy is an interesting phenomenon that raises a lot of questions about US foreign policy, its normative implications are not immediately obvious. For example, a proliferation of bureaucracies could, theoretically, contribute to healthy competition and innovation. It could provide an opportunity for agencies to specialize and collaborate. USAID staff do not necessarily have expertise in every minutia of foreign aid policy, and the ability to work with staff from the Departments of Energy, Agriculture, and even Defense can certainly have its perks. In fact, one important foreign aid tool is the hiring of "contractors" from within the government. For example, if USAID wants to help Mexico improve its food safety, it might create a project and work with the Animal

[11] Ruttan (1996)

and Plant Health Inspection Service (APHIS) or the FDA in implementing it. Such collaborations have led to increasingly unusual agencies, such as the US Postal Service, being involved in foreign aid.

Another possible example of the benefits of fragmentation comes from the MCC described in Section 2.2. The MCC was created in 2004 and specifically designed to be independent of traditional aid and political actors and to focus on best practices. The MCC only delivers aid to recipients who can be expected to do well with it. This is expected to lead to better aid outcomes.

Both of these justifications for aid fragmentation assume a rational, top-down process driving US decisions. If the fragmentation of US foreign aid were unrelated to political processes, then one could surmise that it is driven by policy considerations. When fragmentation is planned and well-thought-out, it could result in better foreign aid practices in the places that need it most.

However, as I show in this book, this is not often the case. When the United States fragments foreign aid, it is often driven by political processes and does not result in better policy outcomes. Through careful data analysis and case selection, this book paints a picture of an internally divided government creating an incoherent bureaucracy in an attempt to gain political traction. In each chapter of the book, I show how the politicization and distributive nature of foreign aid, rather than a rational, centralized approach to policymaking, drives leaders' decisions to fragment the aid budget. I also detail some of the policy incoherence, bureaucratic infighting, and ultimate failures that result.

Policy effectiveness can be difficult to measure. For example, scholars have long debated the effectiveness of foreign aid in achieving policy and development goals. Much of this literature has assumed that foreign aid is intended to promote international development, and early empirical debates surrounded questions of how best to estimate macro-level empirical models.[12]

Scholars now acknowledge that not all foreign aid is designed to promote international development. Most recently, aid scholars have begun to recognize heterogeneity in states' foreign aid goals, and therefore, their

[12] The classic foreign aid effectiveness debate between Jeffrey Sachs (Papanek 1973; Levy 1988; Hansen and Tarp 2000; Sachs et al. 2004; Sachs 2006) and Bill Easterly (Bauer et al. 1976; Boone 1994; Easterly et al. 2003; Rajan and Subramanian 2008) epitomizes this assumption. For a concise summary of this debate, see Radelet et al. (2004).

allocation decisions.[13] This variation in aid allocation has been used to explain variation in effectiveness: for example, donors with geopolitical goals are less effective at achieving development goals because development was never what they were seeking to achieve in the first place.[14] This explains much of the supposed "failure" of foreign aid: some donors use foreign aid for their own policy objectives, rather than to promote international development.

This literature might suggest that donors' objectives are the main factors leading to aid's ineffectiveness. However, if foreign aid is being cynically used to further foreign policy goals, then one would expect that it should *at least* be effective at achieving those goals. Strangely, this is not always the case, as the Afghanistan example in Chapter 6 shows. Even motivated states often spend their aid money suboptimally, effectively undermining their own foreign policy agendas. The literature still struggles to explain why leaders would knowingly create ineffective policy. This includes much work puzzling over the presence of bureaucratic fragmentation.

The costs of a fragmented bureaucracy have long been clear to policymakers and scholars. As a recent OECD report concludes: "Nobody seriously questions the fact that fragmentation is causing massive inefficiencies; there is, however, far less agreement on what needs to be done."[15] US leaders routinely complain about the difficulties inherent in the US foreign policy bureaucracy,[16] and many scholars have noted a negative correlation between foreign aid's fragmentation and its effectiveness.[17] The Center for Global Development (CGD) reports "fragmentation across donor agencies" among its indicators of aid (in)effectiveness in its donor country ratings.[18]

The fragmentation of the domestic foreign aid bureaucracy varies both between and within donor states. Reports by NGOs often put the United

[13] Alesina and Dollar (2000); Berthélemy (2006); Lebovic and Voeten (2009); Bermeo (2011); Heinrich (2013); Dietrich (2016); Bermeo (2017);. Still others acknowledge variation over time in donors' goals, such as Meernik et al. (1998); Lai (2003); Drury et al. (2005); Dollar and Levin (2006); Fleck and Kilby (2006); Bourguignon and Sundberg (2007); Bearce and Tirone (2010); Bermeo (2016).

[14] Stone (2002); Bearce and Tirone (2010); Girod (2012).

[15] OECD (2009, p. 30)

[16] For example, a major part of Condoleezza Rice's attempts to streamline the State Department and USAID was driven by her frustration over the difficulties of measuring funding levels when they were so thinly spread (Rice 2011, p. 341). Rice also details the difficulty of determining the aid spending in some countries, for example Nigeria, for similar reasons.

[17] Acharya et al.(2006); Knack and Rahman (2007); Easterly and Pfutze (2008); Annen and Kosempel (2009); Aldasoro and Thiele (2010); Oh and Kim (2014).

[18] Birdsall et al. (2010)

States near the top of the world's most fragmented aid donors,[19] noting both the spread of its funding and the lack of coordination between individual agencies.[20] However, as I showed earlier in this chapter, the United States has not always been such an underachiever: the bureaucratic fragmentation of US foreign aid waxes and wanes. A deeper dive into the policymaking process can help in unpacking this variation.

2.4 Foreign Aid Policymaking in the US Congress

The process of making US foreign aid policy begins with the preferences of congressional leaders and of the legislators themselves. Congressional leadership, especially that of the majority party, plays an outsized role in US policymaking.[21] They set a legislative agenda by introducing votes on policies that they believe will be satisfactory to the majority of their own party. A majority of bills that are introduced in Congress never make it to a vote. Congressional leaders have many tools at their disposal to forward the bills that they like and, even more important, kill the ones that they dislike.[22]

After legislation is carefully crafted and put forward by leadership, policymakers have a chance to vote on that legislation. Obviously, much behind-the-scenes negotiation happens between these two steps. Leadership generally has a good idea of how many votes it has secured before putting a bill forward. Similarly, legislators are well aware of the contents of a bill before it goes to a vote. This provides legislators with a chance to have some say in the contents of a bill before voting on it.

In short, the legislation that makes it to a vote in Congress is often the product of a compromise between leadership and rank-and-file members. For example, legislators may negotiate with leadership on their ideal tax rate. In the simplest possible world, taxation would be the product of compromise between those who want higher tax rates and those who prefer lower tax rates. Congressional leadership would choose a tax rate near the median member's preference, and that tax rate would become law.

[19] OECD (2009, p. 40)

[20] OECD (2009, p. 65)

[21] For explanations of the role of party leadership, see Cox and McCubbins (1993, 2005).

[22] For example, leaders may choose to assign a proposed bill to many different committees in order to hold up its passage, limit, or allow the often lengthy amendment process, or bypass supermajoritarian processes to allow legislation to pass more smoothly.

The next time Congress met, the tax rate may be readjusted to match the preferences of the new Congress.

Returning to foreign aid, it is possible to imagine a scenario in which legislators are scaled based on their overall support for foreign aid. Some legislators prefer that no money be spent on aid, while others prefer a very high amount. In such a scenario, it would be relatively simple for leadership to create a compromise—they could simply choose some level of foreign aid near the center of that distribution.

Much of the literature on the domestic politics of foreign aid envisions just such a model, in which parties disagree about foreign aid expenditures and come to some compromise. This is for good reason: in many cases, debates surrounding foreign aid are simply a matter of less versus more. For example, work on the politics of US foreign aid tends to focus on the right–left spectrum, citing inter-party differences in preferences and behavior.[23] Cross-national work has also highlighted aid cleavages on a left–right spectrum.[24] Some work has begun to consider how ideology can inform the *type* of aid spent, its effectiveness, or the decision to send aid to certain aid recipients.[25] More recent work has even begun considering ideological variation beyond the left–right paradigm.[26]

However, not all foreign aid preferences can be represented by these ideological models. Legislators with little interest in economic development may nevertheless care about other aspects of foreign policy that can be manipulated through foreign aid. Aid policy offers politicians an opportunity to signal their positions on important debates in domestic politics.[27] Debates about foreign aid often play out like a microcosm of American politics, highlighting salient issues like abortion, fossil fuel development, the banking sector, and public spending in general. As McGeorge Bundy once put it, "the multi-purpose grab bag which is our current foreign assistance program accurately reflects the many and varied purposes of the Executive Branch, the Congress and of public opinion itself."[28] Regardless of their ideological

[23] Travis (2010); Milner and Tingley (2010, 2011); Prather (2014).
[24] Thérien and Noël (1995, 2000); Tingley (2010); Greene and Licht (2018)
[25] Fleck and Kilby (2006); Milner and Tingley (2013); Brech and Potrafke (2014); Dreher et al. (2015); Allen and Flynn (2018).
[26] Gibler and Miller (2012); Mawdsley (2017); Dietrich et al. (2020).
[27] Mayhew (1974)
[28] CQ-Almanac (1975)

bent, legislators have reason to prefer foreign aid policies that directly benefit their constituents and donors.[29]

Instead of arguing about *how much* the government should spend on foreign aid, negotiations tend to involve arguments over *how* the government should spend it. The history of foreign aid outlined previously offers several examples. Legislators debated issues like militarization, the use of foreign aid in states with poor institutions, and the domestic beneficiaries of foreign aid (including agriculture, banks, and exporters). These debates rarely fell along classic ideological lines.[30] As mentioned previously, much of the literature considers these questions from a partisan perspective.[31]

Because legislators' foreign aid preferences can be difficult to map onto a single dimension, leaders face a challenge in negotiations. Rather than finding a simple compromise, they must use their agenda-setting powers to seek policy compromises that appease a great variety of interests. This challenge is at the root of congressional policymaking in foreign aid. As I will describe in later chapters, it is also at the root of bureaucratic fragmentation.

2.5 Conclusion

The United States has been engaged in foreign aid since its founding, but the policy tool has evolved a great deal in the past two centuries. Rather than simple goodwill, foreign aid is now driven by a variety of ideological and economic motivations, some of which conflict with each other. Because of this, developing consensus in foreign aid policy is often a struggle.

In this chapter, I introduced the concept of bureaucratic fragmentation in foreign aid, showing its variation across time, space, and issue area. Although the United States is currently one of the world's most fragmented foreign aid donors, this variation suggests that policy fragmentation is not a necessary condition for US foreign aid. Some aspects of the political process drive it up and down.

[29] Fleck and Kilby (2001)

[30] Of course, there are exceptions, and some legislators *do* argue against aid spending for ideological reasons. However, even when legislators claim to want a decrease in aid spending, they often do not decrease the aid budget when given the chance to do so.

[31] Fleck and Kilby (2006); Milner and Tingley (2013); Brech and Potrafke (2014); Dreher et al. (2015); Allen and Flynn (2018).

In Chapter 3, I develop a theory of foreign aid fragmentation that seeks to explain this variation. Building on this chapter's description of the policy-making process, I will show how leaders' need to build a policy coalition leads to an increase in the number of pet projects. In turn, this leads to bureaucratic fragmentation in the foreign aid budget. I will develop testable hypotheses, which I will evaluate qualitatively and quantitatively throughout the rest of the book.

Chapter 3
Why Congress Fragments Foreign Aid

In this chapter, I develop the theory of congressional bargaining and foreign aid fragmentation. In short, I argue that fragmentation results from motivated leaders' attempts to "buy" the votes of legislators who are on the fence about a foreign policy agenda. One form of side payment, the diverting of funds to bureaucracies and programs that may serve as a particular legislator's pet project, results in fragmentation. This can be considered a form of collective action problem. Although no individual lawmaker benefits from foreign aid fragmentation, many lawmakers have pet projects that are best represented by specific government agencies. As the number of pet projects increases, so does the number of agencies and programs. The result is a fragmented foreign aid policy that no individual lawmaker would prefer.

Two factors contribute to this outcome: congressional *disunity* and congressional *interest*. First, the number of legislators on the fence about a foreign policy agenda increases as Congress becomes more *disunified*. A high level of intra-branch conflict, especially among the members whose votes are most uncertain, increases fragmentation. Second, congressional leadership becomes more determined to pass a foreign policy agenda the more *interested* it is in the policy. A high-salience policy will attract more attention from leadership and rank-and-file members of Congress, thus resulting in a greater need for negotiations and vote-buying. As the unity of congressional moderates decreases and the interest in a policy increases, fragmentation in the resulting policy should increase.

I begin the following sections by recontextualizing the focus on Congress and outlining the definitions and assumptions relevant to the theory. These assumptions mainly revolve around the preferences and actions taken by leaders and members of Congress and the bureaucracy. I then explain the role of the bureaucracy in feeding congressional preferences. The bulk of the chapter focuses on developing a spatial model of congressional vote-buying, drawing from recent vote-buying literature to predict longitudinal variation in the magnitude of vote-buying in Congress. This allows me to derive

Competing for Foreign Aid. Shannon P. Carcelli, Oxford University Press. © Oxford University Press (2025).
DOI: 10.1093/9780197799284.003.0003

testable hypotheses, which I will be using throughout the book to examine the evidence for the theory. I then describe the empirical strategy of the book, which combines quantitative and qualitative analysis of the *disunity* and *interest* hypotheses.

3.1 Congress and Foreign Aid

Scholars have been debating Congress's role in foreign policy for decades. The "two presidencies hypothesis" suggests that Congress has little incentive or ability to manipulate foreign policy.[1] Additionally, foreign aid makes up less than 1% of the total US budget. One could argue that legislators have much larger buckets of money to worry about, and that their constituents have little incentive to educate themselves about a small policy tool like foreign aid.

On the other hand, scholars of US foreign policy agree that economic aid is "the principle vehicle by which [Congress] attempts to influence and make U.S. foreign policy."[2] This is because foreign aid policy "suits the congressional character, always at its most skilled and comfortable with using budgetary decisions as a means of policy control."[3] Because congressional leaders have career and policy aspirations,[4] they have every incentive to wrest foreign policy control from the executive branch, in the form of foreign aid, to pursue their own foreign policy agenda.

Rank-and-file legislators, and their constituents, also have many reasons to care about foreign aid. Milner and Tingley (2015) recently found that economic aid is one of Congress's most powerful foreign policy tools. In contrast to the "two presidencies hypothesis," Milner and Tingley suggest that congressional control varies over different foreign policy tools. When properly motivated, members of Congress can and do manipulate foreign policy. The distributive nature of foreign economic aid, as well as the relative ease of collecting information on aid spending, incentivizes Congress to drive foreign policy through foreign economic assistance. Legislators with preferences over foreign policy are more likely to successfully achieve those preferences if they do so through foreign aid.

[1] See Wildavsky (1966), Hinckley (1994), Marshall and Pacelle Jr (2005), and Canes-Wrone et al. (2008), to name a few.
[2] Pastor (1982, p. 253)
[3] Hinckley (1994, p. 102)
[4] Fenno (1973)

Even beyond the foreign aid realm, Congress's role in foreign policy is easy to underestimate. As Howell and Pevehouse (2007) point out, Congress's role in foreign policy is often invisible. When the president is hamstrung by Congress in foreign policy making, it often results in policies that represent a compromise. The unobserved counterfactuals—policies that *would* have happened if the president did *not* have to contend with Congress—are impossible to see and difficult to guess at. Congress can also manipulate public opinion to drive the president toward preferred policies.[5] The evidence of congressional abdication is easily misconstrued, as new challenges may simply move legislation to new venues, such as appropriations bills.[6] This reliance on appropriations would suggest an even greater role for foreign aid, which is driven largely through appropriations.

3.2 Theory Assumptions

The main theory developed in this chapter, which I call the "vote-buying theory of bureaucratic fragmentation," draws on a few assumptions about leader and legislator preferences. First, I assume that congressional leaders have a foreign policy agenda that involves directed foreign aid spending. Second, I assume the foreign policy preferences of rank-and-file legislators can be both ideological and district-specific in nature. Third, I assume that some bureaucracies are better at achieving some foreign policy goals than others. These can include both ideological and district-specific (distributive) goals. Below, I expand upon and build evidence for these assumptions.

Congressional leadership has a foreign policy agenda. Leaders in Congress differ from rank-and-file members in that they have the freedom and power to seek policy gains rather than simply seeking re-election. This is how Congress is able to create policy.[7] Foreign aid offers congressional leaders an opportunity to make their mark in foreign policy; therefore, they should be relatively eager to craft foreign aid policy that can pass congressional muster.

[5] Kriner and Schickler (2016)
[6] Carcelli (2021)
[7] This idea was first introduced by Fenno (1973) but has since been established in other work, for example by Deering and Smith (1997) and Cox and McCubbins (1993, 2005). More recent work has further highlighted the electoral benefits of policy cohesiveness, especially in foreign policy (Adler and Wilkerson 2013; Curry and Lee 2020; Tama 2024).

Given that some legislators do care about foreign aid, it is worth considering how they develop their preferences. As outlined in the previous chapter, much of legislators' overall support for foreign aid is related to ideology.[8] A devoted libertarian, for example, is very unlikely to support any aid agenda. However, more commonly, support for a foreign aid agenda will depend on *how* the foreign aid is to be spent. Some legislators, for example, have an ideological predisposition toward humanitarian goals, some prefer that aid be used to further the national interest, and still others think that foreign aid should be used to provide trade incentives.[9]

Legislators can also use foreign aid to pursue a district-specific agenda by crafting policies that directly benefit their own constituents and donors. Policymakers who are ideologically indifferent to foreign aid may instead be driven by these distributive considerations. Aid money has concentrated benefits, and legislators whose constituents win a lot of aid contracts tend to be rewarded electorally. Milner and Tingley (2015) note the importance of some foreign aid funding to special interest groups. These can include pharmaceutical companies,[10] agricultural groups,[11] and aid contractors.[12] Similarly, concentrated diaspora groups may push their representatives to support foreign aid projects to constituents' countries or regions of origin.[13] Any of these motivations can lead policymakers to support some foreign aid programs while rejecting others.

Variation in legislators' reasons for supporting foreign aid feeds into the variation in aid bureaucracies themselves. Depending upon legislators' philosophy of aid, the interests they represent, and their preferred level of executive and legislative oversight, they will prefer some agencies over others.

3.3 Bureaucratic Allocations as a Vote-Buying Tool

Legislators who care about foreign aid vary widely in their preferences for how and where foreign aid is used. Fortunately for them, foreign aid funding channels—the bureaucracies themselves—vary just as widely. Three sources

[8] Milner and Tingley (2010); Tingley (2010); Travis (2010); Jeong and Quirk (2019), etc.
[9] Chapter 4 explores some of the motivators behind legislators' preferences for *how* foreign aid should be used.
[10] Suzuki (2020)
[11] Nunn and Qian (2014)
[12] Powers et al. (2010)
[13] Bermeo and Leblang (2015); Prather (2020)

of variation between foreign aid agencies are especially salient. Agencies vary in (1) their foreign aid philosophy or way of conducting business, (2) the special interests that they best represent, and (3) their rules of conduct or oversight. Similarly, legislators who care about foreign aid for either ideological or distributive reasons care about how foreign aid is carried out, which interests are benefiting, and who makes the rules.

First, agencies vary in their philosophies or ways of carrying out aid. USAID, for example, tends to work with a specific set of partners, both within and outside the government, that usually carry out large-scale development projects designed for lasting impact. Legislators wary of public spending on large projects, therefore, might prefer that their aid money be spent elsewhere. President George W. Bush, an enthusiastic proponent of foreign aid, had little loyalty to USAID. The ideology of the bureaucrats, the types of programs that were in place, and the contractors USAID hired made it difficult for Bush and his fellow compassionate conservatives to support the agency itself. He built his flagship aid program, the MCC, to bypass the troublesome USAID altogether, leading to MCC's appeal among other aid-friendly Republicans.

Similarly, even very conservative Republicans support foreign aid programs that involve the Department of Commerce (DOC). The implicit trade promotion and market orientation of Commerce's programs allow fiscal conservatives, who may not otherwise support foreign aid for its policy merits, to vote in favor of programs like the 2015 Electrify Africa Act. In fact, the initial version of this Act was voted down by these conservative Republicans partly due to the bill's lack of an interagency working group, which was later created to include DOC and ensure buy-in from the private sector.[14] Because of the interests already in control of the department, transferring aid authority away from USAID and toward DOC was one way to increase fiscal conservatives' support for foreign aid.

At the other end of the ideological spectrum, the IAF has been criticized for its wild independence and lack of accountability to traditional foreign policy and business interests. Lyne et al. (2006) attribute IAF support among liberal Democrats to the diversity of foreign policy preferences in the government at the time of its creation. Liberals in Congress delegated to the IAF precisely because it was willing and able to circumvent some of Reagan's foreign policies. By channeling some foreign policy funding to IAF agencies, congressional leadership could credibly commit to policy concessions

[14] Anonymous interview with author, April 7, 2016

that liberal legislators wanted. This was precisely because of the IAF's way of doing business: it could only fund grassroots organizations in Latin America. More generally, work by Clinton et al. (2012) found that bureaucracies themselves seem to have ideological preferences, which may lead legislators to choose favorites within the executive branch.

Second, agencies vary in the interests they represent. Research since McCubbins et al. (1987) has demonstrated how special interests can become baked into bureaucracies when lawmakers "stack the deck" in agency creation.[15] Variation in special interest control is also visible in the cases described above: legislators with powerful private-sector interests may be more supportive of agencies that work with the private sector. However, these differences run deeper than that. USAID is known for employing a limited set of "beltway bandits" to help carry out its projects. According to USAID data, 90% of non-government aid contractors in the public and private sectors have worked exclusively with a single US agency for their entire existence.[16] Legislators from districts that represent these important contractors are rewarded by constituents for supporting large-scale foreign aid bills.[17]

However, not all agencies are controlled by this limited group of interests. The IAF, mentioned above, is a small US agency that works only with grassroots projects in host countries. The interests the IAF represents are more likely to be diaspora groups or companies with genuine interest in Latin American development.[18] Another example is the Export-Import Bank (EXIM), which has been criticized for disproportionately representing the interests of large exporting manufacturers, such as Boeing. One may therefore expect EXIM's supporters in Congress to be disproportionately represented by successful exporting districts.[19] Depending on whether a district is represented by contractors, diaspora groups, or exporters, legislators vary in the foreign aid channels they prefer.

[15] For example, Wood and Bohte (2004) find that enacting coalitions design agencies in their own image, Macdonald (2007) notes similar findings, and Clinton and Lewis (2007), Bertelli and Grose (2009), and Clinton et al. (2012) demonstrate the dynamics of agency ideology. Additionally, Lewis (2003) and Miller and Whitford (2016) note the striking variation in agencies' insulation from politics, and Moe (1984) also points out the lengthiness of agency preferences.

[16] Data from EADS (2015).

[17] Powers et al. (2010)

[18] In fact, according to Lyne et al. (2006), the IAF was so resistant to corporate interests that it eventually became embroiled in a scandal involving aid beneficiaries kidnapping American businessmen.

[19] Milner and Tingley (2010)

Third, agencies vary in their rules of engagement. Some agencies face a lot of oversight from the executive and legislative branches, while others face less. Fariss (2010) demonstrates differences in aid programs' accountability to sanctions, and Arel-Bundock et al. (2015) show the consequences of executive and legislative control over foreign aid bureaucracies. Agencies whose heads are appointed by independent commissions, such as the International Development Finance Corporation are less likely than agencies whose heads report directly to the president, such as the Department of State, to pursue the president's foreign policy initiatives. Similarly, agencies whose missions directly invoke international security are less likely to seek Congress's permission or oversight.[20] Depending on a legislator's allegiance to decision-makers in both branches, he or she may find reason to seek funding for one agency over another.

Legislators may even hold foreign aid preferences for more personal reasons. Former USAID administrator Andrew Natsios suggests that family connections can lead legislators to support pet projects. He tells a story about Eunice Kennedy Shriver, prominent philanthropist and sister of Senator Ted Kennedy, pressuring USAID to carry out specific education programs for special-needs students in Guatemala. USAID administrators were hesitant to spend their education budget on this project. However, Shriver was able to use her family connections to enact the policy through USAID. Senator Kennedy later sent a personal letter thanking Natsios for "settl[ing] an issue that was a huge contention in the family."[21] Other USAID staff have offered similar stories, in which personal friends of powerful members of Congress have successfully lobbied for policies requested by friends and family, for example, creating a judicial program in Haiti.[22] At the time of writing, one of the most recent aid packages to Ukraine was partially possible due to one powerful legislator's concern over his military-aged son being drawn into a costly NATO engagement.[23]

It should come as no surprise that legislators often rely on the bureaucracy to enact their preferred policies. The power of the federal bureaucracy is well known in American politics. Up to 90% of American law can be attributed to bureaucratic rulemaking.[24] Because bureaucracies have so much power,

[20] Milner and Tingley (2015)
[21] Peasley (2019, 103)
[22] Anonymous interview with author, May 2, 2016
[23] Speaker of the House Mike Johnson reportedly cited his son's matriculation into the US Naval Academy as one reason for his decision to support the aid package (Edmondson 2024).
[24] Potter (2019, p. 2)

lawmakers often end up lobbying *them* for policy change.[25] Indeed, strong autonomous bureaucracies can even overpower the wishes of the president himself—their ostensible boss.[26] Because bureaucracies are both powerful and diverse, legislators may rely on their agency ties to create their preferred policies.

This bureaucratic power is itself a product of congressional bargaining. Lewis (2003), following Moe (1989), finds that a unified Congress creates autonomous bureaucracies to counter executive excess. Miller and Whitford (2016) build on this work by more directly considering the role of congressional unity in this inter-branch relationship. In a case study tracing the autonomy of the US Federal Reserve, they suggest that its independence was a result of warring factions within Congress being unable to choose a set of bureaucratic instructions on which they could all agree.[27] Research on the role of congressional bargaining in building and maintaining the federal bureaucracy has focused mainly on its *autonomy*, rather than its *structure*, but the parallels are clear: a warring Congress could choose to delegate to multiple bureaucracies as easily as it chooses to create an independent one.[28]

In sum, legislators who care about how and where foreign aid is deployed may have corresponding agency preferences. This does not necessarily mean that any legislator prefers a fragmented foreign aid bill. However, it does mean the legislators care about foreign aid for diverse reasons. They may pursue a foreign aid agenda for ideological or particularistic reasons. They may have a desire to appear altruistic for some cosmopolitan constituents. They may genuinely believe that strategic aid can further the US national interest. Regardless of legislators' diverse motivations for pursuing foreign aid, certain agencies are more adept at furthering certain types of goals. And this provides an incentive for leaders, who want to pass a foreign aid bill but may struggle to collect enough votes, to buy some legislators' votes by shifting bureaucratic allocations. A fragmented aid policy is the unintended result.

[25] Ritchie (2018)

[26] Carpenter (2001, p. 112) cites an example of the US Postal Service denying Theodore Roosevelt's demands that the mail system censor materials from Roosevelt's political enemies.

[27] Miller and Whitford (2016, p. 108–117)

[28] Farhang and Yaver (2016) and Epstein and O'Halloran (1999) make a similar argument but focus on the role of divided government in encouraging certain bureaucratic structures.

3.4 Congressional Disunity and Vote-Buying

Ideology has some bearing on legislators' foreign aid preferences. However, no matter their ideology, a legislator's support for particular funding channels can vary depending on policy and distributive preferences. However, not all legislators' opinions are weighted equally. Understanding the preferences and constraints of the most powerful members of Congress is important to understanding the legislation that results.

As discussed in Chapter 2, congressional leaders are arguably the most important voices shaping legislation.[29] However, setting a strong foreign policy agenda is not always worth the effort for leaders. For low-salience issues, leadership has little incentive to overcome gridlock to pass new legislation.[30] The fight for positive agenda control may not offer enough electoral and policy gains to be worth the costs.[31] This suggests that congressional *interest* should play a role in vote-buying. When leaders are not motivated to exert positive agenda control, they will not do so. Later in this chapter, I will more directly consider the importance of congressional interest in the crafting of a foreign aid agenda.

Assuming leaders are *motivated* to set an agenda, their *ability* to do so depends on the level of agreement—or unity—within Congress. As Evans (2004, page 24) puts it, when Congress "enjoys broad agreement but not unanimity on a policy issue, its leaders may still lack sufficient votes to pass it; under those circumstances, the leadership is authorized to use its powers to bring into line recalcitrant members."

Leaders have several vote-buying tools at their disposal to do just that. Perhaps the most hotly debated form of vote-buying is in congressional earmarks or so-called pork-barrel spending. In this process, legislators seek funding for their own projects to be written into larger spending bills. For example, the infamous "Bridge to Nowhere," a road project proposed to cost up to $450 million[32] planned for a town of 50 people. According to Senator John McCain this was one of thousands of such projects padding a particular

[29] This group can include committee or subcommittee chairs or ranking members, senior legislators, and party leadership. The American politics literature tends to focus on different types of leaders for different time periods and areas of legislation.

[30] This can be especially true during some periods, for example, when unified government puts foreign policy on the back-burner (Wang 2024).

[31] Lebo et al. (2007); Rohde (2013)

[32] Forgey (2015)

highway spending bill.[33] Projects like these allow leaders to build legislative coalitions that move policy forward.[34]

Other forms of vote-buying are less sensational. For example, leaders can appoint supporters to powerful positions,[35] direct party funds to specific political campaigns,[36] and provide funding for pork-barrel projects to members willing to vote along party lines.[37] This type of vote-buying allows Congress to pass legislation, and it puts party members in a good position for re-election. When legislators disagree about the details of legislation, buying their votes through side payments can be a feasible path forward.

However, buying votes through traditional means can be costly. Leaders lack complete information about legislators' true preferences. Every legislator has an incentive to advertise himself as undecided in order to gain the benefits of having their votes "bought." In choosing which legislators to "buy," leaders must consider their own limited information. What's more, vengeful legislators whose projects were not funded may vote against a piece of legislation in retribution. The combination can lead to an expensive over-extension of earmarked projects.[38] This is especially likely in cases where policy has clear distributive implications.

The variety of government agencies involved in foreign aid can alleviate these problems, creating a less costly, and less visible, way for agenda-setters to buy votes. In foreign aid, not all vote-buying need be distributive. As outlined above, many members of Congress have foreign and domestic policy interests in mind when they consider foreign aid bills, whether for personal or strategic reasons. Foreign aid represents an unusual combination of regulatory and distributive policy aspects, which often vary by agency. Leadership may be more willing and able to make small adjustments to the bureaucratic breakdown of a foreign aid bill rather than create costly new pork projects.

[33] Siegel (2008)

[34] Evans (2004)

[35] Deering and Smith (1997)

[36] Jenkins and Monroe (2012)

[37] Groseclose and Snyder (1996); McCarty (2000); Evans (2004); Bertelli and Grose (2009); Alexander et al. (2016); also see , Berry et al. (2010), Hudak (2014), Kriner and Reeves (2015), and others on distributive politics through the executive branch. Because I measure the fragmentation of congressional legislation rather than of policy implementation more broadly, I don't consider these executive-branch tools closely in this work. However, future work on the fragmentation of foreign aid *implementation* should more carefully consider the particularistic preferences of the executive branch.

[38] Evans (2004)

The variation available within the foreign aid bureaucracy can be useful to leaders in the vote-buying process. It can allow leaders to avoid the budgetary and political costs of earmarks, while still allowing fence-sitters to gain something in exchange for their support. Channeling resources to the bureaucracy that best represents a specific legislator's preferences can allow agenda-setters to ensure those legislators' support. Unfortunately, it can also result in inefficient bureaucratic fragmentation in the final bill.

3.4.1 The Role of Moderate Legislators

The theory so far suggests that bureaucratic fragmentation in a foreign aid bill is a by product of the vote-buying process. This, then, raises a question: under which conditions should vote-buying be most prevalent? To answer, I first turn to the existing literature on congressional vote-buying, the consensus of which suggests that moderate legislators are the most common targets of vote-buying. When a legislator falls on the extreme end of her party's ideological spectrum, she is unlikely to be persuaded to change her opinion on foreign aid. In contrast, legislators with more moderate preferences are much more likely to be on the fence. Therefore, they are the least costly votes for leaders to "buy."

American politics scholars have demonstrated this argument both theoretically and empirically. Snyder (1991) introduced a spatial model of legislative vote-buying by focusing on the role of lobbyists.[39] He finds that vote-buyers should direct distributive benefits to their moderate opponents, rather than their heavy supporters.[40] Dekel et al. (2009) generate similar predictions through a slightly more complex model with two competing lobbyists.[41]

[39] Snyder (1991) suggests that "lobbyists" can also be defined as legislative leadership (p. 95), which fits the definition of vote-buyers in this chapter.

[40] Snyder (1991) also makes predictions about the ideal points of vote-buyers and their preferred salience of the issues. This and other asides from Snyder could yield interesting new hypotheses about substitution effects in vote-buying strategies but these are not explicitly considered in this book.

[41] It is worth noting that later work used the condition of two competing lobbyists to theorize the puzzle of leaders buying supermajorities. Groseclose and Snyder (1996) asked why vote-buyers would ever choose to offer side payments to more legislators than is strictly necessary for a majority coalition. They determined that this puzzle can be explained theoretically by the presence of multiple competing lobbyists. When more than one actor is competing for a legislative majority, it can be less costly to prevent recursive bargaining by immediately buying a supermajority of votes. This theory was empirically verified by Wiseman (2004), who found that bills with many competing interest groups, such as appropriations bills, are the most likely to attract super majorities.

Empirical research has validated and extended these theories. Carroll and Kim (2010) find that "policy losers"—legislators who lose out based on policy outcomes—tend to be repaid through more pork-barrel spending in their districts. Jenkins and Monroe (2012) find that median voters are the most likely to be offered campaign funds from party PACs. Alexander et al. (2016) scale up previous vote-buying models and find that having preferences near the chamber median increases a legislator's likelihood of receiving federal outlays for their district.

Extending this literature to draw longitudinal predictions, I argue that the magnitude of vote-buying should depend upon the preferences of moderates in Congress. Specifically, a wide ideological spread of moderate legislators should lead to more vote-buying, and therefore, a more fragmented foreign aid budget.

To see how the composition of Congress may affect vote-buying, consider Figure 3.1, which pictures a hypothetical chamber in which ideological preferences are distributed over a uni-dimensional policy space.[42] In order to pass a foreign aid bill, leaders must win over a majority of members. As previous research would suggest, this often involves buying votes, beginning near the chamber median and working outward until a majority is achieved. The price of a vote is equal to the policy loss that a legislator pays due to policy being further from his or her ideal point. If leaders only need to persuade one legislator to support a bill, the total price of vote-buying will simply equal the policy distance between that legislator's ideal point (p_i) and the resulting bill (p_i – *bill*).[43]

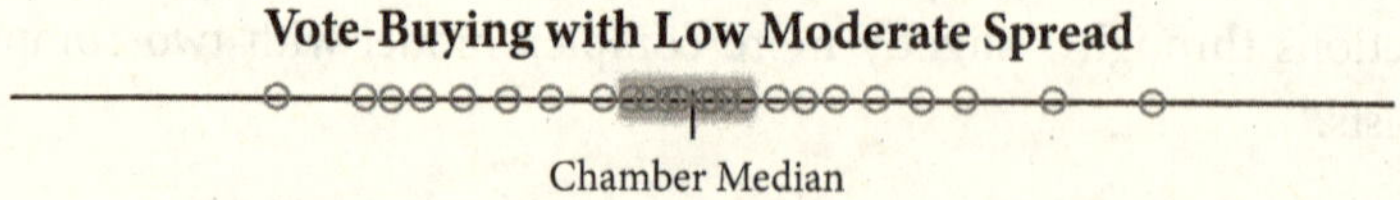

Figure 3.1 The total price of vote-buying is equal to the sum of the prices of each individual vote. When moderate legislators are in relative agreement over the ideal bill, then the price of even the costliest vote will amount to half the distance of this relatively small highlighted region. The total magnitude of vote-buying will be relatively low.

[42] This distribution follows much of the vote-buying literature (Snyder 1991; Dekel et al. 2009).

[43] More accurately, the price of a vote should consider the distance between the bill and the status quo in the policy space, or (p_i – *s.q.*) – (p_i – *bill*). Because leadership will always consider the status quo when developing policy, and because the location of the status quo does not change the *relative* costs of votes, I omit this consideration from this simple model.

It is likely, of course, that leaders will need to persuade more than one legislator to support their agenda. As the number of votes needed increases, so does the total price leaders must pay for their bill to pass. The total magnitude of side payments will be equal to the summation of each vote's price, or $\sum_{i=1}^{n} p_i - \textit{bill}$, where n is equal to the number of votes bought and i indexes each legislator receiving side payments. This suggests that two factors affect the total magnitude of vote-buying in a given Congress: (1) the number of recalcitrant legislators, and (2) the preference distance *between* those legislators. In short, the higher the preference distance between moderate legislators, the higher a marginal price leaders will have to pay for each additional vote. This is true regardless of the number of legislators being offered side payments.

In Figure 3.1, moderate legislators are in relative agreement. The costliest side payment in this example is equal to half the size of the highlighted region. The middle of the ideological distribution of legislators represents a relatively small policy space; therefore, the distance between any moderate voter's ideal point need not be far from the bill itself. In such a scenario, congressional leadership should not find policy consensus to be too difficult. The preferences of the crucial moderates are not very far removed from the preferences of the next logical target of vote-buying.

Now consider Figure 3.2, which depicts a legislature with a *high* ideological spread. In this scenario, the middle section is much more dispersed. The most moderate legislators have been replaced with slightly more extreme counterparts. The range of ideological positions represented by the middle 50% of legislators is much higher than in the previous case.[44] When such a change occurs, "moderates" are all of a sudden not so moderate anymore.

Vote-Buying with High Moderate Spread

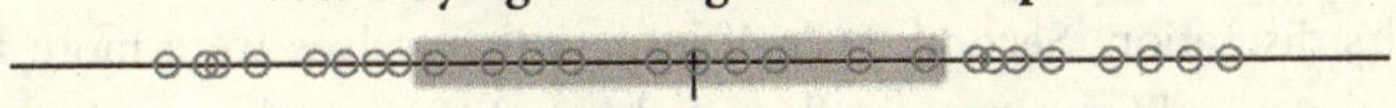

Figure 3.2 In contrast to Figure 3.1, this figure depicts a Congress in which moderates are ideologically diffuse. The cost of buying moderates' votes increases. The price of the costliest vote will again be half the distance of the highlighted region, but in this case the highlighted region is much larger. The magnitude of vote-buying, and therefore the degree of fragmentation, is higher.

[44] There is no particular reason to believe that the size of the middle 50% is more important than, say, the size of the middle third. The crucial part is that the distribution comes from the center of the ideological spectrum. Empirical tests show consistent results with the two measures of moderate-legislator spread.

In contrast to Figure 3.1, in Figure 3.2 the summation of ideological distances will be higher regardless of the status quo. This is especially clear in the price of the costliest votes, represented by the (now much larger) highlighted region. Even if the number of recalcitrant legislators is held constant, the total magnitude of vote-buying is larger when the moderate spread increases. Insofar as vote-buying involves allocating funds to bureaucratic allies of particular legislators, this will increase the fragmentation of foreign aid.

3.5 Congressional Interest and Vote-Buying

The unity of Congress is only important if Congress is actually interested in an issue. When Congress is uninterested, it can either leave the policymaking to the executive branch or not make policy at all. For example, Milner and Tingley (2015) find that Congress is happy to delegate some foreign policy areas entirely to the executive, and Tama (2024) finds that some foreign policy issues lend themselves well to pro-presidential bipartisanship. However, while Milner and Tingley find variation between foreign policy realms, I suggest that congressional interest also varies *within* the realm of foreign aid. Certain types of aid, and certain regions of the world, are more interesting to Congress than others. Therefore, Congress should be more likely to micromanage those areas of foreign aid, leading to vote-buying and fragmentation.

Congressional interest can moderate the role of disunity in two ways. First, when leadership is uninterested in a policy, they are unlikely to spend the resources necessary to pursue an agenda. Instead, unmotivated leaders should be more willing to leave some areas of foreign aid to the executive branch's discretion. Second, even if leaders themselves were more motivated, that would not necessarily entail vote-buying unless rank-and-file members were also interested in the policy area. Legislators with little interest in an area of foreign aid are unlikely to demand pet projects. In this case, congressional disunity is unlikely to lead to fragmentation. In order for congressional vote-buying to lead to bureaucratic fragmentation, both leadership and the rank-and-file members must be interested and invested in the policy.

Some policy areas are inherently more salient to Congress than others. For example, some types of foreign aid are more politically visible to both lobbyists and the public. Additionally, some regions of the world are also more salient than others. The relative salience of certain topics and regions might make them more interesting to leaders and members of Congress. For example, relations with trade partners might be salient areas of debate, creating clear winners and losers within Congress. This variation by area and topic is relevant to the vote-buying theory insofar as it limits the willingness of both leaders and legislators to engage in vote-buying.

I expect vote-buying to be scarce when congressional interest is low. This is true regardless of the unity of congressional moderates. A perfectly unified Congress will be just as likely to ignore an issue area of low interest as a very diffuse Congress.

3.6 Testable Implications

The vote-buying theory of bureaucratic fragmentation leads to a few testable implications, from which I will draw throughout the book. First, bureaucratic fragmentation should increase during times of high congressional *disunity*. That is, when the spread of moderate legislators within Congress is high, vote-buying should increase, leading to an increase in fragmentation.

Hypothesis 1 *When moderate legislators are more ideologically heterogeneous, foreign aid fragmentation will increase.*

Another way to test the mechanisms of the disunity hypothesis is to consider the actions of legislators themselves. Because vote-buying tends to be concentrated in the ideological center of Congress, moderates are the most likely to successfully demand pet projects. This should be visible in their behavior in congressional hearings and debates, the legislation they put forward, and their voting records. Party moderates are overall the *least* likely to "heed the party call" and vote along with their own party's agenda.[45] But according to the theory, this should change when leadership successfully

[45] Minozzi and Volden (2013)

courts their votes: they should be the *most* likely to change their votes in the face of a fragmented bill.

Hypothesis 2 *Moderate legislators should be more likely than non-moderates to successfully introduce pet projects into, and support, fragmented legislation.*

Finally, congressional *interest* plays a clear role in moderating this relationship. When a topic or area of foreign aid is of greater interest to congressional members and leadership, there should be greater supply of and demand for pet projects. Therefore, congressional interest should make vote-buying and fragmentation more likely. This leads to the third testable hypothesis of this book.

Hypothesis 3 *When congressional interest in a topic or geographic area increases, the fragmentation of US foreign aid in that topic or area should increase.*

Various combinations of these three hypotheses will be tested in the empirical chapters of this book. In each of the quantitative chapters, I control for one of the main variables (disunity or interest) and carry out statistical analyses on the other variable. In the qualitative chapters, I choose cases that allow me to vary the value of Congress's disunity and interest in a particular time and policy area. This allows me to examine the mechanisms involved, evaluating whether fragmentation is indeed a result of an attempt by leadership to persuade moderate legislators to support an agenda. A more precise chapter breakdown follows, and Table 3.1 summarizes the expectations of the theory. The theory suggests that bureaucratic fragmentation requires both of the two components: congressional *interest* and congressional *disunity*.

Table 3.1 Summary of theoretical expectations

	Disunity	
Interest	**Low**	**High**
Low	Low Fragmentation	Low Fragmentation
High	Low Fragmentation	**High Fragmentation**

3.7 Empirical Framework

Throughout the remainder of this book, I quantitatively and qualitatively evaluate the vote-buying theory of bureaucratic fragmentation. Chapters 4 and 5 are strictly quantitative: they provide statistical evidence of the disunity and interest hypotheses, respectively. Chapters 6 through 8 provide mixed-methods case studies probing the theoretical mechanisms. The cases vary on the crucial dimensions of congressional disunity and interest. This allows me to demonstrate the mechanisms leading to foreign policy fragmentation in some cases (Chapters 6 and 7) and preventing it in others (Chapter 8). Although Congress is certainly not the only force driving interagency conflict, the case studies provide straightforward evidence of the links between congressional disunity and interest and the resulting fragmentation.

Table 3.2 outlines the values of the relevant variables in the empirical chapters. Although the case studies are largely qualitative, all case study chapters include a quantitative component as well. By analyzing votes on specific legislation surrounding the cases of interest, I am able to demonstrate the mechanisms in more depth. Specifically, in each case, I find that moderate legislators are the most likely to demand and receive their preferred pet projects in specific legislation. The quantitative components of the case studies support the assertion that moderate legislators are the ones driving foreign aid fragmentation.

Chapter 4, the first empirical chapter, selects bills with high levels of congressional interest in order to examine the disunity hypotheses. The evidence in this chapter focuses on variation over time. I find that an increase in congressional disunity, as measured by the spread of moderate legislators' preferences, is associated with greater budgetary fragmentation of foreign

Table 3.2 Summary of quantitative chapters

Chapter	Summary	Disunity	Interest
4	Quantitative Test of Disunity Hypothesis	Variable	High
5	Quantitative Test of Interest Hypothesis	High	Variable
6	Case Study: Fall of the Soviet Union	High	High
7	Case Study: US War in Afghanistan	High	High
8	Case Study: Global HIV/AIDS Relief	High	Low

aid. I also examine legislative voting behavior, finding that moderates are the ones most likely to support this fragmented legislation. This suggests that moderates are the ones whose pet projects are moving forward thanks to the vote-buying that induces the fragmentation.

Chapter 5 provides the second quantitative analysis, this time choosing a period of high congressional disunity in order to focus on the congressional interest hypothesis. Using two novel measures of congressional interest, I find that an increase in the salience of a type of aid or recipient country is associated with an increase in bureaucratic fragmentation.

Chapters 6 through 8 develop in-depth case studies to qualitatively examine the mechanisms. The cases in these chapters vary in congressional interest and disunity. First, Chapter 6 selects a case in which salience and disunity were extremely high. The vote-buying theory would predict high levels of bureaucratic fragmentation. Throughout the case, the qualitative and quantitative evidence make it clear that the fragmentation that resulted came about *because of*, rather than *despite*, congressional interest.

Chapter 7 also presents a case of high salience and disunity. Unlike the case in Chapter 6, this case occurred at a time of divided-party government, which rules out party politics as an alternative explanation. The fragmentation in this case can be clearly traced to congressional disunity, both qualitatively and quantitatively. The new programs created in this case were disproportionately introduced by moderate legislators and designed to build a legislative coalition.

Finally, Chapter 8 shows that vote-buying is not necessary when Congress lacks a strong interest in the topic. The chapter presents a case in which congressional interest was low, while disunity was still relatively high. The resulting fragmentation was relatively low. Interestingly, the political conflicts that existed in this case tended to lie along party lines. This partisanship decreased the need for vote-buying by creating a simple policy coalition. Additionally, the lack of congressional interest in the area was enough to make disunity unimportant. This suggests that both aspects may need to be present for fragmentation to occur.

Combined, these empirical chapters provide quantitative and qualitative tests of all three hypotheses. The quantitative chapters focus on congressional disunity and congressional interest. The qualitative chapters provide a deeper understanding of how these hypotheses lead to the resulting fragmentation. The large-*n* and small-*n* analyses in this book are designed to provide several sources of evidence for the main theory and to show why alternative explanations fail to explain the phenomenon.

3.8 Conclusion: A Theory of Foreign Aid Fragmentation

This chapter outlined the theoretical mechanisms leading from political preferences to congressional legislative bargaining, and, finally, to foreign aid fragmentation. Foreign aid is one of Congress's most powerful foreign policy tools. Congressional leaders, who generally want to have some say in foreign policy, therefore have an incentive to craft and push a foreign aid agenda. They often resort to side payments to induce legislators to support that agenda. These side payments can come in many forms, but one such form is the diversion of funding to smaller agencies, or the creation of new agencies altogether, to draw support. This form of side payment has the unintended consequence of increasing fragmentation in the resulting bill.

This theory explicitly centers foreign policy fragmentation within the legislative branch. It considers intra-branch conflict as the major barrier to foreign policy coherence. Specifically, disagreement among Congress's centrists—the most common pivot points in policymaking—is an important barrier to negotiation. In contrast, it would be possible to center a theory of fragmentation on inter-branch divisions or on simple bureaucratic inertia. I consider these competing explanations throughout the book, finding little evidence that they are driving foreign aid policy. However, these alternative explanations are important to consider, and I will revisit them in each chapter.

Chapter 4

Congressional Disunity and Bureaucratic Fragmentation

This chapter begins the empirical portion of the book with a quantitative test of the *disunity* hypothesis. In this chapter, I hold congressional interest constant by selecting a subset of bills—annual appropriations bills—that are inherently of high interest to Congress. This allows me to isolate variation over time in congressional *disunity*. I measure the heterogeneity of moderate legislators, as well as the voting behavior of moderate legislators, in Congress.

I find both bill-level and legislator-level evidence in favor of the vote-buying theory of bureaucratic fragmentation. I begin by restating the hypothesized expectations drawn from Chapter 3. I then introduce the novel data set that I am using in this chapter. I outline the methods and show the statistical results, which describe variation in foreign aid bills, as well as legislative votes on those bills. I conclude with a consideration of what these findings may mean in the larger context of the book, as well as in American politics.

4.1 Theoretic Expectations

In Chapter 3, I introduced two testable hypotheses that will be relevant in this chapter. First, recall that the magnitude of vote-buying increases with the ideological heterogeneity of moderate legislators. In turn, this vote-buying increases the fragmentation of the resulting legislation. The first hypothesis, therefore, predicts that an increase in moderate heterogeneity should increase budgetary fragmentation.

Hypothesis 1 *When moderate legislators are more ideologically heterogeneous, foreign aid fragmentation should increase.*

Competing for Foreign Aid. Shannon P. Carcelli, Oxford University Press. © Oxford University Press (2025).
DOI: 10.1093/9780197799284.003.0004

The theory also provides a secondary hypothesis, testing the mechanisms at a different level of analysis. Recall the expectations about the congressional beneficiaries of foreign aid fragmentation. According to the vote-buying theory, fragmentation is an attempt to pull fence-sitters into a coalition behind the leadership's agenda, and moderate legislators are the members most likely to be on the fence. This would suggest that moderate legislators benefit most from foreign aid fragmentation because they are seeing their pet projects represented. Therefore, they should be more likely to support legislation the more fragmented it is.

Hypothesis 2 *Moderate legislators will be more likely to vote in favor of a foreign aid bill when that bill is more fragmented.*

These two testable hypotheses provide an opportunity to witness the mechanisms, but they do not provide a real-world definition of bureaucratic fragmentation. In Section 4.2, I more clearly define bureaucratic fragmentation and describe two components of the phenomenon. I then operationalize it, introducing a new annual-level data set of fragmentation in foreign aid appropriations.

4.2 The Two Components of Bureaucratic Fragmentation

As described in Chapter 2, I define bureaucratic fragmentation as a *relatively thin spread of foreign aid funding between many independent bureaucratic agents*. Bureaucratic fragmentation is a complex phenomenon, but two major components are crucial to this definition. First, fragmentation requires the creation of new agencies: its definition presupposes the existence of multiple independent bureaucratic agents. High bureaucratic fragmentation is only possible in the presence of many discrete bureaucracies. As outlined previously, fragmentation was low in 1961, before many of today's foreign aid programs came into existence. In the interim, the United States has created a number of new aid agencies, which has increased aid fragmentation. Although the creation of new aid agencies certainly contributes to fragmentation, it is not the lone contributor. In fact, agency creation can often be a poor measure of aid fragmentation. It is a relatively rare event and is sporadic. Throughout US history, the country has often gone many years without creating an agency and then created several agencies in a single year.

Additionally, not all new agencies contribute to fragmentation equally. New agencies are sometimes created and not used, which diminishes their power to fragment. The relative importance of an agency creation event requires subjective knowledge and can be difficult to measure. Therefore, it is difficult to use agency creation in any quantitative test of bureaucratic fragmentation. Agency creation can be useful as a qualitative measure, and it can provide an opportunity to witness the mechanisms behind the theory as a whole. In later chapters, I do just that. However, in the present chapter I take a different approach by studying another component of fragmentation.

This second component of bureaucratic fragmentation, which is easier to test quantitatively, is the spread of aid funding between existing agencies. Many of the problems associated with aid fragmentation in the literature assume that no single agency is effective in coordinating foreign aid. The problems of fragmented aid tend to stem from collective action problems and lack of coordination between agencies.

Therefore, the spread of funding can be just as important as the number of agencies involved. A hierarchical bureaucratic system, in which several agencies exist but one is the undeniable lead agency, is very different from one in which all agencies are relatively equal. The latter creates more fragmented policy than the former. The spread of foreign aid funding between agencies is more objective and provides a cleaner annual measure. Congress passes foreign aid bills every year, which allows for annual variation and annual observations. Therefore, the quantitative evidence outlined below will be driven by a measure of the spread of foreign aid funding among agencies, rather than the creation of new aid agencies.

4.3 Measuring Foreign Aid Fragmentation

Based on the definitions above, a quantitative test of the hypotheses requires an annual-level dataset of the spread of funding among bureaucratic agencies in foreign aid bills. To create such a dataset, I go straight to the source: congressional appropriations bills. Appropriations bills are pieces of annual legislation that must be passed in order to fund the government. They are written and debated by subcommittees of the Appropriations Committees in the House and Senate. The subcommittee that crafts aid-related appropriations is the Foreign Operations Subcommittee. These bills provide a good source of data for this project because they specifically list agency funding levels, they are consistent over time, and they provide a measure of Congress's preferences. Existing foreign aid datasets do not have these benefits.

A major challenge in measuring aid fragmentation is separating the signal from the noise. In order for a dataset to properly measure aid fragmentation, it must capture the breakdown of independent foreign aid projects by agency for every year since at least 1961, when USAID was first created. Such a long time frame is difficult to find. A recent push by the US government and several international organizations has made government-released foreign aid data increasingly transparent and reliable.[1] Although these efforts have increased data reliability in the twenty-first century, much in-depth foreign aid expenditure data is either lost to history or remains to be dug up.

The state-of-the-art dataset of US foreign aid expenditures is the USAID data development library (DDL) platform. The creation of this platform has rapidly increased data availability and precision over the past decade.[2] However, it remains imperfect. Most importantly, the agency-level data are inconsistent over time and difficult to interpret. USAID's online platform only reports implementing agency data going back to 2001.[3] Its downloadable data are much more detailed, with in-depth records even beyond 1961. However, as these data move further back in time, they become increasingly imprecise. "Unknown" and "USAID Greenbook" (the name of a historical data source) are listed as the most common "agencies" in the early years of the USAID DDL data. It should come as no surprise that this is problematic for anyone seeking a consistent record of changes over time. As data reporting standards have improved over time, so has the precision of agency-level data. Even if no changes to fragmentation were made over the past decades, USAID's DDL would erroneously report increasing fragmentation, due to changing data quality standards over the decades.

Furthermore, aid expenditure data reported through USAID are noisy and don't always represent the reality of bureaucratic relationships. For example, the DDL reports agency-level programs that were in fact controlled by USAID, as being controlled by other agencies. Many US agencies

[1] See, for example, the 2016 Foreign Aid Transparency and Accountability Act (Saldinger 2016) and the Department of State's efforts since 2004 (McMahon 2007).

[2] Ziadeh (2016)

[3] EADS (2015)

use their expertise to serve in a foreign aid contractor role under USAID and other large agencies. For example, the US Postal Service (USPS) has consulted with USAID and the Department of Defense on several mail security projects. USAID's DDL often reports these projects as being independently run by USPS.

However, collaborations such as these, in which smaller agencies report directly to USAID, do not fit into the definition of fragmentation because agencies are not acting independently. The hierarchical structure of these contractor relationships, and the centralized responsibility of USAID avoids the problems associated with fragmentation.[4] An increase in within-government contracting does not represent an increase in bureaucratic fragmentation. The USAID DDL's inclusion of programs such as these finds fragmentation where it does not exist. At best, this leads to random noise, and, at worst, it will systematically bias fragmentation measures in years when within-government contracting was high.[5]

In order to avoid the pitfalls of missing information and noisy agency contracting, I compiled a novel dataset measuring the fragmentation of spending in the annual foreign operations appropriations bills. This dataset offers at least two benefits for studying the fragmentation of US foreign aid over time. First, data availability is consistent over time. Foreign aid legislation has funded various agencies since at least the time of USAID's creation. Unlike USAID's DDL, historical appropriations legislation does not show more missing values for earlier years. Therefore, measures of fragmentation should not change over time simply because of data availability, as they do in the DDL.

Second, the appropriations dataset more accurately measures fragmentation in the independent actions of agencies. Each appropriations bill specifies the total funds for which each agency is ultimately accountable. Rather than including smaller projects that a specific agency simply collaborated on, appropriations legislation only includes the funds that each individual agency controls by legislative mandate. Within-government contracts,

[4] In fact, these relationships might provide a template for overcoming foreign aid fragmentation.

[5] Another source of noise in the DDL data is its sensitivity to bureaucratic vagaries. The executive branch, with its various layers of bureaucracy, has a lot of input into actual spending and delegation decisions, making policy outcomes a noisy measure of congressional will. A cleaner measure of US government intentions for the purpose of this work is the content of the legislation that comes directly from Congress. However, future research can and should begin capturing the determinants of over-fragmentation by the bureaucracy.

and other hierarchical relationships between agencies, will not appear as an increase in fragmentation in this dataset. The data only measure the fragmentation of ultimate agency control.

Finally, this dataset is ideal for this particular theory because it isolates the foreign aid bills that are of greatest *interest* to Congress, allowing me to isolate and test the *disunity* hypothesis. Appropriations bills are one of the most crucial types of legislation in Congress. They must pass in order for government to run at all. Also, in foreign aid, appropriations is one major area through which Congress legislates. If congressional leadership were ever to be motivated to buy votes, it would be through appropriations bills. By using this type of legislation, I am able to assume high levels of congressional interest for all of the bills in the data set.

To create this measure of bureaucratic fragmentation in US foreign aid appropriations, I read and coded all annual foreign operations appropriations bills that Congress has produced since 1961.[6] For each bill, I noted the name of each budget line, the agency of allocation, and the dollar amount appropriated to each line. For example, if a paragraph of the appropriations bill were to read:

> FOREIGN MILITARY FINANCING PROGRAM
> For expenses necessary for grants to enable the president to carry out the provisions of section 23 of the Arms Export Control Act, \$3,650,000,000: Provided, that of the funds appropriated under this heading, not less than \$2,040,000,000 shall be available for grants only for Israel, and not less than \$1,300,000,000 shall be made available for grants only for Egypt.

I would code the program as Foreign Military Financing (FMF), a part of the Department of Defense, and the total amount of aid as \$3,650,000 (in the unit of 1000 USD). This process provided me with a list of every program that Congress has funded since 1961, which I could aggregate to determine the dollar amount to which Congress funded each agency in each year. The unit of the appropriations dataset is the budget code-year, but I aggregated up to the agency-year for the purposes of this chapter. The annual Foreign Operations appropriations bill explicitly funds several dozen programs in

[6] I collected the bill text from Congress.gov; for older bills, I used govtrack.us or obtained the information directly from print archives at the Library of Congress.

twelve unique agencies. On average, 59.9% of appropriations go through USAID.[7] Agencies and funding levels (in billion USD), are presented in Figure 4.1.

Figure 4.2 plots the total economic and security aid appropriated over time. With few exceptions, the trends for security and economic assistance were generally similar until 2000. Both types of assistance increased shortly after Ronald Reagan took the presidency in 1981. That spike lasted until the fall of the Soviet Union, when security aid levels retreated. However, economic aid continued to grow throughout the post-Cold War period. At least half of the Reagan-era spike was driven by an increase in the FMF budget, which was funded at $750 million in Reagan's first year and would rise to $5 billion by George H. W. Bush's presidency. FMF was an important source of funding for Nicaraguan rebels and continues to be used to fund political allies, especially Israel and Egypt.

Another clear trend is the total increase in economic assistance at the beginning of the twenty-first century. There were two reasons for this. First, the George W. Bush era witnessed an increase in conservative interest in foreign aid. Bush himself was a huge proponent of development, health, and humanitarian projects, even those with very little strategic appeal. Second, the attacks of September 11, 2001, and the wars they

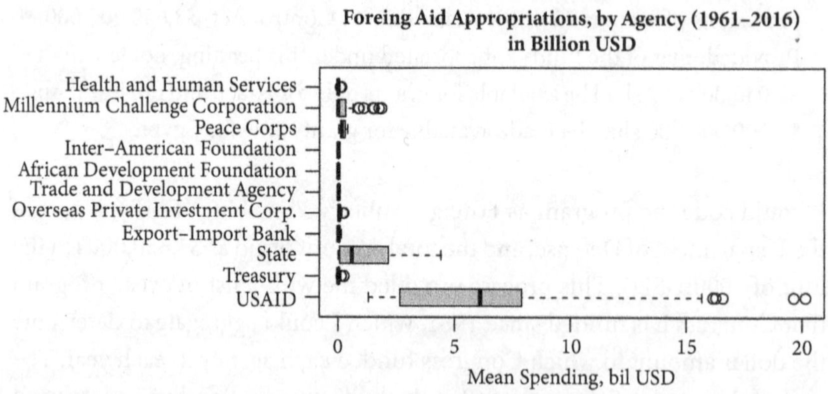

Figure 4.1 Agency-year spending in foreign aid appropriations bills, 1961–2016.

[7] Compare this to the Netherlands, which channels 97% of its foreign aid projects through its Ministry of Foreign Affairs, according to data from AidData (Tierney et al. 2011).

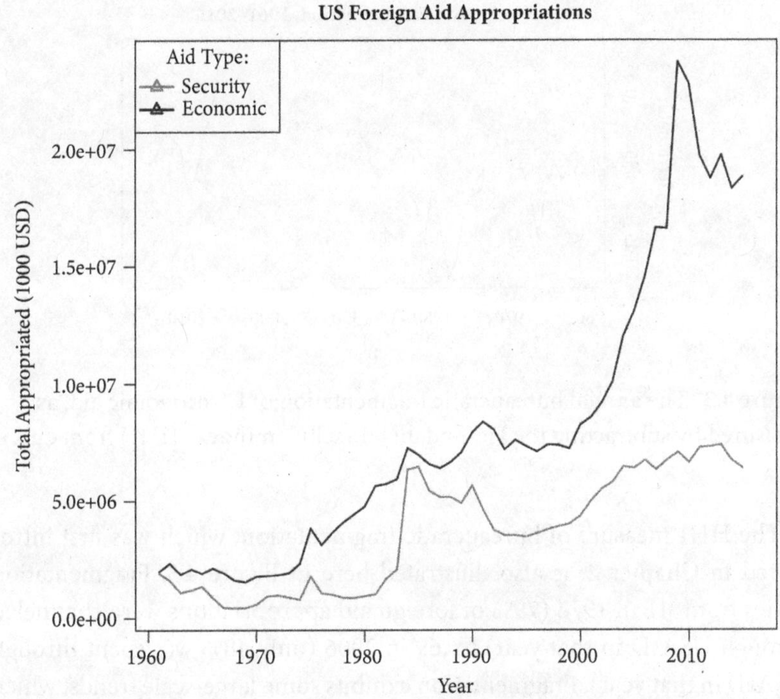

Figure 4.2 Total United States economic and security aid appropriated through the Foreign Operations Subcommittee, 1961–2016.

sparked, increased all international spending. Foreign aid, both economic and security, constituted a large part of the plan to rebuild Iraq and Afghanistan after the wars began. This will become relevant in Chapter 5.

In order to test the hypotheses above, I measure fragmentation by calculating the spread in budget share across all US agencies devoted to foreign economic aid, as measured by the HHI of the Foreign Operations Appropriations budget. The HHI is a common measure of aid fragmentation in the economics literature. It is calculated by summing the squared market share of each firm; therefore, it is bounded by zero and one. A high HHI indicates that one agency has a large share of the total budget, meaning the state has low fragmentation. In order to simplify interpretation, I subtracted the HHI from one to determine the absence of a market monopoly of foreign aid. This value—one minus the HHI—measures the overall fragmentation of Congress's foreign aid budget.

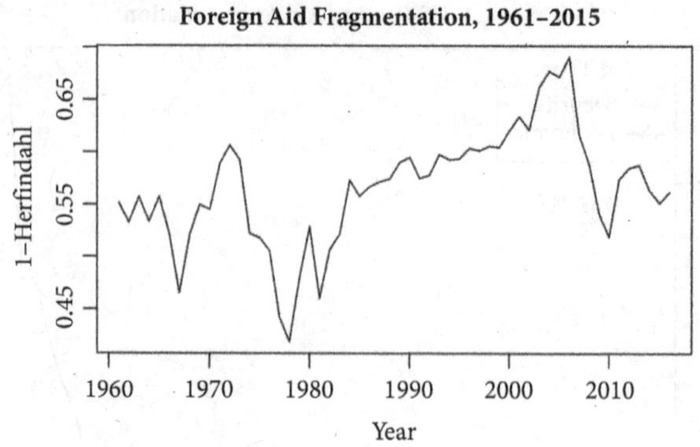

Figure 4.3 The annual bureaucratic fragmentation of US economic aid, as measured by subtracting the Herfindahl–Hirschman Index (HHI) from one.

The HHI measure of bureaucratic fragmentation, which was first introduced in Chapter 2, is also illustrated here in Figure 4.3. Fragmentation varies from .41 in 1978 (79% of foreign aid appropriations were channeled through USAID in that year) to .69 in 2006 (only 48% was spent through USAID in that year). Fragmentation exhibits some large-scale trends, which also follow the trends of party power in Congress.

4.4 Congressional Voting on Foreign Policy

The second hypothesis requires a dataset of legislative votes to complement the previous data set. Figure 4.4 presents data on House roll call final votes for all Foreign Operations appropriations bills between 1961 and 2016, the bills that were used to create the fragmentation data.[8] Each point in the figure represents an individual legislator. The horizontal axis reflects the legislator's mean first-dimension DW-Nominate score, which represents ideological liberalism or conservatism.[9] Lower Nominate scores are associated with more liberal legislators. It should come as no surprise, then, that the blue circles on this figure (representing Democrats) are further left than the red triangles (Republicans).

[8] Data from 1988 to 2001 were generously provided by Crespin and Rohde (2010) and the rest were collected from https://voteview.com. The data set excludes omnibus bills and only includes final votes on foreign aid appropriations legislation.

[9] See Poole and Rosenthal (1991) for more on this measure.

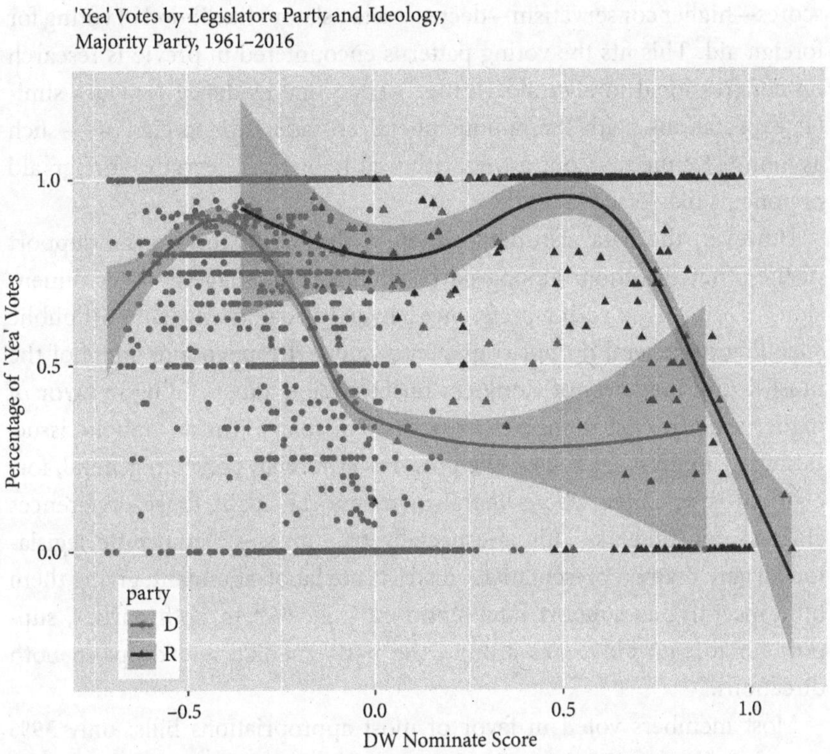

Figure 4.4 Votes on Foreign Operations appropriations bills, 1961–2016, by legislator. Red (Republican) and blue (Democrat) lines represent the smoothed loess curves for each party's ideology-vote relationship.

The vertical axis represents the percentage of Foreign Operations appropriations bills that the given legislator supported during his or her tenure. Note that many legislators fall on either 0 or 1 on this axis. That means that these legislators voted for either none or all of the Foreign Operations appropriations bills. The majority of legislators fall in the middle: they voted "yea" on some bills and "nay" on others. The figure also includes smoothed loess curves for both Republicans and Democrats (in red and blue, respectively). These curves help to provide a sense of the voting behavior among various ideologies. Areas where the curve is higher indicate that legislators with a given ideology more strongly supported Foreign Operations appropriations bills, on average. Note the nonlinear voting patterns in both parties (as evidenced by the single-peaked curves). For both Democrats and Republicans, higher-than-average DW-Nominate scores—higher conservatism—decrease a legislator's likelihood of voting for foreign aid. This fits the voting patterns encountered in previous research on congressional foreign aid voting.[10] Anecdotal evidence provides similar expectations, with the famous liberal crusaders for foreign aid—such as John F. Kennedy—contrasting with well-known conservative foreign aid opponents like Jesse Helms.

However, the data also demonstrate a decline in foreign aid support in the other direction: among party liberals. This suggests other dimensions of foreign aid voting preferences. Even legislators who support public spending in general do not consistently support foreign aid. Some of the most liberal members of Congress reject foreign aid spending in favor of higher spending on domestic programs. For many, it is a symbolic issue. Because Congress often has little power over foreign policy in general, foreign aid is one area where liberal members can make those preferences clear to constituents. This is especially true among Democratic legislators, where many representatives' districts are labor-abundant, giving them little incentive to support interventionist policies.[11] In both parties, support for foreign aid peaks around the party median and drops in both directions.

Most members voted in favor of most appropriations bills: only 39% were "nay" votes. However, the figure highlights some areas of variation. Democrats were more likely to vote in favor of a bill (68.7%) than Republicans (51.3%). Unsurprisingly, members of the majority party were much more likely to vote for a bill than the minority party (72.4% and 45.5%, respectively). What the raw data cannot show is *why* some of these legislators failed to support their parties' agendas, and why others supported bills outside their ideological preferences. This is where the hypothesis tests will be useful.

4.5 Hypothesis Tests

I will use these two datasets to test the two hypotheses outlined above. The first dataset includes annual-level covariates, and the second varies

[10] Fleck and Kilby (2001); Milner and Tingley (2010)
[11] Milner and Tingley (2011)

on the legislator-year. For the first dataset, the dependent variable is the fragmentation of a Foreign Operations appropriations bill. In the second dataset, the dependent variable is legislator votes on those same bills.

To construct the primary independent variable, the size of the moderate policy space, I calculate the interquartile range (IQR) of DW-Nominate scores in a given Congress.[12] I use the legislative voting dataset to test Hypothesis 2. This includes a binary measure of each legislator's "moderation," coded as a 1 if the legislator's DW-Nominate score falls within a given Congress's IQR and 0 if it does not.

The hypotheses require two sets of statistical tests. Recall from Hypothesis 1 that greater ideological heterogeneity increases fragmentation. The statistical model therefore considers the correlation between the ideological range of moderate legislators and fragmentation. Due to the time series nature of the budgetary data, these statistical tests are estimated using an ARIMA (AR1) model. Alternative model specifications can be found in the appendix to this chapter.

The legislative voting model, Hypothesis 2, includes an interaction term. I expect moderate legislators to be the most likely to change their votes in response to vote-buying, as they are the most likely beneficiaries of said vote-buying. Diverting funding to smaller agencies that represent a specific set of interests and policies will increase the likelihood that moderates support a bill i indexes every legislator in the dataset, and t indexes the bills. Models also include state fixed effects for each legislator (i) and congress fixed effects for each bill (t). The estimating equation for the legislative voting model is below, with most variables varying on the legislator-vote (it).

$$Vote_{it} = \beta_0 + \beta_1\, Moderation_{it} + \beta_2\, Fragmentation_t +$$
$$\beta_3\, Moderation_{it} * Fragmentation_t + State_i + Congress_t + \varepsilon_{it}$$

The coefficient of interest is β_3, the interaction between bill fragmentation and the "moderation" of the policymaker. I expect this coefficient to be positive: moderate legislators will be more likely to support more fragmented bills. I used an ordinary least squares model with standard errors clustered at the vote level.[13]

[12] See Poole and Rosenthal (1991) for more on DW-Nominate.
[13] See the Appendix (Section 4.8) for a variety of other models.

4.6 Statistical Results

The results support both expectations of the vote-buying theory. First, foreign aid fragmentation is highest in years in which vote-buying should theoretically be highest: when moderate legislators are spread out and difficult to please through policy change. Second, moderate legislators, who are generally the least likely to support aid legislation, are more likely to support a bill when it is more fragmented. The results and details are outlined below.

4.6.1 Fragmentation

Table 4.1 evaluates Hypothesis 1. It shows that the greater the ideological spread of moderate legislators, the more fragmented the foreign aid budget. Model 1 shows a bivariate relationship between a heterogeneous moderate wing and fragmentation in the resulting appropriations bill. This result holds in Models 2 and 3, which control for other ideological factors and a lagged dependent variable.

The coefficient on Moderate Spread is greater in the models that include control variables. In these models, a one-unit increase in the IQR increases fragmentation by around one unit. In the barest model, a one-standard-deviation change in the independent variable corresponds to a change of 0.03 in fragmentation, a little over half a standard deviation. Even this smaller coefficient relates to a non-negligible substantive effect.

The control variables also show a few trends. The strongest results from the controls have to do with the role of congressional and presidential ideology and party. A more conservative Congress (higher DW-Nominate) leads to greater fragmentation in all models. A one-unit increase in congressional DW-Nominate increases a bill's fragmentation by around 0.2 units. Republicans tend to be more skeptical of foreign aid and prefer that it be used for domestic economic purposes.[14] Therefore, it is unsurprising, although interesting, that a Republican majority would be more willing to bypass USAID and increase the budget, perhaps for things like defense or energy. The presidential ideology and party results are mixed. Although a more liberal president tends to be associated with greater fragmentation, Republican

[14] Milner and Tingley (2010)

Table 4.1 Generalized least squares results using AR(1) model. Models 2–3 examine the correlation between divided-party government and fragmentation.

	Dependent Variable: Fragmentation (1–HHI)		
	(1)	(2)	(3)
Moderate Spread (IQR)	0.366***	0.975**	1.172***
	(0.093)	(0.435)	(0.421)
Divided Govt.		−0.054***	−0.042**
		(0.019)	(0.017)
Inter-Party Distance		−0.730	−1.051**
		(0.546)	(0.520)
Change in Med. Ideology		0.005	−0.002
		(0.057)	(0.056)
Cold War		−0.059	−0.036
		(0.037)	(0.033)
War		0.033*	0.030*
		(0.018)	(0.016)
Maj. Size (House)		0.001	0.001
		(0.001)	(0.001)
Majority SD		−1.071	−0.894
		(0.911)	(0.823)
Number of Agencies		0.002	0.003
		(0.003)	(0.003)
Cong. Median DW-Nom		0.339**	0.364***
		(0.145)	(0.123)
Pres. DW-Nom		−0.209**	−0.160**
		(0.089)	(0.073)
Cong. Party (R)		0.003	−0.008
		(0.037)	(0.033)
Pres. Party (R)		0.306**	0.222**
		(0.120)	(0.098)
Total Aid Budget		−0.002	−0.002
		(0.004)	(0.004)
Year		−0.001	−0.002
		(0.004)	(0.004)
Lagged DV			0.301**
			(0.131)
Constant	0.020	2.979	3.910
	(0.070)	(8.765)	(7.542)
Observations	56	55	55

Note: *p<0.1; **p<0.05; ***p<0.01

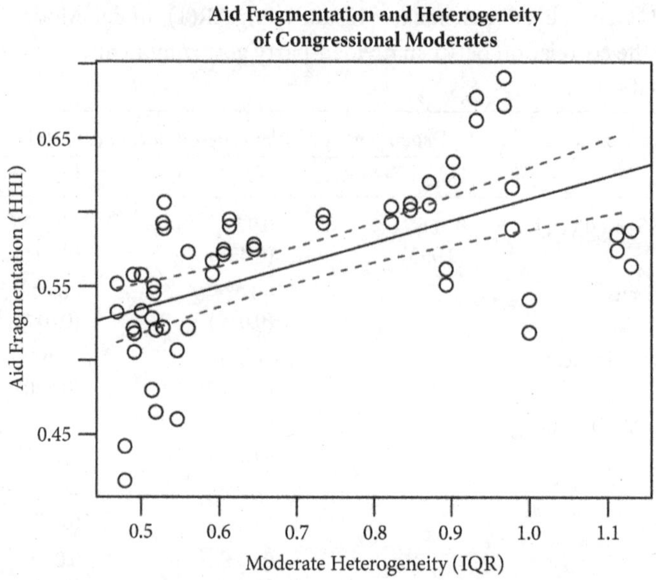

Figure 4.5 Higher ideological heterogeneity among moderate legislators (as measured by the DW-Nominate difference between the 75th and 25th percentiles) is associated with a more fragmented foreign aid bill.

presidents tends to preside during times of greater fragmentation. This suggests that different types of presidents may respond differently to foreign aid bills but can provide little systematic explanation of presidential positions.

Figure 4.5 displays the main results graphically in a scatterplot of all observations. An increase in the size of the moderate region is associated with an increase in bureaucratic fragmentation.

4.6.2 Legislative Voting

The second set of tests examine Hypothesis 2 to explain voting patterns in fragmented foreign aid bills. Model 1 in Table 4.2 shows that, overall, moderate legislators are less likely to support a foreign aid bill, while co-partisans of the president are generally more supportive of foreign aid. This tracks with previous research: moderates are generally the most difficult legislators to convince to follow the party line, and co-partisans of the president tend to be more in favor of providing funding for foreign policy, however

Table 4.2 Ordinary least squares estimates of the interaction between ideological moderation and fragmentation of a foreign aid bill, with standard errors clustered at the state level. Model 1 shows coefficients without interactions. Interactions in Models 2–4 show that moderate legislators are more likely to support fragmented legislation. This is not necessarily true of non-moderates, as shown by the inconsistent coefficient on the "Fragmentation" variable.

	Dependent Variable: "Yea" Vote on Appropriations Legislation			
	(1)	(2)	(3)	(4)
Moderate	0.044**	−0.078**	−0.118***	−0.064*
	(0.019)	(0.037)	(0.034)	(0.034)
Fragmentation	0.538***	0.305	−0.131	−0.633**
	(0.149)	(0.202)	(0.395)	(0.287)
Moderate xFragmentation		0.464***	0.558***	0.470***
		(0.151)	(0.139)	(0.145)
FA Committee			0.086**	0.067*
			(0.040)	(0.040)
App. Committee			0.023	0.035**
			(0.020)	(0.018)
Election			0.003	−0.002
			(0.036)	(0.012)
Aid Budget			4.075	13.901**
			(6.565)	(5.728)
Pres. Party (R)			−0.003	0.017
			(0.038)	(0.210)
War			0.009	−0.082**
			(0.046)	(0.040)
Cold War			−0.094	0.024
			(0.093)	(0.041)
Party (R)			−0.140**	−0.134**
			(0.055)	(0.060)
Constant	0.475***	0.536***	0.737***	0.587***
	(0.037)	(0.045)	(0.158)	(0.036)
Fixed Effects				State, Congress
Observations	13,344	13,344	13,328	13,328
Adjusted R^2	0.021	0.025	0.049	0.172

Note: *p<0.1; **p<0.05; ***p<0.01

the president chooses to spend it. Model 1 also suggests that vote-buying is doing its job: legislators as a whole are more likely to vote for a bill the more fragmented it is.

The interactive coefficients in Models 2–4, show how these votes can change in the face of a fragmented bill. Moderate legislators are more likely to support a fragmented bill than an unfragmented bill. This is true after adding control variables and state- and congress-level fixed effects. In contrast, non-moderates, if anything, are *less* likely to support a fragmented bill (as evidenced by the negative coefficient on "Fragmentation" in Model 4).

The control variables also trend in the expected directions. Placement on the Foreign Affairs and/or Appropriations Committees increases a legislator's likelihood of supporting a foreign aid bill, probably because these committees also give legislators power to include their own pet projects in the legislation. Unsurprisingly, Republican legislators are significantly less likely to support a foreign aid bill than Democratic legislators.

To ease interpretation of the interaction coefficients, Figure 4.6 presents a marginal means plot with predicted probabilities, drawing from Model 3. In this plot I separate majority-party moderates from party non-moderates and calculate each group's probability of voting in favor of a bill given the bill's

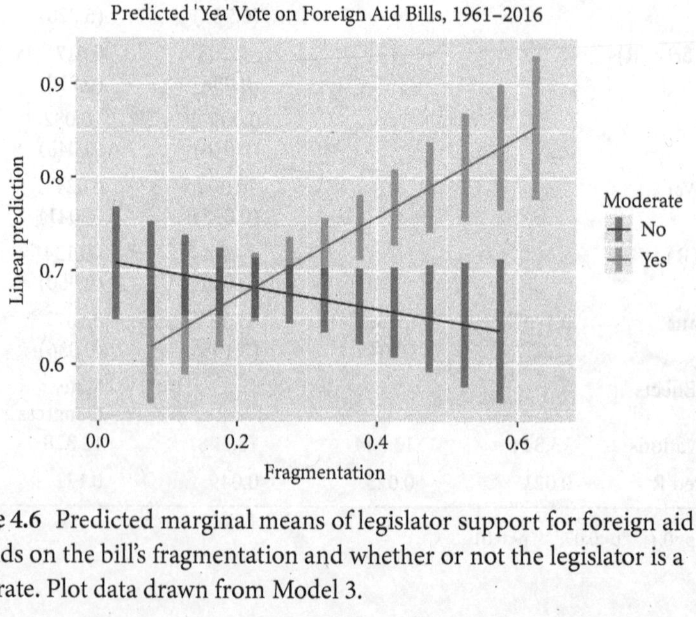

Figure 4.6 Predicted marginal means of legislator support for foreign aid bills depends on the bill's fragmentation and whether or not the legislator is a moderate. Plot data drawn from Model 3.

level of fragmentation. According to this figure, a non-fragmented bill would gain some support from party extremists and little support from moderates. As fragmentation increases, moderates become more likely to support the bill. At a hypothetical fragmentation level of 0.15 (near the first quartile), the two groups are indistinguishable. However, by the time bills reach a fragmentation level of 0.35 (just below the third quartile), moderates are significantly more likely to support the bill than non-moderates.

4.7 Discussion and Conclusion

As a whole, the statistical results support the vote-buying theory of fragmentation. Fragmentation increases with the heterogeneity of moderate legislators. The vote-buying theory is also supported by the legislative voting data. As the theory would suggest, moderate legislators are significantly more likely to support a bill that is fragmented than an unfragmented bill. This implies that moderates are the disproportionate beneficiaries of fragmentation-causing pet projects.

This chapter speaks to the literature on congressional vote-buying in several ways. First, by considering novel methods of congressional vote-buying, the theory suggests that previous work may have underestimated the benefits that parties provide to their moderate members. If earmarks and campaign contributions are indeed substitutes for allocations to pet-project agencies, then the latter may be replacing the former.

Second, this potential substitution effect of earmarks and fragmentation suggests that the recently increasing opposition to earmarks could be driving further government fragmentation. As the use of traditional earmarks loses political viability, leaders will be driven to new methods of vote-buying, including budgetary fragmentation. Tightening the budget could lead to more fragmentation. It is worth considering the costs and benefits of various methods of vote-buying before for swearing off one method altogether.

This theory is potentially generalizable to other policy domains. Foreign aid is not the only policy that combines policy goals with concentrated, particularistic benefits. Nor is it the only policy domain that has suffered criticism for its fragmented nature. Fragmentation of policy instruments pervades much of US government today, even outside of foreign aid. A much-publicized 2011 report by the Government Accountability Office (GAO) brought to light dozens of examples of inefficiencies caused by government fragmentation in foreign aid and elsewhere.[15] Since then, leaders from both parties have been struggling and campaigning to clear up the bureaucracy. However, their efforts have done little to pinpoint the root causes of the problem and have therefore been ineffective. This research suggests that policymakers may have been going about it the wrong way.

The relative absence of systematic research on the political causes of policy fragmentation gives policymakers little information to work with. As government waste increases in salience, both in political campaigns and in congressional oversight, it is up to political scientists to identify the causes of this phenomenon. Public understanding of the roots of the problem would give Congress more room to provide inventive- and evidence-based solutions.

Although this chapter does not offer hypotheses or statistical tests on how to reverse the process of bureaucratic fragmentation, it lays the groundwork toward suggesting potential ways forward. If Congress wishes to better control agencies, leadership must consider the full consequences of how it is overcoming legislative hurdles. In order to create more streamlined foreign policy, leadership has a few options. Congress can create institutions further limiting the domestic policies relevant to foreign aid. This would decrease the number of dimensions on foreign aid votes, thus making intra-party compromise easier. Alternatively, leadership can further attempt to increase bipartisanship, attracting votes from the minority party. Although the government appears a long way off from taking these policy steps, the first step is knowing the sources of the problem.

The strength of these quantitative tests is their ability to track large-scale political trends. The weakness of this approach is the problem mentioned above: the hypothesis tests only show indirect support of the theory. In order to see the theoretical mechanisms more directly, later chapters will take a more qualitative approach. Rather than simply showing large-scale trends, the three case studies later in the book provide more immediate evidence of the theory.

First, however, Chapter 4 introduces a second set of quantitative tests, focusing on the congressional interest hypothesis. While the present chapter

15 Dodaro (2011)

focuses on high-interest legislation—appropriations bills—and examines variation in congressional unity, Chapter 5 will do just the opposite. I will draw from a time period of high congressional disunity—the twenty-first century—and examine variation in congressional interest. I will introduce a dataset that considers variation in congressional interest by issue area and recipient country and measure the resulting levels of bureaucratic fragmentation. Chapter 5 will therefore complement the current chapter by examining the second dimension of the theory

4.8 Appendix

In the appendix below, I report the results from a series of robustness tests and provide more information on the data.

4.8.1 Alternative Model Specifications

Due to the time series nature of the data, the main text in this chapter analyzes the data using an ARIMA model. In this section, I replicate the results using a variety of other models. In Table 4.3, I display results using a multilevel model due to the nested structure of the data, much of which is constant for each Congress. In Table 4.4, I display results using an ordinary least squares model. Finally, due to the censored nature of the data (the fragmentation level can never fall below 0), in Table 4.5, I show the results using a Tobit model. The main findings are robust to all model specifications.

Finally, in Table 4.6 I substitute Newey–West standard errors for the generalized least squares model in the main body of the chapter, as a different method of addressing autocorrelation. I find the results to be robust to both models. As in the ARIMA model, first-order autocorrelation (AR(1)) is appropriate. A first-order Breusch–Godfrey test provides a test statistic of 28.05, with a very low p-value, while a second-order test only increases the test statistic to 28.54. Additionally, the inclusion of a lagged dependent variable in the model decreases the test statistic to 2.33, with a p-value of 0.12.

I also include an alternative set of voting models, using a logit model due to the binary dependent variable. The results of these models, found in Table 4.7, are similar to the ordinary least squares results.

Table 4.3 Results using a multilevel model with Congress random intercepts. Models 1–3 test the correlation between a high IQR of DW-Nominate scores and fragmentation in the resulting foreign aid bill. Models 4–6 substitute the middle third as a measure of moderate spread. Models 1 and 3 include observations for all annual appropriations bills between 1961 and 2016. The rest of the models drop the first observation (1961) due to the inclusion of lagged covariates.

	Dependent Variable: Fragmentation (1–HHI)					
	(1)	(2)	(3)	(4)	(5)	(6)
Moderate Spread (IQR)	0.459***	1.028**	1.195***			
	(0.053)	(0.505)	(0.391)			
Moderate Spread (Mid 1/3)				0.479***	0.807**	0.756***
				(0.052)	(0.330)	(0.286)
Divided Govt.		−0.028*	−0.021*		−0.028*	−0.024*
		(0.015)	(0.012)		(0.015)	(0.013)
Inter-Party Distance		−0.853	−1.129**		−0.694	−0.693*
		(0.623)	(0.489)		(0.471)	(0.411)
Change in Med. Ideology		−0.105*	−0.020		−0.081	−0.014
		(0.062)	(0.067)		(0.061)	(0.065)
Cold War		−0.038	−0.007		−0.047	−0.032
		(0.036)	(0.033)		(0.035)	(0.033)
War		0.047***	0.039**		0.041**	0.033**
		(0.016)	(0.016)		(0.016)	(0.016)
Maj. Size (House)		0.0004	0.001*		0.0002	0.001
		(0.001)	(0.001)		(0.001)	(0.001)
Majority SD		−1.464**	−1.244**		−1.208**	−1.016*
		(0.595)	(0.486)		(0.580)	(0.525)
Number of Agencies		0.002	0.002		0.001	0.002
		(0.003)	(0.003)		(0.003)	(0.003)
Cong. Median DW-Nom		0.394***	0.334***		0.269**	0.225*
		(0.123)	(0.098)		(0.129)	(0.115)
Pres. DW-Nom		0.014	−0.002		0.016	0.006
		(0.015)	(0.013)		(0.014)	(0.014)
Total Aid Budget		−0.004	−0.004		−0.004	−0.004
		(0.003)	(0.002)		(0.003)	(0.003)
Year		−0.002	−0.002		0.001	0.0003
		(0.003)	(0.003)		(0.003)	(0.003)
Lagged DV			0.385***			0.287**
			(0.131)			(0.136)
Constant	−0.040	4.546	4.584	0.011	−0.674	−0.315
	(0.039)	(6.315)	(5.278)	(0.032)	(6.306)	(5.772)
Observations	56	55	55	56	55	55
Log Likelihood	83.887	65.185	67.109	85.088	65.576	66.379

Note: *p<0.1; **p<0.05; ***p<0.01

Table 4.4 Results using an ordinary least squares model. Models 1–3 test the correlation between a high IQR of DW-Nominate scores and fragmentation in the resulting foreign aid bill. Models 4–6 substitute the middle third as a measure of moderate spread. Models 1 and 3 include observations for all annual appropriations bills between 1961 and 2016. The rest of the models drop the first observation (1961) due to the inclusion of lagged covariates.

	Dependent Variable: Fragmentation (1–HHI)					
	(1)	(2)	(3)	(4)	(5)	(6)
Moderate Spread (IQR)	0.459*** (0.039)	1.020** (0.430)	1.209*** (0.390)			
Moderate Spread (Mid 1/3)				0.479*** (0.039)	0.824*** (0.278)	0.756*** (0.263)
Div. Gov't.		−0.030** (0.013)	−0.019 (0.012)		−0.029** (0.013)	−0.023* (0.012)
Inter-Party Distance		−0.794 (0.526)	−1.125** (0.483)		−0.687* (0.403)	−0.691* (0.379)
Change in Med. Ideology		−0.021 (0.070)	−0.038 (0.063)		−0.014 (0.067)	−0.024 (0.063)
Cold War		−0.021 (0.036)	−0.007 (0.033)		−0.035 (0.034)	−0.028 (0.032)
War		0.048*** (0.016)	0.037** (0.015)		0.042** (0.016)	0.034** (0.015)
Maj. Size (House)		0.0004 (0.001)	0.001* (0.001)		0.0003 (0.001)	0.001 (0.001)
Majority SD		−1.663*** (0.524)	−1.307*** (0.483)		−1.312** (0.506)	−1.028** (0.489)
Number of Agencies		0.001 (0.003)	0.002 (0.003)		0.0003 (0.003)	0.002 (0.003)
Cong. Median DW-Nom		0.388*** (0.108)	0.340*** (0.098)		0.252** (0.113)	0.223** (0.107)
Pres. DW-Nom		0.017 (0.013)	−0.002 (0.013)		0.019 (0.012)	0.005 (0.013)
Total Aid Budget		−0.004 (0.003)	−0.003 (0.002)		−0.005* (0.003)	−0.004 (0.002)
Year		−0.002 (0.003)	−0.003 (0.003)		0.001 (0.003)	0.0003 (0.003)
Lagged DV			0.405*** (0.123)			0.312** (0.124)
Constant	−0.040 (0.029)	4.308 (5.988)	5.623 (5.391)	0.011 (0.023)	−1.492 (5.931)	−0.360 (5.596)
Observations	56	55	55	56	55	55
R^2	0.718	0.920	0.937	0.740	0.925	0.936
Adjusted R^2	0.713	0.895	0.915	0.735	0.902	0.913

Note: *p<0.1; **p<0.05; ***p<0.01

Table 4.5 Results using Tobit model with dependent variable censored at 0 and 1. Models 1–3 test the correlation between a high IQR of DW-Nominate scores and fragmentation in the resulting foreign aid bill. Models 4–6 substitute the middle third as a measure of moderate spread. Models 1 and 3 include observations for all annual appropriations bills between 1961 and 2016. The rest of the models drop the first observation (1961) due to the inclusion of lagged covariates.

	Dependent Variable: Fragmentation (1–HHI)					
	(1)	(2)	(3)	(4)	(5)	(6)
Moderate Spread (IQR)	0.459*** (0.038)	1.020*** (0.371)	1.209*** (0.333)			
Moderate Spread (Mid 1/3)				0.479*** (0.038)	0.824*** (0.240)	0.756*** (0.224)
Div. Gov't.		−0.030*** (0.011)	−0.019* (0.010)		−0.029*** (0.011)	−0.023** (0.010)
Inter-Party Distance		−0.794* (0.454)	−1.125*** (0.412)		−0.687** (0.348)	−0.691** (0.323)
Change in Med. Ideology		−0.021 (0.060)	−0.038 (0.054)		−0.014 (0.058)	−0.024 (0.054)
Cold War		−0.021 (0.031)	−0.007 (0.028)		−0.035 (0.030)	−0.028 (0.028)
War		0.048*** (0.014)	0.037*** (0.013)		0.042*** (0.013)	0.034*** (0.013)
Maj. Size (House)		0.0004 (0.001)	0.001** (0.0005)		0.0003 (0.0005)	0.001 (0.0004)
Majority SD		−1.663*** (0.452)	−1.307*** (0.412)		−1.312*** (0.437)	−1.028** (0.417)
Number of Agencies		0.001 (0.002)	0.002 (0.002)		0.0003 (0.002)	0.002 (0.002)
Cong. Median DW-Nom		0.388*** (0.094)	0.340*** (0.084)		0.252*** (0.098)	0.223** (0.091)
Pres. DW-Nom		0.017 (0.011)	−0.002 (0.011)		0.019* (0.010)	0.005 (0.011)
Total Aid Budget		−0.004* (0.002)	−0.003 (0.002)		−0.005** (0.002)	−0.004* (0.002)
Year		−0.002 (0.003)	−0.003 (0.002)		0.001 (0.003)	0.0003 (0.002)
Lagged DV			0.405*** (0.105)			0.312*** (0.106)
Constant	−0.040 (0.028)	4.308 (5.170)	5.623 (4.598)	0.011 (0.023)	−1.492 (5.121)	−0.360 (4.772)
Observations	56	55	55	56	55	55

Note: *p<0.1; **p<0.05; ***p<0.01

Table 4.6 Replication of main findings using Newey–West standard errors.

	Dependent Variable: Fragmentation (1–HHI)					
	(1)	(2)	(3)	(4)	(5)	(6)
Moderate Spread (IQR)	0.459*** (0.128)	1.086** (0.413)	1.195*** (0.407)			
Moderate Spread (Mid 1/3)				0.479*** (0.126)	0.806** (0.307)	0.753*** (0.271)
Div. Gov't.		−0.028* (0.014)	−0.021** (0.009)		−0.029* (0.015)	−0.024** (0.012)
Inter-Party Distance		−0.928* (0.511)	−1.129** (0.488)		−0.698 (0.462)	−0.691* (0.395)
Change in Med. Ideology		−0.088** (0.033)	−0.020 (0.037)		−0.048 (0.039)	0.008 (0.042)
Cold War		−0.025 (0.046)	−0.007 (0.045)		−0.038 (0.037)	−0.025 (0.033)
War		0.054*** (0.013)	0.039*** (0.012)		0.045*** (0.013)	0.033*** (0.012)
Maj. Size (House)		0.0005 (0.0003)	0.001** (0.0005)		0.0003 (0.0002)	0.001 (0.0003)
Majority SD		−1.484*** (0.375)	−1.244*** (0.302)		−1.209*** (0.406)	−1.015*** (0.347)
Number of Agencies		0.001 (0.002)	0.002 (0.002)		0.001 (0.003)	0.001 (0.002)
Cong. Median DW-Nom		0.392*** (0.075)	0.334*** (0.044)		0.256** (0.125)	0.216** (0.082)
Pres. DW-Nom		0.012 (0.010)	−0.002 (0.014)		0.017 (0.011)	0.005 (0.013)
Total Aid Budget		−0.004** (0.002)	−0.004** (0.001)		−0.005** (0.002)	−0.004** (0.002)
Year		−0.001 (0.003)	−0.002 (0.001)		0.001 (0.003)	0.001 (0.002)
Lagged DV			0.385*** (0.140)			0.315** (0.134)
Constant	−0.040 (0.079)	3.067 (4.993)	4.584 (2.931)	0.011 (0.062)	−2.177 (6.091)	−0.747 (3.775)
Observations	55	55	55	55		

Note: *p<0.1; **p<0.05; ***p<0.01

Table 4.7 Replication of legislator-level tests using a logit model. The positive coefficient on the interaction is robust to both methods.

	Dependent Variable			
	(1)	(2)	(3)	(4)
Moderate	0.222***	−0.350***	−0.527***	−0.404***
	(0.077)	(0.135)	(0.130)	(0.146)
Fragmentation	2.570***	1.504*	0.253	−2.962**
	(0.763)	(0.890)	(1.884)	(1.487)
Moderate x Fragmentation		2.294***	2.697***	2.914***
		(0.567)	(0.508)	(0.594)
FA Committee			0.312*	0.221
			(0.188)	(0.223)
App. Committee			0.199**	0.262***
			(0.094)	(0.101)
Election			0.073	−0.031
			(0.166)	(0.064)
Aid Budget			9.942	157.629***
			(31.395)	(39.239)
Pres. Party (R)			−0.077	−1.828
			(0.179)	(1.231)
War			0.056	−0.469*
			(0.205)	(0.244)
Cold War			−0.326	0.054
			(0.454)	(0.251)
Party			−0.584**	−0.647*
			(0.254)	(0.342)
Constant	−0.197	0.074	0.778	0.006
	(0.175)	(0.195)	(0.758)	(0.261)
Fixed Effects				State, Congress

Note: *p<0.1; **p<0.05; ***p<0.01

4.8.2 Extreme Bounds Analysis

To ensure that the results were not driven by model specifications, I used the "ExtremeBounds" package[16] to determine the robustness of the main estimators in the face of various combinations of covariates. The histograms for the year-level and legislator-level models are visible in Figures 4.7 and 4.8, respectively. As is clear in these figures, the coefficient for the moderate range falls significantly above zero with most combinations of covariates. This suggests that the results are not being driven by the variables included in the models.

[16] Hlavac (2016)

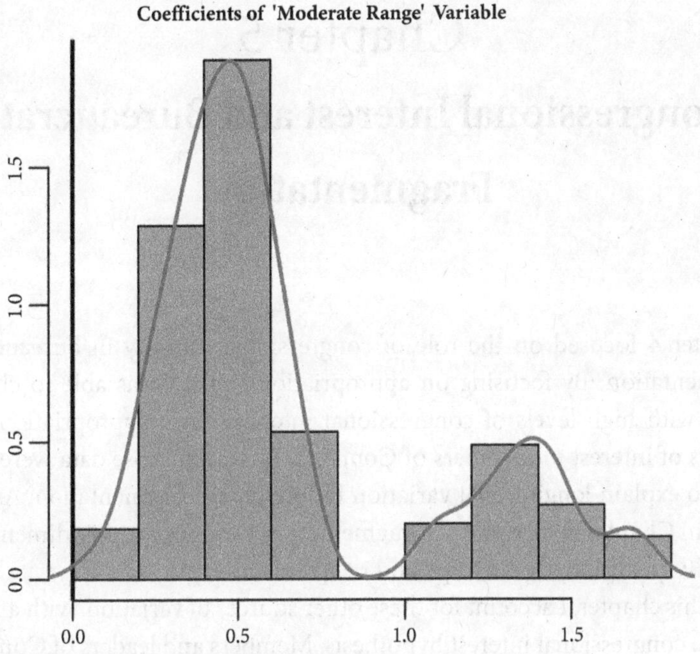

Figure 4.7 Coefficients on "Moderate Range" variable with different combinations of covariates.

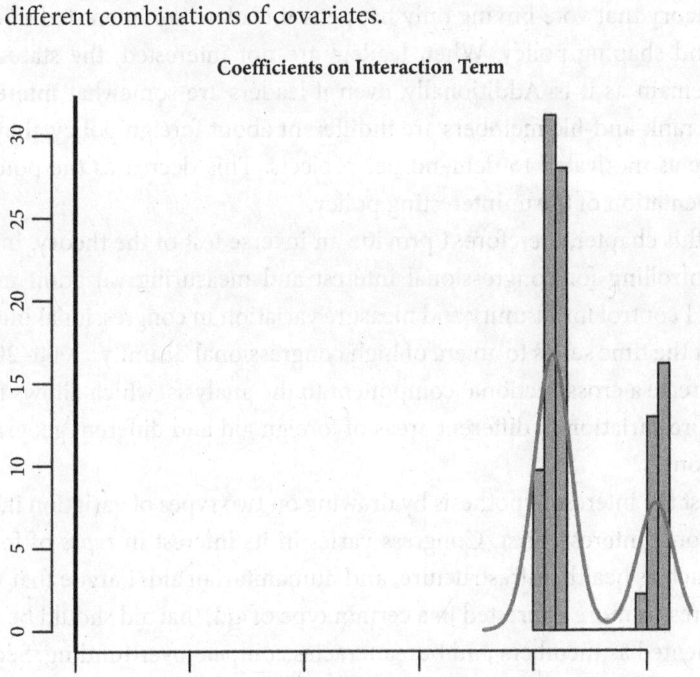

Figure 4.8 Coefficients on interaction variable with different combinations of covariates.

Chapter 5
Congressional Interest and Bureaucratic Fragmentation

Chapter 4 focused on the role of congressional disunity in bureaucratic fragmentation. By focusing on appropriations bills, I was able to choose cases with high levels of congressional interest, since appropriations are always of interest to members of Congress. However, those data were only able to explain longitudinal variation in foreign aid fragmentation. As was clear in Chapter 2, foreign aid's fragmentation varies over other dimensions as well; specifically, by aid type and recipient country.

In this chapter, I account for these other sources of variation, with a focus on the congressional interest hypothesis. Members and leaders of Congress are not equally interested in all areas of foreign aid policy. Recall from the theory that vote-buying only happens if leaders are interested in crafting and shaping policy. When leaders are not interested, the status quo can remain as it is. Additionally, even if leaders are somewhat interested, when rank-and-file members are indifferent about foreign policy, they will not be as motivated to demand pet projects. This decreases the potential fragmentation of the uninteresting policy.

In this chapter, therefore, I provide an inverse test of the theory. Instead of controlling for congressional interest and measuring variation in disunity, I control for disunity and measure variation in congressional interest. I limit the time series to an era of high congressional disunity: 2000–2015. I also create a cross-sectional component to the analysis, which allows me to measure variation in different areas of foreign aid and different geographic locations.

I test the interest hypothesis by drawing on two types of variation in congressional interest. First, Congress varies in its interest in *types* of foreign aid, such as health, infrastructure, and humanitarian aid. I argue that when Congress is more interested in a certain type of aid, that aid should be more fragmented as members and bureaucracies compete over funding. Second, I consider variation in congressional interest in the *recipients* of foreign aid.

Competing for Foreign Aid. Shannon P. Carcelli, Oxford University Press. © Oxford University Press (2025).
DOI: 10.1093/9780197799284.003.0005

Some countries and regions are inherently more interesting to Congress than others. I argue that higher levels of congressional interest in a foreign aid recipient state should increase fragmentation in that country, all else being equal.

The remainder of this chapter develops these recipient- and topic-level measures of congressional interest to test the vote-buying theory of fragmentation. I use panel data and draw largely on cross-sectional variation. The data in all cases provide evidence for the vote-buying theory, showing that higher congressional interest is associated with more bureaucratic fragmentation in foreign aid.

5.1 Measures of Congressional Interest

I created two novel datasets as proxies for topic- and recipient-specific congressional interest in foreign aid. First, I consider the inputs: the factors that drive congressional motivation. Specifically, I look at the levels of foreign aid lobbying from the public and private sectors working in specific topics and mentioning specific aid recipients. I code the identities of authors of lobbying reports involving US foreign assistance and match these categories to the fragmentation of reported aid flows. Second, I more directly measure congressional interest through a form of congressional oversight: congressionally commissioned GAO reports. When Congress commissions a report focused on a specific country, then it is safe to suppose that country is more interesting to Congress. I introduce the data sets in greater detail, and discuss the statistical analysis, below.

5.1.1 Inputs: Congressional Lobbying

Members of Congress become interested in foreign policy for many reasons, such as personal preferences, constituent demands, and lobbyist pressure. In this section, I consider the latter pathway to congressional interest. When companies and organizations lobby for specific foreign policy demands, they can shape the preferences of members. Lobbyists might inform members on the issues relevant to their congressional districts, tug at their heartstrings, or seek to persuade members of a specific point of view. Lobbyists vary in their goals: some wish to increase their organization's foreign aid contracts while others simply want to ensure that vulnerable people are being helped. In foreign aid, lobbyists can come from the private or public sector, they can be interested in broad or narrow aspects, and they can speak to various members of the legislative and executive branches.

Lobbying in foreign aid comes from several sources, such as private companies hoping to profit from foreign aid contracts, NGOs trying to drive aid policy in step with their agenda, or foreign governments trying to increase aid delivery or decrease restriction in their home countries. Lobbying in foreign aid is a big business. A majority of foreign aid lobbying comes from public entities and NGOs. Unlike most lobbying in the US government, 86% of which comes from corporations and trade associations,[1] the private sector only accounts for about half as much foreign aid lobbying as the non profit sector.

The magnitude of lobbying in a given issue area could be both a cause and an effect of congressional interest. The number of lobbyists involved in a specific topic can arise from a variety of sources. Famously, Gray and Lowery (1996) suggest that the size of the special interest community is self-regulating. If and only if there are constituencies not being served by existing interest groups, will new interest groups emerge to represent them. The most important check on lobbyists, according to this thinking, is other competing lobbyists, although regional variables also matter.[2]

If this is true, then lobbying could be a driver of congressional interest. Lobbyists can provide information to lawmakers regarding the viability and popularity of legislation. Not only can this information influence legislative voting,[3] it can also influence which policies are introduced in the first place.[4]

Conversely, some scholars highlight what they call the "demand" side of lobbying, suggesting that lobbyists arrive when Congress is interested in a policy area.[5] Congress itself, according to this research, is a driver of lobbying efforts. For example, congressional hearings, an indicator of congressional interest, can increase the number of lobbyists in an issue area.[6] Berkman (2001) finds that more professionalized legislatures, who often have their own staff to provide them with information that lobbyists would otherwise

[1] De Figueiredo (2004)
[2] Gray and Lowery (1998)
[3] See Hojnacki et al. (2012) for a survey of some of this literature.
[4] Lorenz (2020)
[5] Leech et al. (2005); Baumgartner et al. (2011)
[6] Baumgartner et al. (2009)

provide, are less likely to demand lobbying. This also appears to be true over time in Congress, where staff have decreased over time, with commensurate increases in revolving-door lobbyists.[7]

Regardless of the causal direction, the literature generally agrees that congressional lobbying is an indicator of congressional interest.[8] Another benefit of using lobbying as a proxy for congressional interest involves the targeting of lobbying activity. While the lobbying reports used in this chapter cannot determine which individual members were lobbied, there is much literature suggesting that congressional moderates[9] and agenda-setters[10] are likely targets. There is no reason to suppose that foreign aid lobbying should be any different. According to the vote-buying theory, policy interest by both of these groups can lead to fragmentation. Interest by the leadership leads to a greater incentive to shape policy, and interest among moderates encourages them to seek pet projects. Insofar as those two groups are the targets, their interest in policy will be associated with lobbying.

To develop a list of lobbying reports involving foreign aid legislation, I downloaded data from the LobbyView project[11] that include the terms "foreign aid" or "foreign assistance." This provided me with a list of 1400 lobbying reports submitted between 2000 and 2018. I coded each of the reports for several characteristics. First, I determined the industry in which each lobbyist operated using the NAICS codes listed on their lobbying reports. Next, I determined the foreign aid topic of interest, by industry.[12] Figure 5.1 shows the average annual lobbying expenditures, in millions, spent by foreign aid lobbyists working on each topic of interest. The plot differentiates between public/NGO and private companies, which tend to specialize in different areas.

The category with the greatest annual lobbying expenditures is "Infrastructure." This includes government contractors who take on projects in the developing world, as well as other service companies working abroad,

[7] LaPira and Thomas (2017)

[8] This is true in foreign policy as well, where the constellation of lobbyists impacts the bipartisanship of national security policies (Tama 2024).

[9] Austen-Smith and Wright (1994)

[10] Hojnacki and Kimball (1998)

[11] See Kim (2018) for more information on LobbyView. All United States federal lobbyists are legally mandated to report their expenditures in written reports. The LobbyView project digitizes and sorts information from these lobbying reports.

[12] The universe of topics come from a typology of aid established by the OECD DAC reporting requirements.

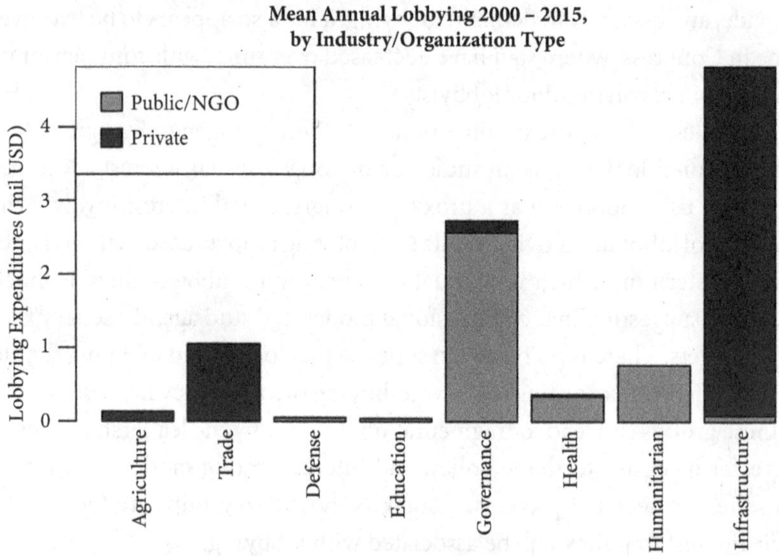

Figure 5.1 Mean annual lobbying expenditures by US companies and organizations working in specific topic areas of foreign aid. Private companies' lobbying is darker, and not-for-profit organizations' lobbying is lighter.

such as those in the telecommunications and banking sectors. Some infrastructure lobbyists are environmentally oriented organizations promoting sustainable development. However, most of the spending on infrastructure lobbying, perhaps unsurprisingly, comes from the private sector.

The "Governance" category is the second-largest. This includes lobbyists concerned with issues of human rights, sanctions, and other organizations seeking to support or coerce foreign governments to carry out specific actions. The largest groups lobbying on governance issues tend to be focused on Israel, such as the American Israeli Political Action Committee. Very few for-profit organizations engage in lobbying for governance-related issues. The non profit sector is also more likely to spend lobbying dollars on "Humanitarian" and "Health" issues. This includes NGOs focusing on disaster relief, refugees, and other issues dealing with basic survival. Nearly all humanitarian lobbying comes from the public sector and NGOs, rather than the private sector. In contrast, a majority of private-sector lobbying falls in the "Infrastructure" and "Trade" categories.

I used the same reports to determine country-level lobbying decisions. For each country, I created a binary measure of whether that country is mentioned in a lobbying report in a given year. Twelve percent of countries are

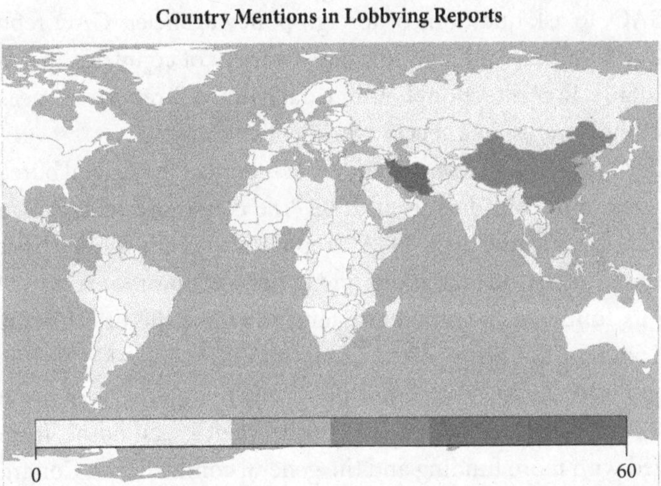

Figure 5.2 Number of times states were mentioned in aid-related lobbying reports from 2000 to 2018.

mentioned in these reports in any given year. The mean country had six mentions over the 18-year period for which data are available.

The state with by far the most lobbying, mentioned in 54 reports, was Iran. Many of the reports discussing Iran involved nuclear weapons and treaties, as well as human rights issues. Israel and China were also mentioned quite often, with 42 and 32 mentions, respectively. All three of these countries involve issues that Congress discusses a lot; therefore, it is understandable that they would be the object of a lot of lobbying. They are also countries of high congressional interest.

For the purposes of the analysis, I counted the number of lobbyists for each topic in each year from 2000 to 2015. I included both private- and public-sector lobbyists in the data set, aggregating to the topic-year and country-year units and running separate statistical models for each. I expect bureaucratic fragmentation at both the topic and recipient level to increase as lobbying increases. Because Congress makes spending decisions one year in advance, I use lobbying data from the previous year to predict fragmentation.

5.1.2 Outputs: Congressional Oversight

Congress expresses interest in specific topics or countries through the oversight decisions it makes. Crucially, Congress can order inspectors, such as the GAO, to ask questions of foreign policy agencies. GAO reports are ordered by Congress and tend to cover a variety of countries and topics in foreign affairs. In this section, I outline data on GAO reports as measures of congressional interest in a specific recipient country.

The GAO is an independent agency that monitors the federal bureaucracy for Congress and considers itself to be "the congressional watchdog"[13] or Congress's "investigative arm."[14] GAO reports are commissioned by congressional committees, who seek audits and reviews of how the executive branch is using its funding. They therefore tend to reflect the priorities of members of Congress. The power of the Comptroller General—GAO's head—has waxed and waned over time, with a politically imposed lack of resources in the 1990s. However, in 2004, the GAO underwent a rebranding, from which it emerged with more funding and the general confidence of Congress.[15]

Since 2011, the GAO has kept an online database of its reports and recommendations. I drew from this database information on all GAO reports involving "international affairs." The GAO data set includes 155 recommendations set by 53 recent GAO reports on the topic. The largest share of these recommendations (54) was directed toward the Defense Department, with the State Department (50) as a close second. USAID (13), DHS (12), and 10 other agencies were also subject to GAO reports. Thirty countries were mentioned in GAO reports.

Based on foreign aid expenditures alone, it is clear that Congress has an interest in the states where it commissions oversight reports. The mean annual aid expenditures to GAO-mentioned countries ($1.2 billion) is nearly an order of magnitude higher than the mean for non-mentioned countries ($190 million). GAO reports could, therefore, be both a cause and an effect of congressional interest. Regardless of the causal relationship, the presence of GAO-commissioned reports can serve as a proxy for congressional interest in a country.

Once again, I am agnostic about the *reasons* behind congressional oversight. Most work that has attempted to explain Congress's decision to conduct oversight has considered the role of divided-party government in spurring congressional action.[16] Kriner and Schickler (2016) expanded this line of analysis but continued to focus on variation over time. Less is

[13] www.gao.gov/about
[14] Kaiser (2007, p. 1)
[15] Kaiser (2007)
[16] Most famously, Mayhew (1991) found no relationship between divided government and the number of important oversight hearings.

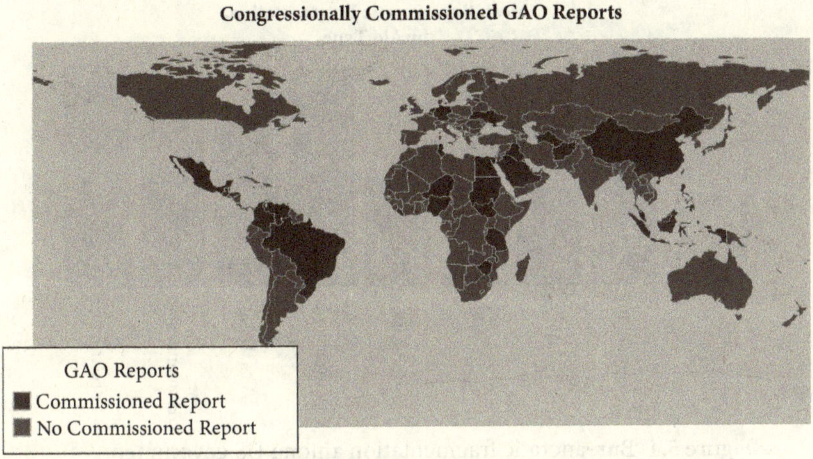

Figure 5.3 Countries that were subjects of GAO Reports, 2011–2021.

known about why Congress would choose to investigate one country versus another. The reasons behind Congress's choice, however, are less important than the fact that Congress makes the choices it does. For whatever reason, Congress investigates some countries more than others. This, I argue, is an expression of congressional interest.

Most GAO reports, even in the area of "international affairs," have little to do with foreign aid topics. Therefore, it is more appropriate to aggregate to country-level variation in these reports. This variation is outlined in Figure 5.3. While countries in every region have been the topic of a report, it appears that Congress shows the most interest in Central and South America and Southeast Asia. In Section 5.2 I investigate how this variation relates to fragmentation.

5.2 Dependent Variable: Topic- and Country-Level Fragmentation

While the appropriations data set used in Chapter 4 provides the most consistent measure of bureaucratic fragmentation over time, it does not include country- or topic-level variation. Therefore, for this chapter I instead draw from USAID's DDL.[17] Due to the concerns expressed in Chapter 4 regarding the reliability of older data, I focus in this chapter

[17] EADS (2015)

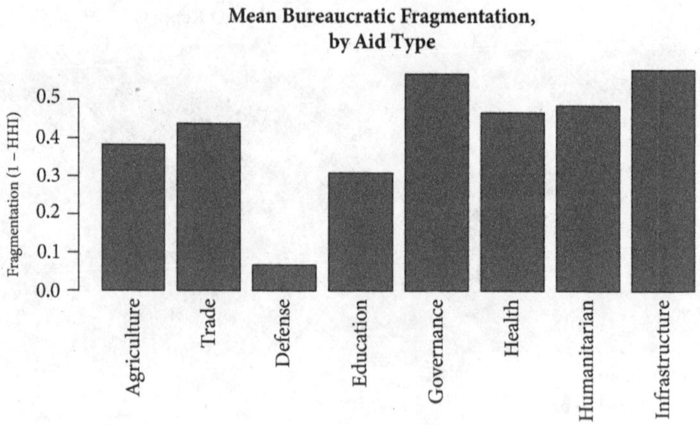

Figure 5.4 Bureaucratic fragmentation among US government agencies' funding for foreign aid projects, by category.

on the twenty-first century (2001 to 2020), when data quality was higher. This period should provide a relatively consistent picture of foreign aid fragmentation.

I disaggregate aid spending by topic and by country. This allows me to develop topic- and country-specific measures of foreign aid fragmentation. To develop the categories of foreign aid interest, I drew from aid categories reported to the OECD Development Assistance Committee (DAC). These categories included "Agriculture," "Commodity Assistance" (or "Trade"), "Education," "Governance," "Health and Population," "Humanitarian," and "Infrastructure."[18] I also introduced a new category to cover security-related appropriations and lobbying, which I call "Defense."

As discussed in Chapter 2, certain categories of foreign aid are performed in a more fragmented manner than others. For example, infrastructure projects are carried out by 13 separate agencies. The mean infrastructure budgets allocated to each agency range from $73 million for the IAF to $11.7 billion for the Department of the Army. In contrast, defense aid has the lowest level of fragmentation, with most aid being spent either through the Defense Department or the State Department. Figure 5.4 displays the topic-level variation, introduced in Chapter 2, once again.

[18] The DAC also includes catch-all categories of "Economic Development" and "Other," but I excluded these from the topic-specific models for being too general for this project.

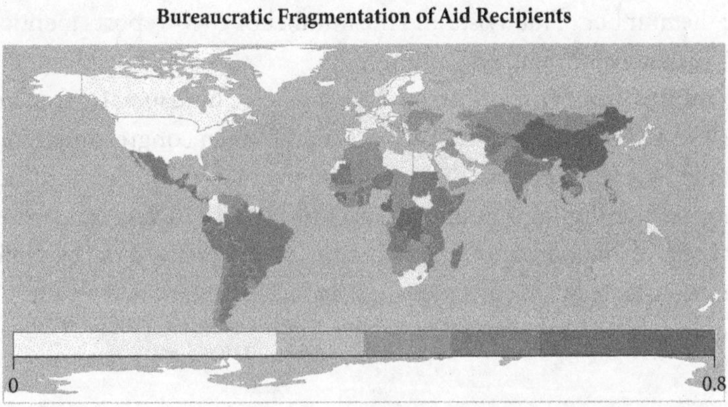

Figure 5.5 Bureaucratic fragmentation (1 – HHI) of foreign aid within recipient states. Darker grey is associated with higher levels of fragmentation.

The other source of variation introduced in Chapter 2 is the bureaucratic fragmentation of US aid within a recipient state. Recipient-level fragmentation also varies quite a bit in this time period. Figure 5.5 once again displays the bureaucratic fragmentation of US foreign aid funding to worldwide recipients, with darker coloring associated with greater levels of fragmentation.

The recipient states with the lowest levels of fragmentation tend to be states with very low foreign aid levels. Small states like Anguilla and Bermuda have only received aid from one US agency, and wealthy states like Canada are unlikely to receive much aid at all. The states with the highest fragmentation levels tend to be in Central America, although the most fragmented US recipient is China. Both measures of bureaucratic fragmentation also vary over time, as was evident in Chapter 4. Therefore, some of the statistical tests reported in this chapter consider the topic-year or state-year as the unit of analysis.

5.3 Statistical Results

The statistical models in this chapter all consider fragmentation (either at the topic or state level) as the dependent variable of interest. The independent variables are the two measures of congressional interest outlined above: the number of lobbyists and the number of GAO reports mentioning a particular topic or recipient country.

The results support the vote-buying theory of bureaucratic fragmentation. All results show a positive relationship between congressional interest in a topic or country and consequent fragmentation of the bureaucracy working on that topic or country. The specific tests, using the two proxies for congressional interest and two units of analysis, are outlined below. Tests are conducted using ordinary least squares estimation, with alternative estimations found in the appendix.

5.3.1 Lobbying

The first set of statistical results consider lobbying as the independent variable, using both the topic-year and country-year units. As shown in Table 5.1, all models demonstrate a positive and statistically significant relationship between lobbying reports and fragmentation. The first three models vary on the country-year, and the last three vary on the topic-year level. Because it is rarer for lobbying reports to mention specific countries, the independent variable in the first three models is binary: coded as 1 if any lobbying reports mentioned the given country in the given year and 0 otherwise. The independent variable in the last three models is the dollar amount (in billions).

When a country goes from not being mentioned in a lobbying report to being mentioned, the fragmentation of its incoming US aid increases by around 0.1. This represents a change of nearly half a standard deviation (0.23) in the fragmentation variable. This number is relatively consistent throughout the models. A billion-dollar increase in spending for a topic of foreign aid increases the fragmentation within that topic by 10 standard deviations. This, of course, is a very large substantive effect.

It is worth considering the coefficients on the time-varying control variables considered in Chapter 4. The shortened time series decreases the power of these variables in some models. First, an increase in the heterogeneity of moderate legislators is positively associated with fragmentation in the topic-level models. This matches the findings from Chapter 4 and supports the vote-buying theory, although it is not robust to the country-year models. The inconsistency of the moderate range variable is unsurprising considering the fact that all years in this time period exhibited a relatively

Table 5.1 Ordinary least squares estimates of lobbying and bureaucratic fragmentation (1 – HHI), standard errors clustered by state. Lobbying variables are lagged one year. Models 1–3 display results for recipient-year models, and Models 4–6 display topic-year results.

	Dependent Variable: Bureaucratic Fragmentation					
	Recipient Fragmentation			**Topic Fragmentation**		
	(1)	**(2)**	**(3)**	**(4)**	**(5)**	**(6)**
Lobbying (Y/N)	0.107***	0.100***	0.102***			
	(0.023)	(0.024)	(0.024)			
Lobbying (bil USD)				22.185***	19.664***	21.982***
				(8.328)	(5.558)	(5.613)
Recipient Aid (bil USD)		0.002	0.002			
		(0.003)	(0.003)			
Aid Approp. (bil USD)		0.002			0.001	
		(0.002)			(0.004)	
GDP (tril USD)		–0.036	–0.036			
		(0.028)	(0.027)			

continued

Table 5.1 *continued*

	Dependent Variable: Bureaucratic Fragmentation					
	Recipient Fragmentation			**Topic Fragmentation**		
	(1)	**(2)**	**(3)**	**(4)**	**(5)**	**(6)**
Battle Deaths (mil)		−0.020	−0.532			
		(0.746)	(0.744)			
Disaster Loss (bil)		40.093***	39.603***			
		(11.268)	(10.704)			
Div. Gov.		0.033***			−0.170***	
		(0.010)			(0.036)	
Mod. Range		−0.054			1.463***	
		(0.066)			(0.239)	
Topic Aid (bil USD)					−0.006	−0.009
					(0.007)	(0.007)
Constant	0.377***	0.367***	0.351***	0.387***	−0.748***	0.307***
	(0.014)	(0.079)	(0.019)	(0.059)	(0.161)	(0.096)
Year Fixed Effects			Yes			Yes
Observations	1714	1664	1664	119	119	119
Mult. R-2	0.032	0.049	0.637	0.067	0.227	0.772

Note: *p <0.1; **p<0.05; ***p<0.01

high moderate range. Nearly all values of the variable in the 2000–2015 time period fall above the *third quartile* of moderate ranges in the previous chapter's data set. Therefore, the precise value of this coefficient is difficult to gauge.

The only country-specific control variable that provides a consistent result is the presence of a natural disaster, which is associated with higher levels of bureaucratic fragmentation. There are a few potential explanations for this finding. First, a natural disaster might increase the complexity of problems in a recipient state, requiring a wider variety of responses. If so, this would suggest that some bureaucratic fragmentation arises from the actual needs of recipient states. However, it is possible that natural disaster damage increases the salience of a country to Congress. It is well known that interest in foreign aid increases after a natural disaster, leading to greater public and private expenditure.[19] Natural disaster damage, therefore, might simply be another proxy for congressional interest. If so, then this finding provides additional evidence for the vote-buying theory.

5.3.2 Government Accountability Office (GAO) Reports

The next set of results considers Congress's commissioning of reports from the GAO. These data draw from 155 reports from 2011 to 2021. The categories of these GAO reports are too broad to draw specific foreign aid topics, as they are not all related to foreign aid. However, they do mention 36 specific countries, and therefore, I use the recipient country as the unit in this analysis, with a binary measure of GAO mentions. When a GAO report was commissioned about a country in the data set, it is coded as a 1; otherwise, it is 0.

Table 5.2 shows the results from the ordinary least squares regression. In all models, bureaucratic fragmentation is consistently associated with GAO reports. This is even true controlling for total US aid spending in the recipient state, GDP, and other variables. When a state is the subject of a GAO report, its overall fragmentation increases by around 0.07. This corresponds to a half-standard deviation increase. Unexpectedly, GDP is associated with a significantly decreased level of fragmentation, suggesting

[19] Büthe et al. (2012)

Table 5.2 Ordinary least squares results showing mean bureaucratic fragmentation of US foreign aid to a recipient country. All variables are aggregated to the country level.

	Dependent Variable:		
	Recipient-Country Fragmentation		
	(1)	(2)	(3)
GAO Reports	0.076** (0.031)	0.080** (0.031)	0.061** (0.031)
Recipient Aid (bil USD)		0.002 (0.020)	0.019 (0.021)
GDP (tril USD)		−0.046** (0.022)	−0.098*** (0.027)
Battle Deaths (mil)			−2.640 (15.842)
Disaster Loss (bil USD)			272.465*** (79.134)
Constant	0.273*** (0.012)	0.289*** (0.013)	0.290*** (0.013)
Observations	195	186	186
R^2	0.031	0.051	0.109
Adjusted R^2	0.026	0.035	0.085

Note: *p<0.1; **p<0.05; ***p<0.01

that aid to larger states is more streamlined. Disaster loss follows a similar pattern as the previous models: it is associated with higher levels of bureaucratic fragmentation.

5.4 Conclusion

In this chapter, I consider a time period in which congressional disunity was relatively high and measure the role of congressional interest in driving bureaucratic fragmentation. I developed two novel data sets to create proxies for congressional interest, by measuring both the inputs (lobbying) and outputs (GAO reports) of Congress. I find consistent evidence for the hypothesis that higher congressional interest leads to a more fragmented foreign aid bureaucracy.

Because of data availability, I am not able to evaluate the congressional interest hypothesis on a longer time series. It is possible that this link between congressional interest and fragmentation is only relevant to the 2000–2020 era. The crude proxies for foreign policy interest developed in Chapter 4 provide some reprieve from this concern. The case studies that I will introduce in the following three chapters will derive from various time periods, providing a wider range of evidence. Chapter 6 takes data from the pre-2000 time period, which should provide especially strong support that congressional interest is not a new phenomenon.

5.5 Appendix

To ensure that the results were not driven by model specifications, I used the "ExtremeBounds" package[20] to determine the robustness of the main estimators in the face of various combinations of covariates. The histograms for the country-level and topic-level models are visible in Figures 5.6 and 5.7,

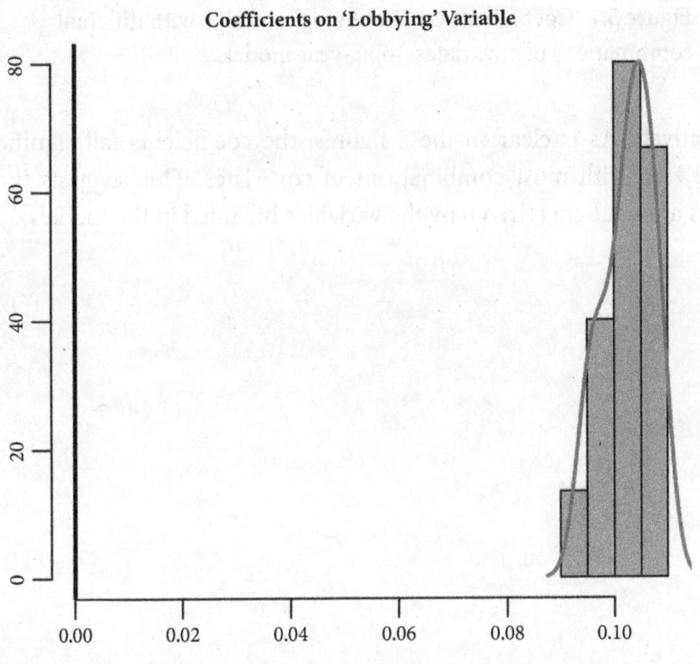

Figure 5.6 Coefficients on "Lobbying" variable with different combinations of covariates, country-year models.

[20] Hlavac (2016)

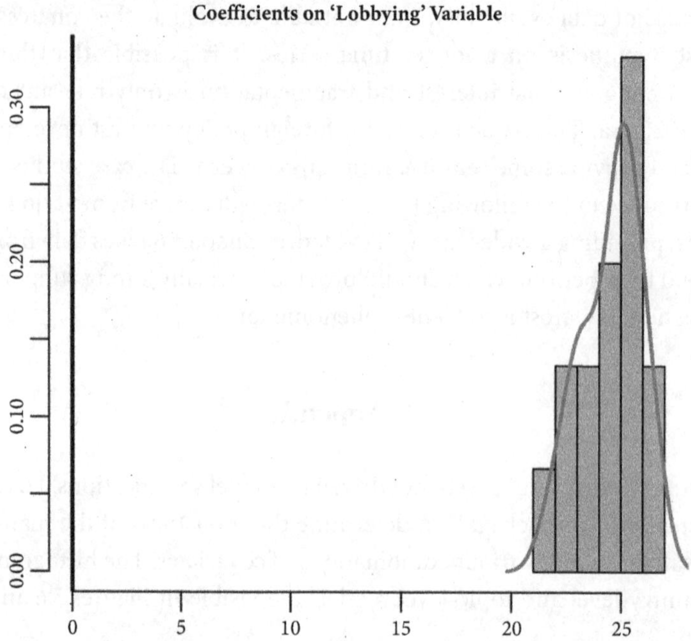

Figure 5.7 Coefficients on "Lobbying" variable with different combinations of covariates, topic-year models.

respectively. As is clear in these figures, the coefficients fall significantly above zero with most combinations of covariates. This suggests that the results are not being driven by the variables included in the models.

Chapter 6

Bureaucracy at War: Fragmentation in the Afghanistan Campaign

In this chapter, the first of three qualitative chapters in this book, I examine the twenty-first century United States nation-building effort in Afghanistan. If bureaucratic cooperation in foreign policy was ever crucial, it was in the wake of the 9/11 terror attacks. The United States had just been gut-punched by an enemy, and public opinion was at its most bipartisan in years. Congressional interest in foreign policy was high. The Bush administration and both parties in Congress were unified in desiring a strong and effective response to the attacks. It was clear to many that a military response alone was not enough: once the inevitable ground victory solidified in Afghanistan, the United States would have a nation to rebuild.

Unfortunately, the nation-building effort in Afghanistan was hampered by bureaucratic conflict from the start. Bureaucracies consistently undermined each other's access to funding, refused to share important intelligence, and failed to coordinate on large infrastructure projects. The classic civil–military disagreements were exacerbated by infighting between USAID, State, Justice, Treasury, Agriculture, and other cabinet agencies. This was especially problematic in stabilization and counternarcotics programs, which were particularly salient to political actors and required a great deal of collaboration. As the first Acting Ambassador after the US occupation, James Dobbins, lamented in his memoirs, operations from the start were immediately divided into "fiefdoms."[1]

This bureaucratic fragmentation occurred because of, rather than despite, congressional interest. Congress's "mercurial" interest in Afghanistan[2] created a situation in which agencies sought congressional allies for their own operations rather than Congress overseeing the operation as a whole. When agencies disagreed with either each other or the White House,

[1] Dobbins (2008, p. 135)
[2] Keane (2016b, p. 137)

Competing for Foreign Aid. Shannon P. Carcelli, Oxford University Press. © Oxford University Press (2025).
DOI: 10.1093/9780197799284.003.0006

they often appealed to allies in Congress. In turn, politicians in both the House and the Senate took sides in bureaucratic debates, clinging to specific agencies whose policies the legislators supported. The end result was a failure of executive and legislative leadership and oversight. Rather than encourage the different bureaucratic agencies to cooperate, Congress created incentives for further bureaucratic battles over funding and attention.

To explain the fragmentation in Afghanistan, this chapter draws on first- and second-hand accounts, statements in congressional hearings, and voting and amendments data from Afghanistan-specific legislation. Although Congress was not the only force leading to a fragmented bureaucracy in Afghanistan, it certainly did not ameliorate the phenomenon. In the remainder of this chapter, I first lay out the theoretical expectations from the vote-buying theory of fragmentation. I then introduce the case and demonstrate the level of fragmentation in Afghanistan. I consider the role that Congress played in both appropriations and oversight. With examples from congressional appropriations and oversight hearings, I link the actions of Congress to the interagency conflict that resulted. I show that Congress was not apathetic about Afghanistan, that congressional moderates were powerful in demanding specific Afghanistan appropriations, and that Congress's disunity and interest in Afghanistan eventually led to ineffective, scattered policy.

6.1 Theoretical Expectations

The vote-buying theory suggests that bureaucratic fragmentation should be greatest when congressional disunity and congressional interest are high. The Afghanistan case offers high levels of both. Much of the early Afghanistan War took place in an era of high moderate heterogeneity, leading to congressional disunity. Between 2001 and 2014, the IQR of ideology never dipped below 0.9, keeping it above the 76th percentile of the 1961–2016 period.

Additionally, this was clearly a case of high congressional interest. After the attacks of 9/11, Congress provided broad bipartisan authority to President Bush to go after those responsible. It quickly became clear that the responsible parties were located in the mountains of Afghanistan. The invasion of Afghanistan reflected congressional interest in the area. Congress conducted dozens of hearings on the subject and allocated a staggering amount of funding toward the state-building effort.[3] These all provide evidence of congressional interest. Fragmentation, therefore, should be high according to the vote-buying theory.

6.2 Bureaucratic Conflict in Afghanistan

The bureaucratic conflict in the Afghanistan campaign is well documented. Scholars, journalists, and policymakers bemoaned cross-agency chaos throughout the war. From the very start of the campaign and the very top of government, coordination problems were evident. Memoirs by major US policymakers like George W. Bush, Donald Rumsfeld, Condoleezza Rice, Robert Gates, and Hillary Clinton all complain of difficult interagency dynamic during the war.[4] As one post-invasion analysis put it, "the real issue was not going to war with the Army we had, but going to war with the bureaucracy we had."[5] According to an autopsy by three prominent policymakers,

> Despite thirteen years of experience—and innumerable opportunities to learn lessons from both successes and mistakes—there have been few significant changes in our cumbersome, inefficient and ineffective approach to interagency operations in the field.[6]

Such a lack of organization can hamper foreign policy,[7] and the war in Afghanistan is no exception. Interagency frustrations were not unique to high-level decision-makers with big jobs and big egos. They trickled down to the operational level as well. If anything, interagency coordination became even more of a struggle at lower levels of bureaucracy. According to an interview with a former USAID Mission Director,

> There is a lot of discussion of interagency agreement at the policy level. The problem is when strategy gets down to the operational level. Each agency does their own thing instead of having the operational levels work together.[8]

[3] Crawford (2019) estimates the total cost of the war to the United States to be over $2 trillion.

[4] Bush (2011, p. 88); Rumsfeld (2011, p. 527); Rice (2011, p. 22); Gates (2014, p. 92); Clinton (2014, p. 24)

[5] Hooker Jr. and Collins (2015, p. 231)

[6] Blair et al. (2014, p. 11)

[7] See also Stephenson (2007) for an example of this process in the Iraq War.

[8] Fishstein (2014, p. 5)

Every agency blamed the others for the strife. For example, some State Department representatives believed that "AID staff was not very enthusiastic about their plans being checked by other agencies such as State Department,"[9] while USAID representatives complained that "ambassadors were yelling at USAID because they were receiving complaints from Petraeus."[10] Foreign service professionals charged with stabilization complained that they "[n]eed a bureaucratic home for these [stabilization] experts and their bullpen of detailees."[11]

Among other issues, a rivalry between the Departments of State and Defense set the groundwork for a poor working relationship. One troubling example of breakdown in civil–military relations involved a 2003 dispute in which US bureaucracies supported rival Afghan warlords. When USAID ended assistance to two northern warlords, other US agencies continued to provide them with aid. They spent much of their aid money on "tanks, artillery, and ground forces," which the two warlords used to battle each other, resulting in over 1000 casualties.[12]

However, the civil–military divide does not explain all of the interagency conflict in Afghanistan. Civilian agencies tasked with different aspects of the war also often struggled to cooperate. According to Hooker Jr. and Collins (2015),

> Poor horizontal collaboration was a major performance impediment because so many of the subsidiary objectives and tasks in the war on terror—such as attacking terrorist leaders, countering their narrative and promoting ours (that is, strategic communications), and interrupting terrorist financing—depended upon interagency cooperation.[13]

While a common government complaint, the lack of bureaucratic collaboration in Afghanistan went beyond the typical problems. Bureaucrats themselves exacerbated these problems by creating even more new bodies to compete with existing ones. When Zalmay Khalilzad was appointed Ambassador to Afghanistan in 2003, one of his first actions was to set up a parallel organizational structure called the Afghan Reconstruction Group (ARG). This group, which consisted of private-sector experts, mirrored the expertise of various members of USAID and was considered

[9] State 2/9/16, p. 1
[10] USAID 11/10/16, p. 2
[11] Fishstein et al. (2016b), p. 4
[12] Tomsen (2013, p. 632)
[13] Hooker Jr. and Collins (2015, p. 203)

to be a direct reflection of Khalilzad's lack of respect for USAID as an organization. Working with the ARG presented a major challenge for USAID representatives,[14] and tension between the two groups was high.[15]

The problem of bureaucratic battles was not unique to the development and nation-building projects. Bureaucracies tended to silo their intelligence materials, either purposefully or due to bureaucratic inertia. Intelligence coordination was an early problem at the highest levels. Secretary Rice recounts an incident at a high-level meeting in which President Bush demanded to know who was taking the lead on an issue, and the CIA and Defense representatives pointed at each other.[16]

One general complained that "the CIA was not sharing all of their information with the Department of Defense or the rest of the Intelligence Community for that matter."[17] Another senior officer noted that,

> There was a massive communication challenge caused by the U.S. bureaucracy—a function of the competitive environment in the US for raising resources and the number of different agencies who felt they had a role to play. The result was that the DEA would not speak to CFC Alpha Command Intelligence Centre... INL had different information and each institution felt they had a hand to play. It was a dog's breakfast with no chance of working.[18]

This failure to share intelligence in Afghanistan became especially problematic when different agencies began working with different allies to collect often-faulty intelligence. The CIA took much of their information from ISI, Pakistan's intelligence service, which is infamously connected to the Afghan Taliban. At the start of the war, these connections allowed the ISI to trick the CIA into allowing the so-called Evil Airlift, in which the United States stood by while thousands of Taliban and ISI troops flew out of Kunduz. This operation was attributed to Cheney, who took charge without communicating with the State Department. Either out of ignorance or due to misinformation, then-Defense Secretary Rumsfeld later denied that it had ever happened.[19]

[14] Fine (2016)
[15] Neumann (2009, p. 11)
[16] Rice (2011, p. 92)
[17] Fishstein et al. (2016d)
[18] Sopko (2018, p. 226)
[19] Tomsen (2013, p. 606–607)

6.3 Bureaucracies in Counternarcotics

One of the areas in which agencies clashed the most was in the problem of Afghanistan's opium trade.[20] Part of what made counternarcotics policy in Afghanistan so difficult was the trade-offs that it created. The costs and benefits of Afghanistan's opium market were difficult to measure. On the one hand, it is an economic booster: in 2017, the opium trade was estimated to have created more than half a million jobs in Afghanistan[21] and contributed to the creation of a lot of infrastructure. On the other hand, the opium trade in many ways exacerbated the insurgency, especially regarding the problems of corruption and lack of government legitimacy.[22] It is likely that much of the Taliban's funding was driven by opium sales. Also, opiate addiction was a serious problem throughout Afghanistan, which by 2013 produced 90% of the world's opiates and had the highest rate of addiction in the world.[23]

Policymakers at all levels disagreed about the ideal course of action when it came to counternarcotics. On the ground, among high-level bureaucrats, and within Congress, the narcotics issue rarely saw much agreement. Eradicating crops, targeting traffickers, providing alternative incomes to farmers, and closing borders all seemed like promising solutions to different groups of people. This does not, however, mean that there were no right answers.

Certain policies, in a certain order, are thought to benefit the counter narcotics efforts more than others.[24] Specifically, experts point to the importance of the *sequencing* and the *collocation* of counternarcotics activities. First, it is important that donor efforts to support farmers be carried out *before* efforts to eradicate crops. This is for the simple reason that eradication without support can cool farmers to the entire nation-building effort. Unfortunately, different agencies were in charge of different parts of this policy. Ensuring that the sequence of events follows an ideal template requires some collaboration between USAID, the Defense Department, and the State Department's Bureau of International Narcotics and Law Enforcement Affairs (INL). Such collaboration was difficult in Afghanistan, to say the least.

[20] Keane (2016a)
[21] Sopko (2018, p. 5)
[22] Sopko (2018, p. vii)
[23] Qadiry (2013)
[24] See Sopko (2018) for a summary of expert opinion on counternarcotics policy.

Experts also highlight the importance of the *location* of counternarcotics activities. If the United States were to support farmers in one district and spray farmers' crops in another district, the two activities would not create a harmonious policy. Instead, it may exacerbate tensions between different districts and between farmers and the United States. Unfortunately, this is exactly what the United States did in Afghanistan. Once again, the lack of communication between bureaucracies made it all but impossible to carry out a coherent, effective counternarcotics policy.

Instead of a centralized effort, different agencies highlighted the importance of, and carried out, different policies. Everyone agreed that the counter insurgency effort would be strengthened by a decrease in the opium trade: not only did opium provide funding for the Taliban and fuel government corruption, but it also decreased the land that could be used for growing food.[25] Where agencies disagreed was on the proper role of carrots versus sticks in the process. Some argued that a focus on negative incentives would only push people toward the Taliban and so would be counterproductive.[26] Others argued that forcefully cutting off the Taliban insurgency's major funding stream would be an important tool in winning the war.[27]

The INL was an early (and consistent) supporter of strong eradication efforts, up to and including aerial spraying of chemicals from planes and helicopters.[28] However, the Pentagon was wary of policies that might put soldiers in the way of wrathful farmers. Along with USAID, the Pentagon preferred alternative development programming, in which the United States would encourage farmers to plant other crops instead of lucrative poppies.[29] The Defense Department was also hesitant to spend much energy on counternarcotics at all, thinking that stability would lead to improved governance, which would itself decrease the drug trade. Beyond that, through the DEA, the Department of Justice managed training of the Afghan National Police and raided drug production sites. Meanwhile, the Treasury Department targeted the financing end of the Afghan drug trade, establishing the Afghan Threat Finance Cell.[30]

[25] However, as we will see, the level of importance of narcotics to the counter-insurgency effort was hotly debated.
[26] Fishstein (2014)
[27] Pain (2011)
[28] Sopko (2018, p. ix)
[29] Some suggested substitutes that arose, with various success, included saffron and wheat.
[30] Sopko (2018, p. 71)

As a result of these disagreements, US counternarcotics policy was often unpredictable and tenuous. When coalition forces first arrived in Afghanistan, the UK was initially charged with counternarcotics.[31] In 2001, opium production in the Taliban-controlled south was very low, because the Taliban (bowing to Western pressure) had successfully banned the crop in the previous year. Most of the existing opium planting was happening in the north of the country and was not funding the Taliban.

As the UK began its work of eradicating opium production in the north, three things happened that shifted and supported opium production. First, opium prices skyrocketed due to the decrease in supply. Second, the Taliban insurgents in the south lifted their ban on poppy production. Both of these forces shifted the opium market south, to the Taliban-controlled regions. Third, many of the UK's programs had the side effect of further incentivizing opium production. In an effort to encourage eradication, the British had begun offering rewards to farmers who could demonstrate that they had destroyed their opium crops. Instead of decreasing opium production, this had the effect of encouraging more farmers to plant poppies, so that they could then destroy them and collect a reward. The initial push to decrease opium production, in sum, was not effective.

Worse, the initial moves to decrease opium actually ingrained opium production in precisely the places where the United States did not want opium to be. As the opium market thrived in the south, so did the insurgents who were drawing from those economic sources. By 2003, the United States essentially took control of the operation, at least in the southern provinces. By 2005, Congress had ensured US control by increasing the counternarcotics budget to well above what the UK was willing to spend.[32] The programs offered by the United States, however, were hardly more coherent.

Once the United States took de facto control of counternarcotics efforts, the initial plan was to take direct action on poppy eradication. Ambassador Neumann, along with the INL and even President Bush, planned to spray poppy fields from the air to directly manage the problem. However, this plan immediately faced several powerful detractors. First, Afghan President Hamid Karzai was vehemently opposed to the idea, which

[31] See Sopko (2018, p. 39). This division of powers made sense at the time because a majority of the UK's opium trafficking originated in Afghanistan, whereas only 1% of US heroin originated there (Sopko 2018, p. 14).

[32] Sopko (2018, p. 66)

was incredibly unpopular among the Afghan public. For similar reasons, General McChrystal and the British eventually came out against the idea of spraying.[33] Because the United States needed permission from its allies—and couldn't even get permission from its own bureaucracy—the plan of spraying was scrapped.

It remains unclear how prominent poppy spraying actually was in those early days. In 2003, farmers in Southern Afghanistan claimed that the United States was spraying their fields. The local population grew furious, as did President Karzai. While the United States officially denied carrying out aerial spraying, it remains unclear whether parts of the US government were still involved in spraying well into 2004. In a recent interview, then-USAID Mission Director Patrick Fine confessed that he himself still didn't know the extent of spraying by other agencies.[34]

6.4 Congress and the Bureaucracy

Congress had every motivation to ensure the existence of a stable bureaucracy in Afghanistan's reconstruction. They had funding sources and oversight capabilities. They had political incentives to ensure that the Afghan War remained short and successful. However, Congress did not use this power to encourage interbranch harmony. If anything, Congress used its power to *exacerbate* the interagency conflict in Afghanistan. An ad hoc appropriations process encouraged agencies to continually fight over funding at the congressional and operational levels. And oversight hearings highlighted the tendency of legislators to take sides in the bureaucratic battle *de jour*, rather than providing bureaucrats with an incentive to resolve disputes on their own.

Congress was certainly capable of using its appropriations and oversight powers to manage bureaucratic disagreements to the advantage of US outcomes in Afghanistan. One prominent example, Congress's decision to fund the building of mine-resistant ambush protected vehicles (MRAPs) provides a powerful counterexample to the bureaucratic battles discussed elsewhere in this chapter. MRAPs were a controversial tool in Iraq and Afghanistan, but not because of their effectiveness. MRAPs were effectively designed to deter and manage one of the deadliest weapons in Afghanistan,

33 Berry (2018)
34 Mark (2018)

improvised explosive devices (IEDs). The technology that US troops were using at the beginning of the war, armored humvees, were poor at protecting troops. Field commanders and low-level military leaders working on the ground consistently pushed for new technologies to better support soldiers.

This led to a bureaucratic battle within the Defense Department when it became clear that higher-level officers were strongly opposed to the purchase of expensive armored vehicles. They argued that such equipment would be wasteful, as its use after Iraq and Afghanistan would be limited. MRAPs were absolutely necessary protection against IEDs, but senior officials worried about their usefulness in future wars that would not involve IEDs. Secretary Bob Gates sided with the field commanders, pushing for MRAPs. He accused the high-level officers concerned about future usefulness of suffering from what he called "next war-itis."[35]

In this case, congressional interest was high but disunity was low. This allowed Congress to act unitarily and decisively. Gates was able to convince the congressional Armed Services Committee to support his push for more MRAPs. Congress not only demanded the funding of MRAPs in appropriations legislation, it also made clear that it would not be decreasing other areas of funding to get it, creating a win-win for both sides. High-level military leaders had to let go of their criticisms when Congress made it clear that there was no trade-off: Congress would fund both MRAPs *and* the preferred technologies of military leadership. In short, rather than taking sides and worsening bureaucratic divisions, Congress used its power to resolve the dispute.

The results were staggering. In late 2007, nearly 60% of US casualties in Iraq were the result of IEDs. Within a year, that number decreased to 5%. This was despite the fact that insurgents were ramping up their IED numbers and technology during the same time period. The MRAPs are estimated to have cut US casualties by as much as two-thirds.[36]

A few factors made it easier for Congress to soothe bureaucratic battles in this particular case. First, there was a clear electoral incentive that applied to every member of Congress—the elusive national interest was at play in the MRAP case. No single legislator had an electoral incentive to support a policy that led to the deaths of US troops. While many bureaucratic battles involve trade-offs, this battle only required that legislators be willing to

[35] Gates (2009, p. 3)
[36] Hooker Jr. and Collins (2015, p. 232–233)

spend some money on military equipment. Also, high support for President Bush made it easy for legislators to vote for wartime funding.[37]

It also didn't hurt that MRAP spending provided Congress with an excuse to expand military spending—a consistent source of domestic pork in foreign policy.[38] MRAPs were built by companies in several US districts, providing an opportunity for several legislators to provide jobs back home. Therefore, coming down on the side of MRAPs was good politics for many members of Congress.

The quick resolution of the MRAP controversy contrasted with the entrenched bureaucratic battles going on in the rest of Afghanistan. Policymakers were well aware of the problem. There have been many suggestions for streamlining the bureaucratic process in Afghanistan and similar wars.[39] One Inspector General report argued for the creation of a new independent agency called the U.S. Office for Contingency Operations, which would enforce coordination between Defense, State, and USAID.[40] The report noted a series of ad hoc agencies that were created as the government carried out operations in Iraq and suggested that institutionalization could improve these relations.[41]

In congressional hearings, aid workers and bureaucrats implored Congress to step in and consolidate the budget. One telling piece of testimony came early in the conflict, during an Afghanistan security oversight hearing in October 2003. In this hearing, experts asked Congress to increase the power of the US ambassador, with one expert arguing that the lack of ambassadorial coordination power:

> has added to the bureaucratic disunity, confusion and red tape which have undermined our economic, humanitarian, democracy and security programs in Afghanistan.[42]

Unfortunately, this testimony did not reach many policymakers' ears: it was scheduled during a separate Senate vote, and the committee room was nearly empty at the time. It is unclear whether it would have made a difference, but the legislative schedule provides insight into the priorities in Congress.

[37] Jeong (2020)
[38] Milner and Tingley (2015)
[39] See, for example, Serafino (2012, p. 22) for a summary of suggestions and implementations.
[40] Bowen (2010)
[41] It is worth noting that both the State and Defense Departments strongly opposed the idea.
[42] S. Hrg. 108-320 - Afghanistan: in Pursuit of Security and Democracy, 108th Cong. 320 (2003) (Statement of Prepared Statement of Hon. Peter Tomsen, Former United States Special Envoy and Ambassador to Afghanistan, 1989–1992, United States Ambassador to Armenia, 1995–1998)

6.4.1 Appropriations

As demonstrated in the MRAP example, the appropriations process is one of Congress's most powerful tools in both foreign and domestic policy.[43] Congress could have wielded that tool to improve inter agency relations, such as by demanding a chain of command on the ground, or prioritizing one or two main agencies to allocate funding to the others. Instead, Congress passed appropriations legislation that increased inter-agency competition and provided little guidance on how to defuse it.

What's more, Congress earmarked funding to members' preferred projects and programs to such a degree that discretionary funds for those on the ground was low and highly coveted. This made it even more difficult to find policy consensus within the executive branch. Bureaucrats consistently asked Congress for more freedom and consolidation in appropriations. One USAID employee complained that USAID was forced to prioritize funding based on whatever Congress thought were the most important issues at the moment. This resulted in bureaucrats "gaming the US congressional political system," rather than dealing with the actual problems the United States was trying to solve in Afghanistan.[44] The appropriations process provided an opportunity for Congress to help consolidate objectives on the ground. Instead, legislators took sides and contributed to inter-agency conflict.

The more that Congress earmarked legislation to specific projects and programs, the less leeway central actors had to allocate on their own. In early budget negotiations, Ambassador Neumann, along with USAID's Thomas Johnson, pointed out the lack of actual funding to carry out US objectives. According to Ambassador Neumann,[45] "congressional requirements (also known as earmarks) for spending on humanitarian and other areas considerably limited the funds actually available for reprogramming to the areas we recommended." Congressional earmarks, which were disproportionately designated by moderate legislators, served as stumbling blocks to bureaucrats throughout the Afghanistan campaign.

Although Congress was unified in its interest in Afghanistan, large-scale disunity made it difficult to pass an appropriations bill that all legislators could agree on. Congress's solution, drafting several small "emergency" appropriations bills instead of one large one, created the first difficulty in managing a functioning bureaucracy. In the first year of the conflict,

[43] Indeed, according to Carcelli (2021), much of Congress's foreign aid guidance is delivered through appropriations.
[44] Fishstein et al. (2016c), p. 1
[45] Neumann (2009, p. 43)

Congress appropriated funding to Afghanistan in five separate pieces of legislation, in addition to three separate authorizing bills. This made it difficult for bureaucrats to know how much funding to expect and, crucially, to plan for future projects. It provided an incentive to jealously guard bureaucratic coffers, further siloing budgets. Secretary Rice pushed to end Congress's reliance on supplementary appropriations, but to little avail.[46]

Another contributor to interagency conflict was Congress's refusal to waive the so-called Bumpers Amendment. This amendment prohibited foreign aid from funding any projects that could compete with US companies in world markets. This prohibition significantly detracted from policy options in Afghanistan. For example, USAID could not encourage Afghan farmers to develop agricultural products that would compete with US producers. This created interagency conflict, as USAID was responsible for enforcing this policy, which annoyed other agencies that were not aware of the amendment.[47]

Others asked Congress to use appropriations bills to mandate a clear chain of command among agencies. Ryan Crocker, who served as Ambassador early in the war, suggests that the United States needed a "legislatively dictated plan" to lay out which cabinet agencies should carry out which functions, lamenting that "we never came up with a serious structure to affect coordination."[48]

Members of Congress were not deaf to these requests. In 2004, Congress mandated the creation of a "Coordinator for Reconstruction and Stabilization."[49] Also around that time, Congress was debating the Stabilization and Reconstruction Civilian Management Act. This bill, first introduced in 2004, was designed to create a National Security Council office specifically designed to mandate a chain of command, as Rice and others had requested. It was finally passed in 2009, after much of the early war had already been fought. However, the bill was poorly written and did not have the intended effect. First, as had been the case in previous attempts to consolidate the bureaucracy, it failed to demand any White House–level leadership.[50] As one critic argues,

> the empowerment of some sort of interagency overseer failed to consider where the coordinator would come from—the civilian or military

[46] Neumann (2009, p. 41)
[47] Keane (2016b, p. 129)
[48] Fishstein et al. (2016c, p. 5)
[49] Serafino (2012)
[50] Keane (2016b, p. 170)

> realm—or what authority the position would have had with respect to each agencies. Prima facie, there did not seem to be any means of compelling any of the agencies to obey this mysterious figure... this solution, which reflected the importance Congress attached to Afghanistan's drug problem, failed to understand how deeply competing agency cultures are implanted within the bureaucratic machine.[51]

Not all legislators were equally responsible for the interagency fragmentation and conflict. As the theory suggests, moderates drove many of the processes described above. As an example, I consider the very first appropriations bill that Congress provided after the events of 9/11. On November 19, 2001, Congress introduced the "Department of Defense and Emergency Supplemental Appropriations for Recovery from and Response to Terrorist Attacks on the United States Act." This act sought to provide the first source of emergency funding for the new war. In it, Congress mentioned 35 different agencies and considered 235 amendments. Of these amendments, 131 were introduced into debates and 115 eventually made it into the bill.

Figure 6.1 outlines the passage rate of amendments in the bill. Fully three-quarters of legislators who successfully introduced amendments (and 78% of those whose amendments eventually passed into law) were moderates, whose DW-Nominate scores fell between the first and third quartiles of Congress. In a bivariate regression model, having a moderate sponsor increased the passage rate of an amendment by 17%. Even in this crucial policy area at a crucial time, leadership had to strongly consider the preferences of congressional moderates.

Even more telling are the *types* of amendments that moderate legislators successfully put forward. Figure 6.2 outlines the mean final passage rates of three categories of amendments that were introduced in the bill: oversight, spending, and new programs. "Oversight" amendments relate to regulatory questions and technical language. "Spending" amendments include domestic pork and military procurement. "New Program" amendments are those that introduce new programs. Moderate and non-moderate legislators were equally likely to get oversight and spending-related amendments passed. If anything, oversight amendments were more likely to be passed

[51] Keane (2016a, p. 301)

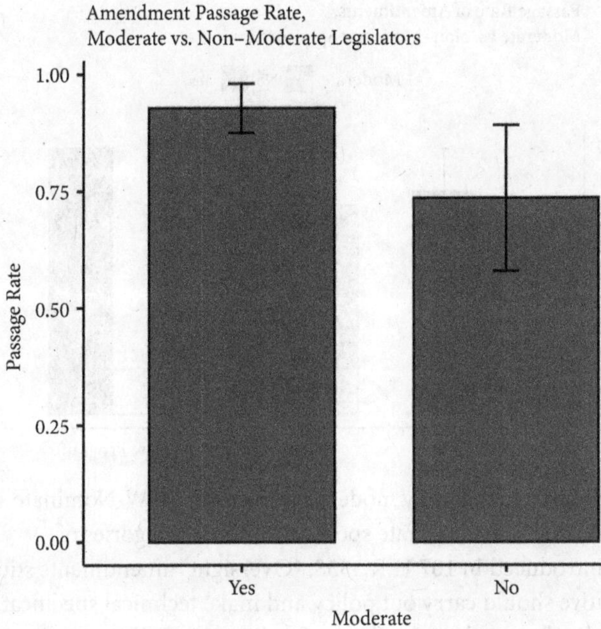

Figure 6.1 Passage rates of 107 H.R.3338 amendments introduced by moderate (those with DW-Nominate scores within the IQR) versus non-moderate sponsors. The mean passage rate is significantly higher (p = .02) for moderates (92.8%) than non-moderates (73.5%). This suggests that moderate legislators were more successful at getting their amendments into the final bill. Error bars represent 95% confidence intervals.

when they came from non-moderates. However, *no* new programs offered by non-moderates made it into the final bill.

Only two new program amendments made it into the final bill, three were officially introduced, and seven were initially offered. The new programs that made it into the bill had very different purposes, but they were both designed to appease constituents. The first program was Senate Amendment 2339, introduced by Democrat Debbie Stabenow from Michigan. With a DW-Nominate score of –0.34, Stabenow's ideology fell well within the moderate range and to the right of the Democratic mean (–0.36). The program she created, titled the "Unity in the Spirit of America (USA) Act," was designed to "establish a program to name national and community service projects in honor of victims killed as a result of the terrorist attacks

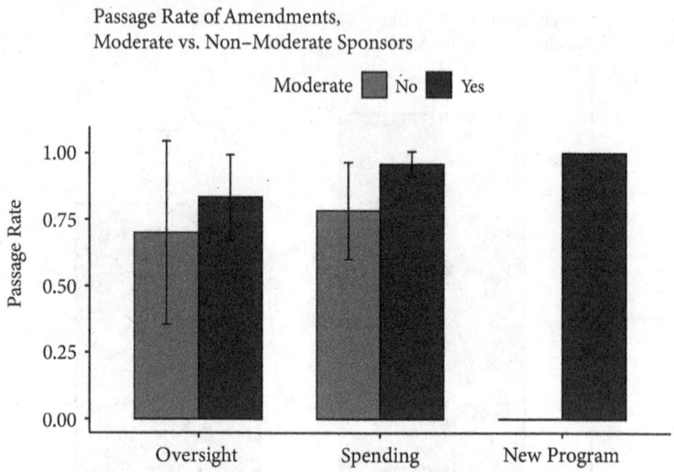

Figure 6.2 Final passage rates by moderate (those with DW-Nominate scores within the IQR) and non-moderate sponsors of three categories of amendments introduced in 107 H.R.3338. "Oversight" amendments stipulate how the executive should carry out policy and make technical specifications to the bill. "Spending" amendments allocate funding to specific projects, programs, and military procurement. "New Program" amendments introduce new programs within the bill. Moderate legislators were no more likely than non-moderates to successfully pass oversight amendments. However, they were significantly more successful at passing spending provisions ($p = 0.06$), and all new program amendments that passed into the law were offered by moderate legislators. Error bars represent 95% confidence intervals.

on September 11, 2001."[52] Stabenow describes her motivation for the creation of the act as an attempt to help constituents honor the victims of 9/11, claiming:

> "Many people came up to me in Michigan after the attacks and asked: What can I do? I have given blood, I have donated to relief efforts, but I want to do more... Then a constituent of mine, Bob Van Oosterhout, wrote me with [this] idea..."[53]

This example illustrates the diversity and strength of congressional opinions regarding Afghanistan. Unlike many traditional earmarks, this program did not financially benefit any particular member of Stabenow's constituents. In fact, it is a program than any legislator could presumably have spearheaded.

[52] Senate Amendment 107–2439
[53] Cong. Rec. Vol. 147, No. 178 (Dec. 20, 2001), S13832–S13856

The high level of congressional interest in relation to all things Afghanistan provided an incentive for Stabenow to promote this program. Because of her moderate status, she was able to claim credit for a low-cost tribute to a popular cause.

The second amendment that created a new program in the bill is a more straightforward example of vote-buying to provide goods to a congressional constituency. It was introduced by Senator Arlen Specter, a Republican from Pennsylvania. Once again, Specter qualified as a moderate legislator, with a DW-Nominate of 0.07, within the IQR. Specter's amendment expedited the creation of a national security program called the "intelligent transportation infrastructure system" (ITS).[54] Housed within the Department of Transportation, ITS is a program that "leads collaborative and innovative research, development, and implementation of intelligent transportation systems to improve the safety and mobility of people and goods."[55]

Specter supported this program for traditional parochial reasons. The initial deployment area for this program was to be in his home state of Pennsylvania; specifically, "in the 2 largest metropolitan areas in the Commonwealth of Pennsylvania."[56] This amendment would provide up to $2 million to two of his largest constituencies. It is no wonder that he worked to push it through the bill. Since these initial projects, ITS has gone on to carry out countless other safety, efficiency, and other projects in other districts. It is now a well-established bureau within the Department of Transportation. Once again, a moderate legislator founded a program that supported his constituents first.

This amendment also provided an example of another phenomenon common to this bill: a number of the amendments mention specific executive agencies that are not traditionally related to national defense. The amendments in this bill mentioned 35 government agencies, including every branch of the military, several cabinet-level departments, and others. A majority of the agencies mentioned were defense-related. Of the introduced amendments, 58.8% mentioned a branch of the military or the Department of Defense, while only 13.7% mentioned any other agency.[57] This is understandable, given that the bill is geared toward defense spending. Amendments that mentioned other types of agencies tended to be less relevant to the bill and more likely to be funding specific pet projects.

[54] Cong. Rec. Vol. 147, No. 169 (Dec. 7, 2001), S12586

[55] DOT (n.d.)

[56] An Act To authorize funds for Federal-aid highways, highway safety programs, and transit programs, and for other purposes. Public Law 105–178. U.S. Statutes at Large 112 (1998).

[57] The remainder did not explicitly mention any government agency.

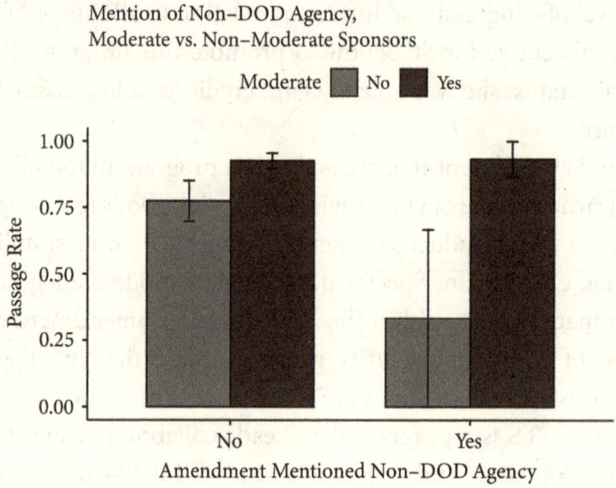

Figure 6.3 Final passage rates by moderate (those with DW-Nominate scores within the IQR) and non-moderate sponsors of amendments introduced in 107 H.R.3338. Moderate legislators were more likely than non-moderates to successfully pass all types of amendments. However, the difference in passage rates are especially marked for amendments that mention a non-military US agency. These amendments are more likely to be funding programs outside of the immediate relevance of the bill. This suggests that moderate legislators are more likely to receive their preferred pet projects. Error bars represent standard errors.

Figure 6.3 shows the passage rates of legislation by sponsor ideology and mention of non-Defense bureaucracies. These trends provide more evidence for the vote-buying theory. Insofar as the mention of non-Defense agencies is a proxy for the creation of pet projects within the bill, they should be more successfully introduced by moderates. In line with the theory, moderates were significantly more successful in passing these types of amendments than non-moderates. In fact, a large proportion of the difference in passage rates between the two groups seems to be driven by nontraditional amendments. Moderates are more disproportionately successful in passing amendments that mention non-Defense agencies than those that do not.

Throughout the Afghanistan campaign, Congress wrote dozens more bills appropriating funding for Afghanistan. Collectively, these bills contain thousands of amendments. It is telling that the first emergency appropriations bill to emerge after 9/11 was so scattered, and that moderate legislators were able to demand their preferred projects even in this early period.

6.4.2 Oversight

Along with appropriations, congressional oversight also incentivized bureaucratic conflict. Congress took its oversight role in Afghanistan very seriously, clearly caring a lot about the issue. Congressional hearings about the Afghanistan campaign served two purposes: they allowed members of Congress to question the administration and others about the aid projects, and they allowed bureaucrats to bypass the administration and directly lobby Congress for the funding and stipulations that they were not able to get out of the executive branch. The latter function led to an uptick of bureaucratic infighting, some of it performative. Because Congress had so much interest in Afghanistan, it unwittingly provided yet another forum for disagreement, and even misinformation, between agencies.

Congressional hearings, of course, addressed all of the major issues of Afghanistan, but they focused on the issues that were more interesting to members of Congress. For example, Congress held a lot of hearings about counternarcotics. For domestic political reasons, the drug issue was important to many members of Congress. Much of the interagency confusion in counternarcotics could be attributed to an excess of congressional oversight. Although members consistently demanded better interagency cooperation, they tended to side with one agency or another and often did not agree among themselves about the best strategy. In this way, congressional involvement exacerbated interagency differences as agencies fought for resources. Sometimes this even extended to interagency debates about the reality on the ground in Afghanistan. .

Legislators naturally care more about some issues than others, leading to more competition between bureaucrats. In his memoir, Ambassador Neumann went even further to suggest that the policy options available to the United States were driven by congressional whims.[58] In arguing for poppy spraying, he noted the importance of political realities in the United States, which made it difficult to delay or ignore the immediate issue of narcotics production. Although some policy experts believed that building capacity on the ground was a necessary step to take before eradicating poppy crops, Neumann argued that order of events was not possible for political reasons. Congress's political incentives drove bureaucrats' decisions, rather than bureaucrats' expertise driving Congress's preferences.

[58] Neumann (2009, p. 61)

In contrast, many crucial projects fell by the wayside because Congress had little political incentive to fund them. Ambassador Richard Armitage lamented:

> Congress's want of 'feel good' items that proved that the US was engaged in development, such as medical clinics and schools. [Armitage] contrasted this sharply with the legislative branch's aversion to less glamorous infrastructure development programmes, such as sewerage plants and electricity grids, and highlighted the difficulty that the State Department faced in Afghanistan when trying to balance practical solutions with congressional musings.[59]

The scattershot nature of congressional oversight hearings is clear in a 2007 hearing titled "Afghanistan on the Brink: Where Do We Go From Here?"[60] In this hearing, several members addressed the growing issue of opium production in southern Afghanistan, and the number of distinct opinions expressed was as high as the strength of those opinions. Members suggested everything from blanket legalization (p. 5), to developing new mycoherbicides (p. 5), evoking shame and dishonor on traffickers (p. 2), creating new intelligence platforms (p. 6), manual spraying (p. 6), a DEA ride-along program (p. 10), capacity-building (p. 22), importing Afghan opiates (p. 24), building infrastructure (p. 40), improving security (p. 43), decreasing global demand (p. 50), and creating a stronger sense of nationhood (p. 51). Congressman Jim Costa put it best at the end of the hearing when he said "the best thing we could do as a committee is really force our folks to really come up with a plan. And frankly if we do not lead by example... I do not see it happening" (p. 53).

This plethora of congressional ideas did not emerge from a vacuum. Bureaucrats within the executive branch actively sought congressional allies to promote and fund their preferred policies. One example is the role of Afghan Counter Narcotics Minister Zarar Ahmad Osmani's testimony in persuading Dianne Feinstein, chair of the Senate Caucus on International Narcotics Control, to support the use of province-level "Food Zones" in countering poppy growth. According to a former committee staffer, Feinstein was:

> all over the map when it comes to drug policies in Afghanistan, including buying the crop. Much is a function of advice of her staff and who she talks

[59] Keane (2016b, p. 136)
[60] Afghanistan on the Brink: Where Do We Go From Here? 113th Cong. (2007)

> to and finds convincing. [In] 2013 she found Osmani an "engaging" and committed partner and that he made a good case for the Food Zones.[61]

In other words, the testimony of an Afghan politician was enough to persuade one member of Congress to virulently support a policy tool she had previously never heard of. She even wrote a letter to Secretary Clinton to demand the expansion of this tool. This is not a unique story. This type of personal connection was important in helping legislators determine their specific policy preferences in Afghanistan.

The Osmani example is notable for an another reason as well: like many bureaucrats jostling for congressional funding, his testimony cherry-picked information to make his preferred policy tool appear more valuable. The Helmand Food Zone initiative that Osmani was pushing was more controversial than his testimony would suggest. Even as INL was extolling its virtues, USAID's Office of Agriculture was warning of the negative consequences of Food Zones, which tended to push poppy production further into the desert, where they depleted natural resources and still contributed to the narcotics industry.[62]

Because of the incentives to connect with legislators, bureaucrats often strategically manipulated the information that Congress received. The bias this created further exacerbated interagency relations. For example longtime INL chief Robert Charles may have deliberately made British and DOD-driven outcomes look worse than they were in order to persuade Congress to allow his preferred policy of aerial spraying.[63] In response to Secretary Rice's decision to shift INL policy away from aerial poppy spraying, Charles appealed directly to Congress.[64] He argued for what some considered unreasonably high eradication targets in order to denigrate the UK's policies and ensure that Congress would support his policy.[65]

Agency representatives also used different sources of information to highlight the truths that they found to be most convenient. First, it was unclear how much of the insurgency's funding really came from narcotics. Agencies who focused on counternarcotics, especially the INL, made much of the premise that terrorists were benefiting from the drug trade. Members of Congress were swayed by this diagnosis, often parroting INL's talking

[61] Fishstein et al. (2016e), p. 1
[62] Sopko (2018, p. 124)
[63] Berry (2018)
[64] Keane (2016b, p. 146)
[65] Sopko (2018, p. 86)

points in committees. In reality, however, the link between narcotics and the Taliban was tenuous.[66]

Another data point that was consistently under question was the extent of poppy cultivation in Afghanistan. The UN Office on Drugs and Crime (UNODC) had a good relationship with the INL and reported eradication numbers that some considered highly suspect.[67] In congressional testimony, DOD officials tried to dissuade members of Congress from relying on UNODC data, but many legislators were convinced by INL's information. The information wars between the agencies made it difficult to create policy compromise.

Interagency battles over policy and information played out in congressional hearings. Rather than seek consensus, members of Congress tended to take sides in these battles based on very little information. This led to support and funding for agencies that were able to convince Congress of their agendas. In turn, this created incentives for bureaucracies to turn up the conflict. Congressional leadership, which itself struggled to forward a legislative agenda, could not easily find consensus among the congressional rank and file. The lack of interagency cooperation was inextricable from the conflicts going on within Congress.

6.5 Conclusion

The Afghanistan case provides evidence of the two mechanisms of the vote-buying theory. First, the disunity hypothesis predicts that the fragmented bureaucracy in Afghanistan is driven by dysfunction within Congress and lack of control of congressional leadership. It also predicts that congressional moderates contribute disproportionately to the bloated bureaucracy by creating their own projects and funding nontraditional agencies. Evidence from appropriations amendments and oversight hearings suggest that this is the case. Moderate legislators' demands for pet projects were driving fragmentation in Afghanistan.

Second, this case provides evidence for the interest hypothesis. The bureaucratic conflicts that took place in Afghan reconstruction happened not *despite* congressional interest in the area but *because* of it. The salience of the issues encouraged members of Congress to pick sides in bureaucratic

[66] Keane (2016b, p. 144)
[67] Fishstein et al. (2016f)

battles, which incentivized bureaucracies to continue battling in search of congressional allies. The policy areas in which Congress was the most active, such as counternarcotics, were the areas with the worst bureaucratic battles. This is no coincidence. Congressional hearings and first-hand accounts make clear the degree of chaos that Congress sowed in the Afghanistan campaign.

The proliferation of pet projects in the Afghanistan case created devastating consequences for the United States. Because members of Congress were so insistent on their own preferred pet projects, and leadership had little power to overcome them, Congress was unable to manage bureaucratic tensions effectively. This contributed to an already toxic combination of interagency conflict and lack of authority that was already wreaking havoc in Afghanistan

This case also suggests interesting normative implications about the role of Congress in the waging of war. According to Rossiter, the executive needs to be a "constitutional dictator" during wars in order to decrease the danger of "the excess of deliberation and compromise."[68] This chapter suggests another reason the executive may be better equipped to carry out functions during times of war. If Congress finds itself incapable of harnessing bureaucracy at exactly the time it is most important to do so, then executive dominance might be one possible solution. Because Afghanistan was one of the first so-called complex crises, it could serve as a warning sign to future Congresses trying to meddle in foreign aid in war zones.

This chapter focused on wartime bureaucracy and mainly considered the disagreements between existing agencies. How do these processes carry over when the United States finishes its wars? And where do new agencies come from in the first place? The next chapter considers the role of bureaucracies in a peaceful transition. The end of the Cold War coincided with many changes in US bureaucracy, including an increase in the number of aid agencies. The process of crafting new agencies in times of peace mirrors the processes described in this chapter. In Chapter 7, I trace the creation of new agencies in the former Soviet Union, finding that the vote-buying theory is generalizable outside the fog of war.

[68] Rossiter (1948, p. 288)

Chapter 7

Bureaucracy at Peace: Fragmentation in the 1992 FREEDOM Support Act

The previous chapters focused mainly on the spread of foreign aid funding among, and competition between, existing bureaucracies. But this presupposes the existence of multiple bureaucracies. In this chapter, I trace the creation of several new foreign aid bureaucracies and programs through the 1992 FSA. I find that the creation of new agencies and programs was driven by the same factors described in previous chapters. Leaders attempting to forward a foreign policy agenda provide side payments to moderate legislators in the form of new agencies and programs. In turn, these moderates choose to support the final legislation.

Recounting the development of the FSA tells what should now be a familiar story. Fragmentation was driven by congressional bargaining during the legislative process, much of it through amendments. Leaders who wanted to pass the FSA were constrained by rank-and-file legislators with diverse motives. Because 1992 was a recession year and an election year, legislators were especially primed to make demands for their constituencies. Agenda-setters began offering side payments to fence-sitting legislators, many of which involved writing the creation of new programs and agencies directly into the bill. This process drew these fence-sitters to the bill. As the number of these smaller programs increased, centralization and authority decreased, leading to collective action problems in the final enactment of the legislation.

In the following sections, I first present the theoretical expectations for this case and then introduce the legislative sources of fragmentation within the bill itself. First, I discuss the Senate bill and its amendments, which created most of the new programs within the FSA. Although the Senate did not record a vote on the final legislation, the decisions of key senators on the specific amendments proposed can provide insight into their opinions of the legislation. Additionally, a dive into the debate transcripts allows me to see who sponsored the amendments in the first place. Second, I outline the two

Competing for Foreign Aid. Shannon P. Carcelli, Oxford University Press. © Oxford University Press (2025).
DOI: 10.1093/9780197799284.003.0007

versions of the bill that the House voted on. The first version received the most votes, although an important moderate group of legislators who voted against the first House bill ended up favoring the final legislation. Finally, I outline the general provisions of the various versions of the bills and point out key differences that drove changes in voting. I conclude with an update on how the FSA and its programs are faring today and what we can learn from this and other fragmented legislation.

7.1 Theoretical Expectations

The FSA is a case of high congressional disunity and high interest. Congressional disunity in 1992 was already quite high due to recent party realignments and polarization. Rather than making it easier to find compromise, these shifts made it more difficult to find consensus among moderate legislators—crucial for creating large-scale policies. As will become clear below, congressional interest was very high due to the recent global shock of the fall of the Soviet Union. Leadership was highly motivated to create legislation that would inform US-Russian relations for years to come. It was important to everyone in government to get this right.

The FSA's contribution to overall fragmentation should be high according to the vote-buying theory of bureaucratic fragmentation. Additionally, the theory would predict that fragmentation in the FSA should come about a result of scattered pet projects designed by the leadership to appease moderate legislators who are on the fence about the bill.

As expected, this case provides a great deal of support for the vote-buying theory. The debates, hearings, and amendments provide example after example of moderate legislators demanding, and receiving, their favored pet projects. These pet projects' contribution to the fragmentation of the bureaucracy is quite clear. In contrast, non-moderates, even powerful party elites, found it difficult to forward their own projects related to this bill. All of this points to the idea that fragmentation in the FSA was driven by leadership appeasing moderate legislators by supporting their pet projects.

7.2 Background on the FREEDOM Support Act

The end of 1991 witnessed an unprecedented international event: the sudden fall of the Soviet Union. When Congress returned to session in January of 1992, legislators began debating how best to address this change in international reality and support the democratization of the former Soviet Union (FSU). While it was clear that some sort of foreign aid legislation would soon be in the works, several members of Congress were concerned about timing. It was important to pass a bill that would last. However, many members, along with the president himself, were now facing an election year and a bad economy. Both the importance and the sensitivity of FSU policy at this moment promised a rocky beginning for any legislation attempting to aid such a controversial region.

After years of pushing the Republican Party to channel more aid toward the region, Democrats saw this international event as an opportunity to push their legislative agenda further than ever before. Democratic leadership finally managed to find enough support to convince President George H. W. Bush to introduce and support legislation to fund FSU democratization. The FSA was this legislation. It authorized a $410 million bilateral aid package intended to help former Soviet states to recover from communism and build private enterprise. It also created various partnership programs between the US and post-Soviet states and increased the US share to the International Monetary Fund by billions.

The once-powerful Senate Foreign Relations Committee had failed to pass an authorization bill for almost a decade. In a recession year, public support for foreign aid was at a lull. Civil unrest after the Rodney King trial was just beginning to sweep beyond Southern California, and the Persian Gulf War was winding down, further increasing the salience of domestic over foreign policy. Party leadership was beginning to take more control over voting decisions. It was therefore important to the Foreign Relations Committee to take advantage of this opportunity to shape US foreign policy.

The legislation that resulted represented a diverse set of bargains on many levels. Issues from the environment to bank bailouts to domestic spending were discussed within the framework of this legislation. With many of its programs still existing today, the FSA has been one of the most influential and controversial pieces of foreign aid legislation in the past few decades, shaping the foreign aid landscape. Its creation, and the creation of the many new programs that came with it, provides the opportunity to uncover intricate details about the making of legislation and voting on Capitol Hill.

Despite its prominence, the FSA was not a perfect bill. Specifically, it was and still is commonly considered an exceptionally fragmented piece of legislation. A set of audits by the GAO in the mid 1990s reported a lack of coordination of programs and authorizations in the bill. According to the

GAO, the FSA encompassed 19 government agencies with often overlapping agendas and competing priorities and did not offer much guidance on who was in charge. While Congress did implement coordination mechanisms, even these overlapped and competed. Among GAO's strongest criticism was the lack of agency coordination:

> The Coordinator's role has been further complicated by the existence of serious disagreement between agencies over various aspects of the program. USAID, a primary implementing agency for Freedom Support Act programs, has been involved in numerous disputes with other government agencies over money and policy... disputes between USAID and other agencies have required the Coordinator's Office to spend an excessive amount of time dealing with high-level political battles over small amounts of money instead of spending time developing program goals and objectives.[1]

The GAO's findings highlighted the complex structure for overseeing the broad variety of programs under the FSA. It found competing jurisdictions, with some sets of programs falling under no jurisdiction at all. Figure 7.1 visually outlines the GAO's findings regarding the complex structure of FSA programs.

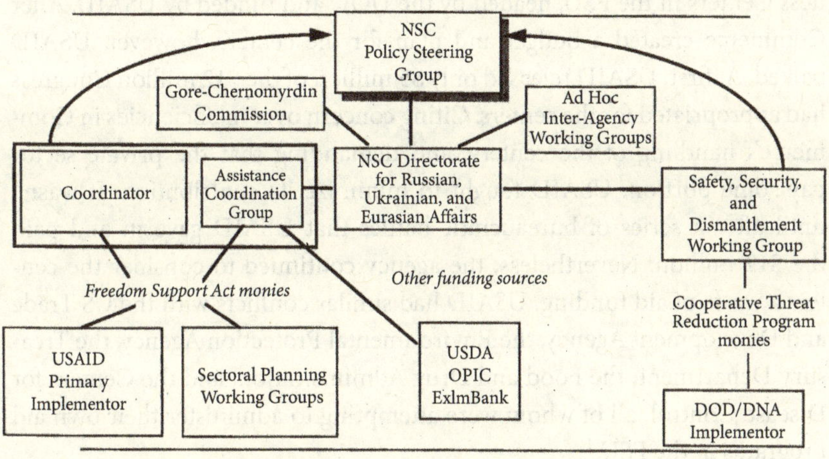

Figure 7.1 FSA coordination, from Johnson (1995a, p. 11)

[1] Johnson (1995a, p. 4)

The bill text even fragmented coordination responsibilities. According to the GAO

> [the] Freedom Support Act states that the Coordinator is responsible for coordinating U.S. government activities and policies with respect to the states of the FSU; however, the Freedom Support Act also gives responsibility to the Secretary of Commerce for coordinating export promotion, and to the Secretary of the Treasury for coordinating activities related to U.S. participation in international financial institutions.[2]

Not only did the FSA legislation encompass an unusual assortment of existing agencies and programs, it also created entirely new ones. A series of foundations, bureaus, funds, and interagency coordination groups came to life through this legislation. Some of these fit better into the existing aid framework than others. For example, the FSA mandated the creation of new Science and Technology Centers in the FSU, to be run by the Department of Energy. These programs were originally carried out and funded exclusively and effectively by the National Laboratories, but Congress later stepped in and mandated that the programs use their own funding source and involve the private sector. According to aid coordinators, this led to confusion and decreased cooperation among agencies.[3]

Another new program authorized by the FSA was a set of American Business Centers in the FSU, headed by the DOC and funded by USAID. After Commerce created a budget and plan for the centers, however, USAID balked. At first, USAID released only $5 million of the $12 million Congress had appropriated for the centers. Citing concern over inefficiencies in Commerce's handling of the centers, and demanding that the private sector pay some portion, USAID fought to minimize its contribution. It wasn't until after a series of bureaucratic battles that USAID gave in and paid the $12 million. Nevertheless, the agency continued to consider the centers a waste of aid funding. USAID had similar conflicts with the US Trade and Development Agency, the Environmental Protection Agency, the Treasury Department, the Food and Drug Administration, and the Centers for Disease Control, all of whom were attempting to administer their own aid programs in the FSU.[4]

[2] Johnson (1995a, p. 26)
[3] Johnson (1995a, p. 31)
[4] Johnson (1995a)

After the GAO's original report, USAID made an effort to work more closely with other agencies. Later, in 1995, the programmatic inefficiencies were being managed more carefully, but the fragmentation of the original bill was still wreaking havoc on FSU aid programs. A later GAO audit once again pointed out ongoing problems among bureaus within the Department of State.[5] Interagency cooperation in the FSU has waxed and waned since these reports, but, according to one prominent aid expert, the FSU and similar programs were the beginning of today's uptick in fragmentation.[6]

Overall, the number and severity of these anecdotes suggest that the FSA served to fragment foreign aid implementation in the FSU. Unlike many programs, it spread aid funding among several agencies, started new projects without carefully considering their authority and placement, and created a coordination nightmare for USAID and the Department of State. This was driven by the dozens of pet projects written into the bill, through the creation of or delegation to new and competing bureaucracies. Below, I show that these pet projects were driven by moderate Democrats, who would be the most likely to vote against their party. As the vote-buying theory suggests, in the case of the FSA, fragmentation was a consequence of a motivated leadership with an unclear hold on power giving legislators what they wanted in order to pass an important bill.

7.3 Empirical Strategy

The theory makes clear predictions about which legislators should benefit from the vote-buying process leading to the FSA's fragmentation. The fragmented bill combined a collection of smaller programs, some of which may have served as pet projects for certain legislators. The empirical results in Chapter 4 confirm that moderates are the legislators whose pet projects are most likely to be represented. These are the legislators who would otherwise be least likely to vote with their own party.

Two elements specific to the FSA allow me to estimate which actors most favored its fragmentation, and therefore to discern which legislators benefited from the fruits of that fragmentation. The first element is related to voting. Several votes took place in both chambers of Congress, with varying effects on fragmentation. On the Senate side, the chamber

[5] Johnson (1995b)
[6] Anonymous interview with author, July 17, 2017

considered dozens of amendments, some of which would create more programs. Determining which senators sponsored which amendments will offer some insight into who stood to gain from the programs. On the House side, two separate votes confirmed two versions of the FSA. The second version, which came out of the conference committee with the Senate, included new programs that were not a part of the House version. This led to an ultimately more fragmented bill, which received support from a different set of representatives. Comparing voting on these two versions of the House bill provides an opportunity to see which representatives stood to gain from the programs that were added.

The second set of factors that will help to determine who benefited from the specific programs are more qualitative in nature. They come from elite interviews, congressional hearing and debate transcripts, and summaries of the legislation. Although not all members of Congress attended hearings and debates on the legislation, the statements of the ones who did can tell us a lot about preferences along the political spectrum. Similarly, the success and failure of the specific programs that these legislators supported can be explained in the theoretical framework. Reading legislators' statements and reactions offers more insight on who was benefiting from fragmentation.

In the following sections, I outline estimation strategies for determining the winners and losers of fragmented programs in the FSA. I show that the most successful programs were not necessarily those espoused by powerful legislators, which would be surprising without the theoretical explanation outlined in this book. Instead, the ability of a proposed program to be included in the final bill is related to the ideology of the legislator who supported the program. Programs introduced by powerful but extreme legislators often failed to make it into the final legislation. Instead, legislators with moderate ideologies were the most successful in gaining funding and support for their programs. The fragmentation among programs visible in the FSA, therefore, is largely a result of moderate legislators demanding payment for their acquiescence. The specific details of the programs, as well as the identity of their supporters, confirm this pattern.

7.4 The Three Votes of the FSA

Like most legislation, the FSA was impossible to resolve with a single vote. Both chambers of Congress created their own versions of the bill, which leaders then reconciled after both bills passed the floor. Both chambers then had to schedule a second vote to pass the final version into law. The first vote for both chambers is recorded in the congressional record. However, the second votes, after leaders reconciled the bills' differences, are not as well recorded. Instead of collecting written votes, the Senate cast and passed their second vote by voice ballot. There is no record of which senators supported the final version of the bill. However, the House cast a recorded vote for the final version, allowing for a comparison of representatives' votes in each version.

The House and Senate versions of the FSA differ slightly for ideological and institutional reasons. First, the House at the time was slightly more liberal than the Senate, with median DW-Nominate scores of –.2 and –.15, respectively. This resulted in less trust of the Republican president, George H. W. Bush. As a result, the House version of the bill provided less discretion to the executive than the version that eventually emerged from Congress. However, the Senate version of the bill was much more fragmented than the House version. The fragmentation was not driven by House members' distrust of the executive branch.

Second, unlike the Senate, every member of the House of Representatives was up for re-election. This made the immediate domestic implications of the FSA more salient within the House, especially among liberal Democrats. The House nearly failed to pass the legislation because of some members' insistence on passing domestic spending bills first.[7] This was a less salient concern in the Senate, where only a third of members were up for re-election. Finally, House leadership was able to pass their version of the FSA through a "closed rule," meaning no amendments were allowed after the committee stage.[8] This allowed the House to boast a "cleaner" bill, with fewer amendments and less outside influence. The Senate version, forced to consider floor amendments, included more scattered legislative content.

The final version of the bill deleted many of the amendments that the Senate had favored, and it weakened some of the strings that the House had attached. The compromise by both chambers echoes the vote-buying theory. The specific programs instituted by the FSA served to bring in moderate legislators who were hesitant to shift the status quo. When comparing votes between and within bills, it becomes clear that the fragmentation created by

[7] Chicago Tribune (1992)

[8] Interestingly, the closed-rule decision was somewhat of an accident: most of the idea's opponents happened to be held up at a news conference when the floor decision was made (CQ-Almanac 1992a).

the FSA was largely a tool to make the bill more palatable to moderates in Congress, especially in the Senate.

The FSA was first introduced in the House, but the Senate leadership was the first to push it as an agenda item, and the first vote took place in the Senate. This is partially because debate in the Senate was less intense than in the House. Fewer senators faced an imminent re-election race, making them less inclined to grandstand against foreign spending. This mostly affected Democratic legislators, many of whose constituents demanded more government support for domestic programs.

The lack of imminent elections minimized the primacy of domestic spending for senators. Unlike the House, whose leadership only managed to pull a 60% majority, over 79% of the Senate voted in favor of the bill. The Senate vote was also more bipartisan than the House, with 82% of Republicans voting in favor of the legislation (compared to only 58% in the first House vote). Whereas the DW-Nominate scores of "yea" and "nay" voters in the Senate did not differ significantly, supporters and opponents in the House significantly differed ideologically. All this led to a smoother bill passage in the Senate.

This is despite the fact that the Senate faced a more complicated institutional process to pass the legislation. Unlike the House, Senate rules did not allow for a quick, amendment-free passage. The Senate had to accept amendments from both the committee and the floor as a whole. This led to some changes to the Senate bill. The Senate recorded 81 separate amendments during floor debate. These were in addition to the amendments that had been added during committee debate, which are not recorded. These Senate amendments played a large role in shaping the coalition in support of the bill, as well as the bill itself. The first task in analyzing the Senate's actions on the FSA, then, is to consider these amendments.

Based on the wording of the amendment and the substance of the debate in the Congressional Record, I coded each amendment by type.[9] I coded four types of Senate floor amendments to the FSA: Politics, Security, Earmark, and Program. *Politics* amendments involved domestic discretionary and legal issues that had little international or distributional bearing and did not specify new programs. They include specification of funding amounts, reporting requirements, and conditionality. Of the 81 total amendments, 21 were coded *Politics*. *Security* amendments dealt with foreign policy issues

[9] The Appendix lists the amendments and their summaries in the legislative record.

rather than domestic politics. Most were short on debate, unless they dealt with a controversial foreign policy issue. A plurality of amendments, 29, were coded as *Security*. *Earmarks* were amendments that either dealt specifically with distributive issues or were transparent in their domestic distributive consequences. A Florida senator introducing an amendment about Cuba is an example. Only 14 of the 81 amendments were coded as *Earmark*. Finally, *Program* amendments are the ones specifically introduced to authorize the creation of a new program within the FSA bill. These are the amendments most responsible for the overall fragmentation generated by the FSA legislation. Of the 81 introduced amendments, 17 were designed to create new programs.

According to the vote-buying theory, new programs should be disproportionately created to appease moderates. This would obviously imply that moderates introduced a higher proportion of the *Program* amendments. This does appear to be the case. A full 23.5% of all *Program* amendment sponsors came from the majority-party moderates. In contrast, only 12% of other amendments came from that ideological space.

The complexity of new programs, and the fragmentation that they could create, was not lost on senators at the time. One clear point of conflict in the Senate debate was the sheer number of priorities in the bill. From the start, the FSA contained a detailed list of programs, many of which overlapped and duplicated existing ones. When challenged by a senator about the overwhelming number of new programs in the bill, an administration official responded:

> I am ready to commit euthanasia on projects that do not get off the ground. But... you have colleagues up here in the House who have specific interest in this and sometimes, the price for doing business for us is to include on the list some things that maybe you or I would not in a vacuum, have on this list.[10]

Senators from both sides of the aisle expressed initial concern that the bill was becoming too fragmented. During a joint hearing, Democratic Senator Patrick Leahy asked the administration, "How do we avoid frittering away our aid in tiny programs all over the former USSR?"[11] Specifically, Leahy criticized the administration for its promotion of a new Democracy

[10] US Senate (1992, p. 46)
[11] US Senate (1992, p. 61)

Corps, which would function similarly to the Peace Corps but focus volunteer recruitment on business executives, who would work directly with local enterprises. Leahy was not a moderate, and clearly this was not his pet project; he had little to gain from this and other new programs that would eventually buy the votes of more moderate legislators.

For their part, Republicans reported skepticism about programs like the new Educational Exchange Endowment. Senator Trent Lott pointed out during debate that the US government already administered a number of similar exchange programs:

> ... such as the Fulbright Scholarship Program, the Samantha Smith exchanges, the Ben Franklin fellowships. To fund the additional programs contemplated by this amendment could jeopardize the continuation of these very highly successful programs in operation now. There simply is not enough money to go around.[12]

The fragmented design of the FSA was not a loss for everyone. To the contrary, some legislators derived district-level benefits from individual projects funded through the bill. For example, Senator Bob Kerrey, a moderate first-term Democrat from Nebraska, created a new Department of Agriculture–based business exchange program that would "increase demand among farmers not only for bulk grains, but also for feed products."[13] In his congressional testimony, Kerrey credited the Land O'Lakes corporation with helping to develop the program. In fact, Land O'Lakes had already been running similar business exchanges at its own expense. This new funding source offered a boon to midwest companies like Land O'Lakes even as it complicated the overall infrastructure of US foreign aid.

Despite hesitation from both parties, many amendments that further fragmented foreign aid passed through the Senate with little difficulty. As long as they were supported by crucial moderate senators, fragmentation of the foreign aid budget was considered a necessary evil. Another theme of the amendments to the Senate bill was an increase in power given to the DOC. According to Senator Kasten, a moderate Republican and supporter of Commerce's programs "we have tried through hearing after hearing, through letter after letter, time and time again to try to get this point across, and

[12] Cong. Rec. Vol. 138, No. 98, S9591, July 2, 1992
[13] Cong. Rec. Vol. 138 No. 98, S9591, July 1, 1992

it wins sometimes in Commerce, and then it loses in State."[14] The explicit inclusion of Commerce in the final FSA bill served to appease Kasten and other moderate Republicans.

Just as notable as programs that were *included* in the Senate bill are those programs that were *excluded*. Powerful senators' pet projects were often excluded when those senators did not need to be convinced to support the legislation. Senator Joe Biden, a powerful member of the Foreign Relations Committee, pushed for inclusion in the bill of a "SEED Foundation," modeled on the IAF and providing grassroots funding for small projects in Eastern Europe. Not only was Biden's foundation excluded from all versions of the final FSA legislation, it had also been ignored three years before in a previous bill.[15] It is initially puzzling that such a powerful senator would be unable to push through a program that he supported. However, the vote-buying theory predicts just such an outcome. Senator Biden's DW-Nominate score during the 102nd Congress, at –0.33, fell outside the range of moderate legislators. He therefore required less convincing and appeasement than other legislators. The final bill would move toward Biden's ideal point, and he would (and did) support it, regardless of whether his pet project was included.

Legislators' voting decisions provide more evidence for the theory. Most Democrats were in favor of this legislation. It represented a new frontier of foreign aid, creating programs to develop democracy in states that were previously controlled by a communist superpower. Most of those programs did not previously exist. Senate votes are represented in Figure 7.2. The region between the first and second quartiles is shaded for ease of interpretation.

As is clear from Figure 7.2, moderate Democrats were much less likely to vote in favor of the FSA than any other Democrat (see the number of blue dots at the vertical zero axis). This is because the FSA drove policy further from their own ideal points. Many moderate Democrats would have been content to extend existing aid programs in the FSU. Unlike Republicans, moderate Democrats did not need to vote for the legislation to support their president. In the absence of any pet projects or new programs, even more of these moderate Democrats would probably have voted against the legislation.

[14] Cong. Rec. Vol. 138, No. 97, S9476, July 1, 1992

[15] U.S. assistance to the new Independent States. Hearings, 102nd Congress, 2nd Session. March 19, 1992. Washington, G.P.O., 1992. (S.Hrg.102-671)

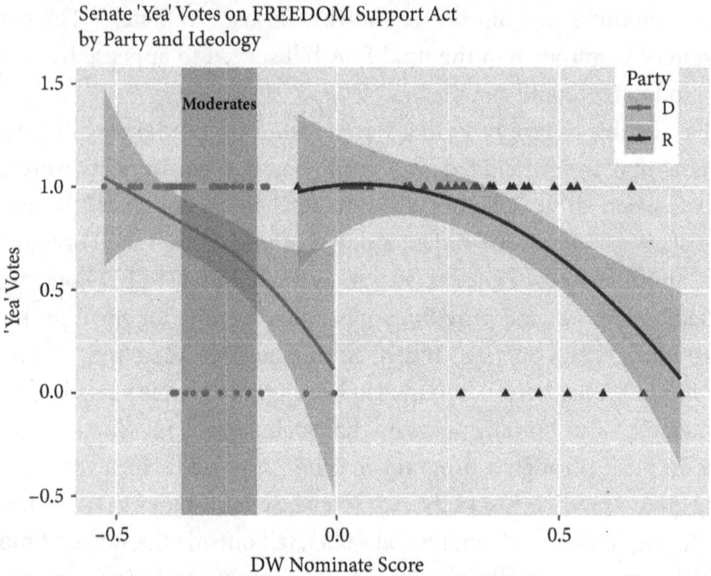

Figure 7.2 Senate roll call votes on the FSA, by DW-Nominate score and party. Dark (Republican) and light (Democrat) lines represent smoothed loess curves for each party's ideology-vote relationship. The highlighted region denotes moderate policy space within the Democratic Party.

After the Senate vote, the House crafted and voted upon its own version of the FSA. As mentioned above, the FSA faced more dissent in House of Representatives than it did in the Senate. This dissent came from across the political spectrum. While liberal Democrats pushed for more domestic and less international spending, conservative Republicans questioned the wisdom of funding our former enemies at all. Much of this dissent can be attributed to election anxiety. Of the 20 senators who had opposed the FSA, 11 were facing an election in that year.[16] Because all House members were facing an election, even the most liberal ones had reason to be wary of foreign aid spending.

This difference in liberal votes is clear from Figure 7.3. Unlike the Senate bill, the House bill was unable to attract some of its most liberal members. The moderate ideological area has little bearing on support for the bill, although it is notable that support decreases throughout most of the moderate region.

[16] CQ-Almanac (1992b)

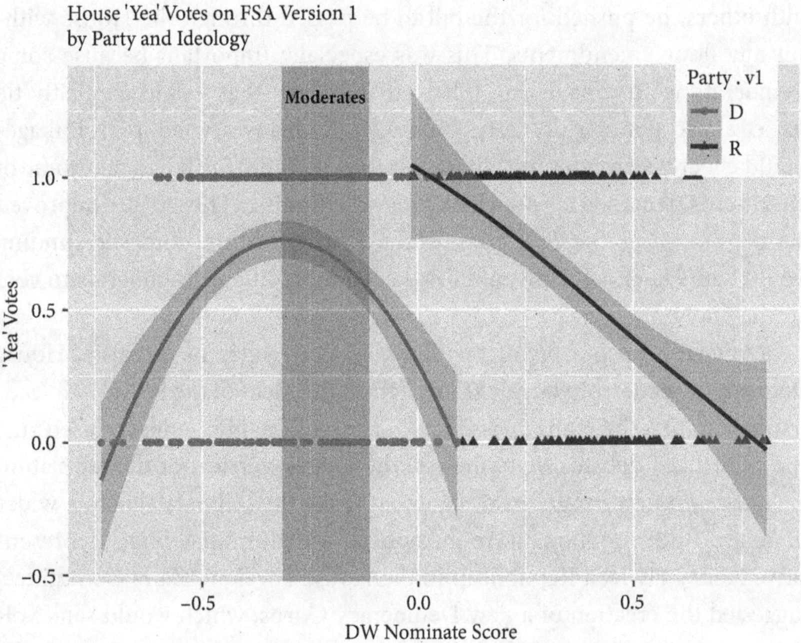

Figure 7.3 House roll call votes on the FSA, by DW-Nominate score and party. Dark (Republican) and light (Democrat) lines represent smoothed loess curves for each party's ideology-vote relationship. The highlighted region denotes moderate policy space within the Democratic Party.

The House of Representatives recorded two separate votes on the FSA: first, on the version of the bill that the House itself had created, and second, on a final version that resolved the differences between the chambers. Two major differences between the two versions of the bill stand out. First, the final bill is less detailed than the version that the House initially wrote and passed. Many representatives were skeptical of the Bush administration and wanted to maximize their oversight while minimizing Bush's discretion. Many accused the administration's bill of being too vague and asking for too much.[17]

Second, the House bill was more streamlined. As Representative Hamilton contested, "several of the Senate amendments were 'overlapping, contradictory, and would create layer upon layer of new bureaucracy.'"[18] Along

[17] Crossettes (1992)
[18] Tarnoff (2004, p. 27)

with others, he pushed for the bill to be passed through the House without any floor amendments. This was especially important because some Democrats were considering killer amendments that would explicitly tie Soviet aid to popular domestic programs. As many argued, such linkages would effectively render the bill impassable. By June, Bush had met some of the House's demands for domestic program funding. This greatly improved the prospects for the FSA passing the House.[19] More domestic funding would come later, which would draw even more liberal Democrats to vote for the final bill.

Despite the misgivings of members on both sides of the aisle, House Democratic leadership largely favored the basic ideas of the FSA. With leadership support, the House passed its version of the bill under a closed rule and with little debate. Nevertheless, the House version of the legislation included two new programs designed to make the bill palatable to a wider audience. Both programs were introduced in committee. First, Representative Henry Hyde, a Republican in the House Foreign Affairs Committee, suggested the creation of a new Democracy Corps, which would send volunteers to rural regions to help build democratic institutions. Second, the committee chairman, Dante Fascell, pushed through the addition of science and technology centers to promote peaceful nuclear power. Both of these programs made it to the final bill, although with less importance attached to them than in the House version.

Unsurprisingly, the structure of the FSA aid package was more conservative in nature than many liberal House Democrats would have preferred. Even House Democratic leadership was split on the bill, with Majority Whip David E. Bonior arguing that the FSA should not be passed until the president agreed to an unemployment benefits package. Republicans were similarly split, with mixed statements even from within the Bush administration. Deputy Secretary of State Lawrence S. Eagleburger argued that "money indiscriminately pumped into the region could hinder reform and promote the very dependencies that have for too long existed in these countries."[20] Despite a group of liberal Democrats and conservative Republicans opposing the bill, the FSA passed the House with minimal difficulty.

After both the House and the Senate passed their own versions of the FSA, representatives from both chambers met to compromise on a final bill. This

[19] Tarnoff (2004, p. 31)
[20] CQ-Almanac (1992a)

conference committee was short, as was the Senate deliberation about the final bill. The House, however, remained skeptical of the FSA, especially the negotiations that had led to the final bill version. According to a later report by the Congressional Research Service:

> The one issue on which the largest number of Members weighed in with their views concerned which programs and activities to support. Whether the intent was to establish a program leading more effectively and efficiently to the goals of democracy and free-markets, to benefit U.S. business or, in some cases, their own districts, or to boost programs reflecting pet interests, Members frequently expressed their own set of priorities of where the money might best be spent.[21]

Many of the programs that had been introduced into the earlier versions of the bill remained. However, the House did manage to decrease the number of specific programs that senators had slipped in as amendments, along with giving up control over its own programs. The final bill included 13 general categories of programs, providing significantly less detail on how they were to be carried out.[22] As expected, the final bill represented a compromise for both branches.

Simplifying the Senate's bill, while important to some, was not the House leadership's main priority. The House had decreased executive control in its version of the bill, and it intended to keep those controls in the final version. House debate over the final bill largely followed that of the first bill, although national security issues were now more prominent than domestic programs, which had been partially addressed in separate legislation. The final version lost votes in the House. While the first vote had passed by 255–164, the second House vote received only 232 votes. Most of the votes lost in the final version were from the most conservative members. Moderates, however, were more likely to vote for the second, more fragmented, version than the first. Their colleagues in the Senate had introduced programs that they supported.

Moderate Democrats were just as likely as liberal Democrats to change their vote in favor of the final bill. This is surprising given that the acceptance of domestic spending conditions, set by the liberal wing of the party, was by far the most important change. Of the 28 legislators who increased

[21] Tarnoff (2004, p. 27)
[22] Tarnoff (2004, p. 26)

their support (either changing from an "abstain" to a "yea" or a "nay" to anything else), 11 came from the moderate and 11 from the liberal wing of the Democratic Party. Only 6 were Republicans. Once again, moderate legislators disproportionately got something out of the final bill—perhaps due to the work of their moderate colleagues in the Senate.[23]

Unlike the House, the Senate passed the final bill by voice vote and with no debate. Although some senators did not see their pet projects in the final bill, the legislation did manage to represent many interests in some way. No programs were excluded entirely; however, some were relegated to executive discretion or merged into a paragraph describing other existing programs. The senators whose amendments were not included, whether those were political or programmatic, put up little fight in the final vote.

7.5 Discussion and Conclusion

The creation of the FSA provides several opportunities to witness the vote-buying theory's mechanisms at work. First, the legislators who most complained about the creation of new, redundant programs were the ones most likely to vote for the bill anyway. Some of them even attempted to push their own new programs into the legislation, but the agenda-setters crafting the bill would not allow just any legislator to introduce a new program. Instead, a disproportionate number of new programs were created by the moderate legislators. This suggests that the inclusion of these programs was necessary to gain moderates' support. Second, an important mechanism by which new programs were introduced was through the amendment process. The House version, which was able to pass without amendments, was much less complicated.

The experience of the FSA informed future aid legislation and US responses to democratization. The programs and funds created by the bill continue to be used in appropriations bills today. In 2009, the FSA was combined with another program to create the Assistance for Europe, Eurasia, and Central Asia account. In the past decades, coordination of FSA

[23] Recall that the House voted the amendment process down, making it more difficult for House moderates to demand new agency creation through their own amendments. The negotiations on the House side, therefore, took place mainly through back channels, which are more difficult to count and measure.

programs has improved, although it might be said that Eastern Europe's democratization process has stalled.

Later funding programs to the FSU would fragment aid in similar ways. However, there is reason to believe that agency coordination has improved. It is no coincidence that this happened as the salience of the FSU waned in the early 2000s.[24] In fact, the FSA is now serving as an example of how coordination in other foreign aid realms can be improved. Despite early problems, there is a chance that internal conflicts can be resolved. When Congress loses interest in a region, bureaucratic coordination is easier to achieve.

Just as the large-scale trends support the idea that foreign aid fragmentation is an unintended byproduct of vote-buying, this chapter shows that bargaining on individual bills can follow the same trend. Rather than being an individual choice by lawmakers, foreign aid fragmentation is a byproduct of congressional bargaining—an unwanted but necessary outcome. In the case of the FSA, no individual legislator wanted the bill to be fragmented. However, many legislators wanted their pet projects to be funded. Although not all legislators were successful in promoting their pet projects—most notably, Senator Joe Biden failed to realize the creation of his SEED Foundation—some were. Disproportionately, moderate legislators managed to get their pet agencies into the final bill. After enough pet agencies were added, the FSA became a fragmented mess, with confusing accountability mechanisms and an unclear leadership structure. The mechanisms that were introduced in previous chapters played out in the case of the FSA.

This chapter and Chapter 6 suggest that fighting against foreign aid fragmentation can be a difficult task. However, in Chapter 8, I show that fragmentation is not a foregone conclusion. When Congress is either unified or uninterested in a policy area, bureaucratic conflict can be minimized. The case of the fight against HIV/AIDS in sub-Saharan Africa provides an example of bureaucratic cooperation and streamlined policymaking. Like the more recent successes in the FSU, when Congress loses interest, bureaucratic efficacy can improve.

[24] It is yet to be seen whether the increase in salience since Russia's invasion of Ukraine will change this.

Chapter 8

A Success Story: The President's Emergency Plan For AIDS Relief

The previous chapters paint a pessimistic portrait of US foreign aid and foreign policy. In both case studies, Congress deformed foreign aid bureaucracy to a degree that left high- and low-level bureaucrats unable to cooperate. However, foreign aid need not be so ineffective. According to the vote-buying theory, when congressional interest is low, leaders have little incentive to micromanage foreign aid, and legislators have less interest in pet projects. This lack of interest can result in lower levels of bureaucratic fragmentation and, counterintuitively, better foreign aid policy.

In this chapter, I present a case that has often been hailed as a success story in US foreign aid, the US response to the AIDS epidemic in sub-Saharan Africa. This initiative, introduced in 2003 as the President's Emergency Plan for AIDS Relief (PEPFAR), was quickly codified into law and continues to drive the US health aid policy agenda. In the case of AIDS relief, Congress was uninterested in becoming as deeply involved in the day-to-day mechanics of aid. This relative lack of congressional interest decreased both the number of pet projects and the incentives for bureaucracies to compete with each other over funding. Although bureaucratic battles existed even in this case, they were not exacerbated by Congress. This kept policy running relatively smoothly. Congressional oversight did not take sides, and bureaucratic fragmentation was minimized.

This case also suggests an intriguing additional component to the theory. Although the theory chapter was agnostic about the identity of the leaders driving policy, I generally assumed that the majority party, which has the power to block unwanted legislation, has the most influence. However, in the PEPFAR case, the power of both parties to whip their own members into negotiating blocs was crucial to policy success. Because both Democratic and Republican leadership were able to control their own members, most congressional bargaining happened at the party, rather than the individual, level. Because of this, most amendments and divisions were

Competing for Foreign Aid. Shannon P. Carcelli, Oxford University Press. © Oxford University Press (2025).
DOI: 10.1093/9780197799284.003.0008

partisan, rather than reflecting individual vote-buying. The importance of the minority party leadership in decreasing fragmentation is clear in this case. The importance of party power fits with cross-national work on the phenomenon, which finds that states with institutions that empower party leaders have less fragmented aid bureaucracies.[1] The role of parties is worth considering further in future research.

In this chapter, I first introduce the case and outline the expectations hypothesized by the theoretical framework. I describe the levels of the independent variables—congressional interest and congressional disunity—during the creation of PEPFAR. Next, I outline the legislation that created PEPFAR and show the role of moderate legislators in demanding pet projects—in this case, very little. I then describe the outcome in this case, a low level of bureaucratic fragmentation and interagency conflict. Finally, I conclude with some lessons that policymakers can and have drawn from the PEPFAR case, and consider how these lessons can be carried over into struggles with current-day health epidemics.

8.1 Case Summary

In his State of the Union address on January 29, 2003, President George W. Bush surprised many by highlighting the global tragedy of HIV/AIDS. Bush asked Congress to appropriate $15 billion over the following five years to fund his new Emergency Plan for AIDS Relief, which later become known as PEPFAR.[2] Bush's ambitious agenda involved preventing millions of AIDS infections through education campaigns and medical interventions and increasing the number of AIDS patients using life-sustaining drug treatments by millions. The breadth of this agenda was unlike anything Congress had ever appropriated for such a goal before.

In response, Congress quickly drafted legislation matching Bush's priorities. This legislation was largely bipartisan—it was co-sponsored by Republican and Democratic members in the House and Senate. The first PEPFAR-related bill was the United States Leadership Against HIV/AIDS, Tuberculosis, and Malaria Act of 2003, or the Leadership Act. The Leadership Act promised $15 billion between 2004 and 2008, mainly for the fight

[1] Carcelli (2023)
[2] Bush (2003)

against HIV/AIDS. It was passed quickly, with only two months between the bill's introduction and the president's signing.

Initially, Bush was concerned that Congress would take too much interest in this initiative, piling on pet projects and drowning out the purpose of PEPFAR. He insisted on keeping the initiative a secret from the public and, especially, from Congress. In fact, Bush was explicitly concerned about members of Congress demanding pet projects within the legislation. President Bush could have written the theory section of this book with his explanation that:

> If word leaked out there would be a turf war among government agencies for control of the money. Members of Congress would be tempted to dilute the program's focus by redirecting funds for their own purposes. I didn't want PEPFAR to end up hamstrung by bureaucracy and competing interests.[3]

Once he finally announced the initiative, Bush appointed Randall Tobias, a pharmaceutical executive, to the role of Global AIDS Coordinator. Legislation empowered the State Department to create the Office of the US Global AIDS Coordinator and Health Diplomacy (OGAC). OGAC centralized PEPFAR funding through a single US bureaucratic entity. This created a streamlined structure through which to carry out the policy.

Initially, high-level bureaucrats did battle for control over PEPFAR. Tommy Thompson, then Secretary of the Department of Health and Human Services, jockeyed for control over OGAC, peeving USAID. According to then-USAID Administrator Andrew Natsios, Thompson was surreptitiously pushing legislation that would allow the department to make country-level decisions without having to work with the State Department. This, of course, would dilute the power of the State Department, and Secretary Colin Powell was furious when he learned about Thompson's attempts.[4]

This is an example of a phenomenon that should look familiar. Like in previous cases in this book, bureaucrats attempted to use Congress as a wedge in interagency battles. However, unlike in the previous case studies, in this case Congress did not take the bait. Because congressional interest in the HIV/AIDS epidemic was relatively low, there was little incentive for Congress to micromanage the situation and side with any agency. Instead,

[3] Bush (2011, p. 453)
[4] Natsios (2019, p. 77)

Powell and Thompson had to work out their disagreements on their own, resulting in a more streamlined bureaucratic process.

OGAC has since been lauded for both its reach and its control over country offices. Each of the states selected as a priority country are given a single leader within the embassy, which controls all of the agencies included in the funding. This allows all of the agencies involved in OGAC to work together and clarifies which projects are provided to which agencies. PEPFAR was reauthorized in 2008 with similarly high levels of bipartisan support. It continues to be a popular program and wins high praise among the development community.

8.2 Theoretical Expectations

In contrast to highly salient issues like the Afghanistan War and the fall of the Soviet Union, global health tends to be of little concern to Congress. This becomes apparent when looking back at the data from Chapter 5. The category of "Health Aid" received very little attention in Congress. Between 2000 and 2014, health-related entities only accounted for around 15% of aid lobbying expenditures. Most of that lobbying took place after 2008, with almost no health-related organizations filing lobbying reports before 2003.

The sub-Saharan African region receives even less attention from Congress. Of the thousands of hearings in the 2002–2018 period, only 15 focused on any sub-Saharan African country. In comparison to the other case studies in this book, which involved major, high-profile international events, PEPFAR provides an example of low congressional interest.

Congressional disunity, on the other hand, was relatively high in 2003. If disunity on its own were enough to drive bureaucratic fragmentation, then it would be difficult to make theoretical predictions in this case. However, disunity does not have many consequences in the absence of congressional interest. Leaders will only be willing to buy votes, and legislators will only demand pet projects, when they are interested in a policy. Additionally, *intra-party* unity in this case was relatively high.

The vote-buying theory would predict low levels of bureaucratic fragmentation. Because congressional interest in the AIDS epidemic was relatively low, leaders were willing to allow the president to take the lead in crafting the policy. Leaders in Congress had little incentive to expend a lot of resources attempting to shape policy. Additionally, few rank-and-file legislators had reason to hold out their votes in exchange for pet projects. Low levels of congressional interest, according to the theory, should lead to low levels of fragmentation.

8.3 The Leadership Act

The 2003 Leadership Act designated OCAG and authorized funding for PEPFAR. This bill was bipartisan and made it through Congress quickly. Only 25 amendments were offered in this bill, 11 of which made it into the final act. The House was able to pass the bill much earlier than the Senate, giving the chamber an advantage in setting the final legislation.[5] Ten of the 11 amendments that made it into the final bill came from the House side. The bill contained few pet projects, and most amendments came not from on-the-fence moderates but from partisan leaders seeking ideological consensus.

The Leadership Act involved bipartisan negotiation and compromise. A majority of the debate surrounding PEPFAR was strictly partisan, rather than being about program specifics. Intra-party agreement, on both the Republican and Democratic side, was high, and inter-party disagreements dominated the debate. As exhibited in Figure 8.1, ideology played the greatest role in the decision to support the bill. In both parties, more conservative members were more likely to vote against the bill than more liberal legislators.[6] This matches the stereotypical depiction of humanitarian aid as a policy that appeals to liberal ideology.

Although Democrats were more likely to support the legislation, one of their main criticisms was Republicans' hurry to push it through Congress. President Bush wanted to announce the legislation at a G8 summit scheduled for early June, hoping that the announcement would prompt other leaders to join the effort.[7] Republican leadership was willing to rally behind the president in this goal, which required whipping the conservatives in their own party. Democrats made a point of protesting the hurried timeline.

[5] Sorrells (2003a)

[6] The only Democrat who did not support the legislation was Rep. Eugene Taylor, a blue dog Democrat from Mississippi.

[7] Sorrells (2003c)

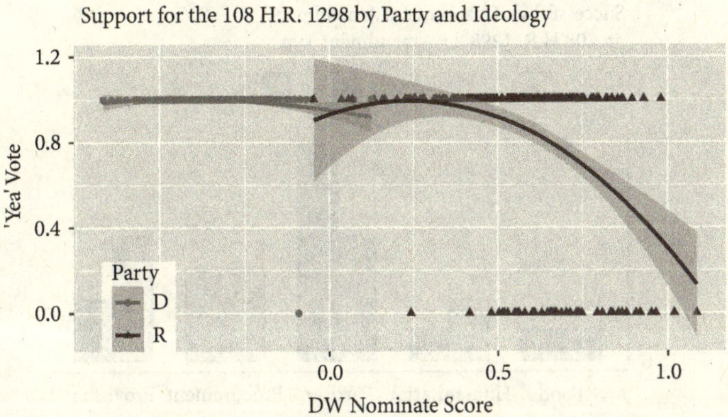

Figure 8.1 Legislators' votes in support of the 2003 Global Leadership Act, plotted against their DW-Nominate scores. Dark pyramids represent Republican legislators, and light circles, Democrats. The dark and light lines represent smoothed loess curves for Republican and Democratic legislators, respectively. More conservative members of both parties were less likely to support the bill.

Nevertheless, most of the House amendments in the final legislation were introduced by conservative Republican lawmakers, who were generally less supportive of the bill as a whole.

Figure 8.2 categorizes the amendments introduced in the bill. The final passage rate of these amendments was generally low. But it is worth considering the differential passage rates of different types of amendments. First, only a few amendments involved traditional topics of foreign aid, such as food and humanitarian issues. These amendments tended to steer away from the topic of global health, although the discussion of food-aid-related amendments did note the links between nutrition and ability to survive disease. Later criticisms of the Leadership Act attacked the inclusion of food aid, arguing that it represented "pet development causes" in a supposed health bill.[8] Procurement-related amendments, arguably the most likely to represent vote-buying, were even less successful. These amendments tended to revolve around the types of medication the government would purchase for the fight against HIV/AIDS.

The "Provisions" category mainly includes amendments proposing increases and decreases in funding. However, two of the provisions did

[8] Loewenberg (2008)

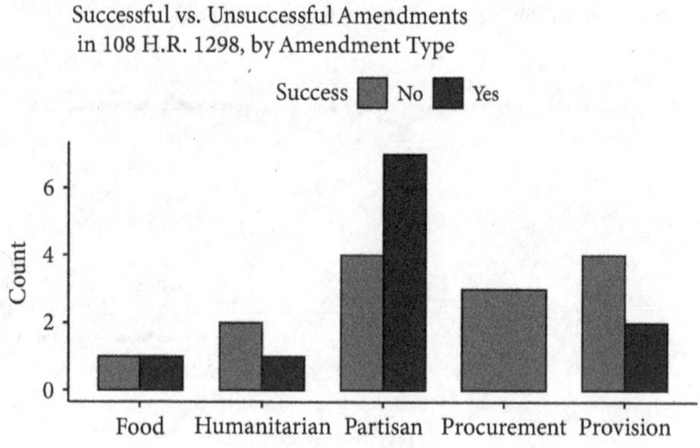

Figure 8.2 Counts of successful and unsuccessful amendments, by type. By far the most common type of amendment introduced was partisan—in this case, it had to do with controversial family planning issues that tend to be ideologically polarizing.

mention more specific preferences about how the money should be spent. Senator Chris Dodd introduced a failed amendment seeking to expand PEPFAR's reach to the Caribbean region, and Senator Sheila Jackson-Lee successfully sought a "sense-of-Congress" amendment to encourage the private sector to help in the fight against HIV/AIDS. The Dodd amendment would have created fragmentation at the country level, if not necessarily bureaucratic fragmentation. The fact that it did not make it to final legislation highlights the leadership's ability in this case to maintain a streamlined bill.

A majority of the amendments introduced and successfully passed into legislation were partisan in nature. "Partisan" provisions in this case were those that dealt, directly or indirectly, with the issue of various means of birth control: how much to limit and fund organizations promoting the use of condoms and even abortions. This included provisions involving the role of an NGO called the Global Fund to Fight AIDS, Tuberculosis, and Malaria (or simply "The Fund"). The Fund has been a major source of inter-party controversy in issues of global health. Democrats pointed to its effectiveness at fighting diseases, but Republicans were leery of The Fund's willingness to work with China despite the country's support for compulsory abortions.

The final bill represented a compromise between these two opposing perspectives. As President Bush would later complain, "both sides charged that we were imposing our values—religious fundamentalism if you asked one camp, sexual permissiveness if you asked the other."[9] The compromise fell toward the Republican side, with language in the final bill requiring that one-third of funding be devoted to abstinence education, a favorite of Christian evangelicals.[10] However, Republicans had originally sought to explicitly prioritize monogamy and abstinence over condom distribution. The one-third level, therefore, represented a compromise between the two parties.

The only amendment that passed in the Senate provides an example of the partisan bargaining in this bill. This amendment, introduced by the ranking Democrat on the Foreign Relations Committee, provided debt relief for the countries hardest hit by the HIV/AIDS epidemic. The amendment was not meant to buy the votes of any recalcitrant legislators. It was not introduced by a moderate, nor did it introduce any new programs or provide support for any specific constituency. This amendment served the simple purpose of making the bill more palatable to Democrats, easing inter-party negotiations.

Not all legislators were pleased about the lack of vote-buying in this legislation, but leadership in both parties managed to suppress criticism. In finalizing the negotiations, Senator Bill Frist encouraged his fellow Republicans to avoid the vote-buying seen in previous bills, arguing "We can't let the perfect be the enemy of the good."[11] This standpoint was not as popular among Democrats, with Senator Barbara Boxer even complaining during debate that "the fix is in. All amendments are being voted down because of the President's schedule."[12] However, Democratic leaders were more willing than their rank and file to negotiate with Republicans. They managed to pass a single amendment into the bill, which was enough to create a bipartisan compromise. Because of the low salience of the issues, a slightly disgruntled Democratic rank and file was willing to accede to the timeline.

Another indication that inter-party bargaining was more prominent than vote-buying in this bill comes from a look at amendment sponsors. In contrast to the bills outlined in previous chapters, only five of the 25 amendments introduced in the Leadership Act were sponsored by moderate legislators. Of those five "moderate" amendments, three passed into law and two were rejected. This means that only three of the eleven amendments in the final legislation were initially introduced by legislators whose

[9] Bush (2011, p. 454)
[10] Boyd (2015)
[11] Sorrells (2003b)
[12] Cong. Rec. Vol. 149, No. 73 (May 15, 2003), S6481

DW-Nominate scores fell within the IQR. Of those amendments, two were partisan in nature. The only moderate amendment that passed into law that is not officially coded as partisan was Joe Biden's humanitarian debt relief amendment. As discussed previously, this amendment was also quite partisan. This all suggests that buying the votes of moderate legislators was not high on leaders' minds during the passage of this bill.

Just as important as what was included in the legislation is what was *excluded*. Specifically, the modest bill did not make any claims about larger national issues. In common parlance at the time of PEPFAR's creation was the idea that the AIDS/HIV epidemic was a national security issue. Because human security was often wrapped up into national security, the George H. W. Bush and Clinton administrations had begun discussing the AIDS epidemic in that way. In 2000, the UN Security Council officially labeled HIV/AIDS as a global security threat.[13]

Bush's plan was a clear deviation from that trend. His 2002 National Security Strategy only gave HIV/AIDS a passing mention, though it was clearly an important issue for his administration. Though counterintuitive, downplaying the issue turned out to be a wise strategy. Conceptualizing health as a national security concern was certain to increase Congress's interest. Therefore, the vote-buying theory would suggest that the Bush administration's decision to downplay any security aspects could have been PEPFAR's saving grace. Had the issue gained greater congressional interest, it is likely that the entire effort would have been mired in bureaucracy like many other areas of foreign aid.

8.4 Bureaucratic Fragmentation in PEPFAR

PEPFAR was and continues to be considered a successful foreign aid initiative. Rather than inviting interagency conflict and bureaucratic dysfunction, OGAC has created streamlined policies within recipient states, successfully communicating agendas with recipients and other donors and carrying out complementary policies. While the roll-out has never been perfect, many mistakes have been addressed through consequent legislation, and many of the initial and later issues were not related to bureaucratic fragmentation.

[13] Dietrich (2007)

OGAC is headquartered in the Department of State and includes representatives from all relevant agencies. This office is responsible for maintaining the focus of PEPFAR through policy development and holistic program oversight. At the country level, PEPFAR develops parallel interagency teams that work together to make local operational decisions. These teams are led by the relevant US ambassador and involve foreign service officers from each relevant agency.[14] OGAC was deliberately kept as a small office, serving as a coordinator rather than a new agency in its own right.[15] OGAC also puts a lot of work into integrating country teams with the central office. The central office holds weekly teleconferences with all stakeholders in country offices.[16]

Internal government audits of PEPFAR have not dug up much interagency conflict. For example, the USAID Inspector General conducted a review in 2008, shortly before PEPFAR's first reauthorization. The review specifically praised the office of the Global AIDS Coordinator for its effectiveness in interagency management. The report claims that the office "fosters an attitude that minimizes interagency jealousies, respects the strengths of other agencies, and promotes frictionless cooperation."[17] This is high praise coming from an often hostile counter-bureaucracy.[18] Although this and other reports did have criticisms of the program, bureaucratic cooperation has largely been lauded as one of PEPFAR's strengths.

Where critics have brought up coordination issues, they tend to discuss OGAC's ability to coordinate with other health specialists. For example, a 2008 Congressional Research Service report suggested that the HIV/AIDS office should bring in more experts on tuberculosis, due to the common comorbidity of the two diseases.[19] Congress addressed some of these inter-disease coordination issues in later legislation.

Although interagency conflict in PEPFAR programs appears to be minimal, those working on the ground have certainly reported some interagency disagreements. However, the resolution and impact of these disagreements differs starkly from the other cases examined in this book. This is largely because PEPFAR-related agencies are unlikely to find motivated congressional allies, forcing them to resolve disputes on their own. For example, in

[14] Orza et al. (2007, p. 70)
[15] Orza et al. (2007, p. 83)
[16] Orza et al. (2007, p. 86)
[17] USIG (2008, p. 7)
[18] Natsios (2011)
[19] Moss (2009)

a 2019 interview, Robert Clay, USAID's PEPFAR Administrator from 2008 to 2011, lamented that:

> we didn't have clarity between the two dominant players—CDC [Centers for Disease Control] and USAID. So every day there would be these issues that would come up about [who is] doing what. Why was CDC taking lead on this—or CDC would come and say why is USAID doing this. There was just a lot of negotiation between the two agencies.[20]

At the same time, Clay noted some of the benefits of these inter agency rivalries. Although turf wars could be frustrating, he argued, they incentivized USAID personnel to maximize their own agency's productivity. The interagency negotiations often led to competition between USAID and the CDC in dimensions that were easy to measure. He suggests that:

> in some ways the interagency rivalries demanded the best. I think USAID's staff were always feeling like they were on the edge and having to really perform at a very high level in order to survive in the PEPFAR environment. So I think it was a strong incentive for USAID to do its best.[21]

Some interagency conflict in PEPFAR was perhaps unavoidable. But the difference between PEPFAR and other areas of foreign aid was that Congress did not increase or exacerbate interagency tensions. Regardless of their preferences, all agencies involved in PEPFAR were willing and able to work together. As previous chapters have noted, this is not always the case.

Indeed, even when agencies initially disagreed on strategy, they were often able to find consensus. For example, CDC and USAID initially preferred long-term strategies focusing on prevention, while the State Department preferred to prioritize treatment of HIV-positive patients. This could easily have turned into a bureaucratic battle, like the interagency disagreements in Afghanistan counternarcotics. But it did not, for two reasons. First, agencies were willing to compromise based on scientific information. When Dr. Anthony Fauci from the NIH teamed up with members of the National Security Council to communicate the ability of HIV treatment drugs to minimize transmission, USAID was willing to back down from its stance.[22]

[20] Clay (2019, p. 46)
[21] Clay (2019, p. 48)
[22] Natsios (2019, p. 79)

Second, and perhaps even more importantly, Congress was clear and unitary about the priorities that it wanted the bureaucracy to pursue. In its authorizing legislation, Congress mandated a specific breakdown of funding between the competing objectives of prevention and treatment. Unlike in previous cases, members did not have strong, divergent opinions on the relative importance of the two objectives. This was partially due to high levels of intra-party agreement. Because parties were negotiating as blocs, there were only a few salient issues of disagreement. In contrast to other cases, Democrats and Republicans were able to settle on a few debates, which were negotiated through a few amendments. A proliferation of pet projects, and a bloated bureaucracy, were not necessary to pass the legislation.

Had Congress, or the parties themselves, been less unified, it is easy to imagine a counterfactual case in which USAID and the CDC would each find their own congressional champions and continue the battle indefinitely. This would mirror the Afghanistan counternarcotics case, in which each member of Congress chose the bureaucracy that they wanted to side with, resulting in a mess of policies. The fact that members of Congress were uninterested in picking sides in this case suggests that party leaders were effective in managing their somewhat uninterested rank and file.

8.5 Conclusion: A Foreign Aid Success Story

Foreign aid fragmentation is not an automatic process or a foregone conclusion. Different areas of foreign aid exhibit different levels of fragmentation. The global fight against the HIV/AIDS epidemic is one area in which federal bureaucracy has worked well as a unit and successfully overcome hurdles. PEPFAR is often considered a success case as a foreign aid agenda. Part of this is due to the strong centralization of policymaking authority into a single office in a single agency, the Department of State's OGAC.

Even in the PEPFAR case, Congress was not able to do away with all interagency conflict. Bureaucrats on the ground still complained of inter-agency disagreements. However, Congress did not serve to *worsen* inter-agency conflict—if anything, they often stepped in to solve it. Two mechanisms led to this state of affairs. First, the salient bargaining in PEPFAR's implementing legislation took place between party blocs. Party leaders on both sides had a lot of power over their rank and file because most legislators had little personal interest in the issue of public health in sub-Saharan

Africa. The amendments and provisions in the bill, therefore, served ideological goals rather than being used to buy votes from individual legislators. Second, because individual members of Congress did not pick sides among different bureaucracies, the agencies had to make their own decisions, leading to better policy.

The legislation considered in this chapter contrasts with previous chapters in interesting ways. Specifically, amendments in the PEPFAR authorization were used for very different purposes than in previous chapters' legislation. This suggests that amendments can play different roles under different types of legislation. Specifically, in cases where inter-party disputes are high, earmarks and amendments need not be attached to pet projects. Instead, earmarks can serve to ease inter-party compromise. This suggests that party discipline may play a role in the congressional disunity mechanism. This tracks with cross-national work on aid fragmentation, which has found that strong parties can keep a more manageable bureaucracy.[23]

Because of the positive role of parties, PEPFAR provides an optimistic case for the role of partisan polarization in foreign policy. Even when congressional leadership does not speak for both parties, it is possible for congressional unity to take place *within* parties. Because Democrats could whip Democratic votes and Republicans could whip Republican votes relatively easily, there was little need to fund individual pet projects in PEPFAR legislation. This case provides a more flexible definition of congressional unity. The role of parties is worth considering in further detail in future work.

The success of PEPFAR can be carried over into other areas of foreign aid policy. Because of the narrow scope of the policy, many legislators were uninterested in requesting pet projects. Such narrow foreign policy legislation is not unique to the PEPFAR case. In fact, Congress has long been moving toward smaller, more contained foreign aid authorization bills. If this trend continues, it may be possible to pass legislation in which fewer legislators want a piece of the pie. This could create an opportunity to decrease the number of pet projects in foreign aid and foreign policy.

However, it is worth noting that the very aspects of PEPFAR that made it so successful can also create other unintended externalities. Because of its strong targeting of a specific disease, PEPFAR was able to escape the proliferation of pet projects faced by other aid programs. However, there is evidence

[23] Carcelli (2023)

that targeting aid toward a specific problem or issue can make it difficult for donors to address other issues. The diversion of resources spurred by PEPFAR, for example, may have had small negative effects on other areas of health in target countries, increasing infant mortality.[24] All of the costs and benefits of targeted aid are worth studying and considering when developing new strategies in future aid policies.

[24] Lee and Izama (2015)

Chapter 9
Conclusion

In this final chapter, I take the opportunity to consider the broader implications of the book's findings. I begin by summarizing the previous chapters, which combine to describe a US Congress that is constantly and, often unwittingly, shaping foreign aid bureaucracy. Next, I consider the implications for current and future research on foreign aid and foreign policy. I describe how future work could address the weaknesses of this book to improve scholarly understanding of the processes at work. I also consider two alternative theories common to the foreign policy literature, neither of which provide satisfactory explanations for the findings described in this book. Finally, I conclude by considering the trade-offs faced by the US government in crafting foreign policy. The policy implications of these findings encompass various branches of the US government but can also be relevant to other countries' attempts to carry out foreign policy. I describe these implications with the hope that future scholars and policymakers will be able to apply this research to new cases and contexts.

9.1 Book Summary

United States foreign policy is a complex phenomenon—too complex for any single book to fully describe or explain. The causes of suboptimal foreign policy are many and come from all areas of government as well as from US allies and adversaries. This book takes just one subset of foreign policy concerns—fragmentation of the US foreign aid bureaucracy—and makes a case for one of its many causes. By focusing on Congress's role in shaping the foreign policy bureaucracy, I introduce a new way of thinking about foreign aid and foreign policy.

By now, it should be clear that Congress can play a large role in US foreign policy outcomes. When members of Congress are especially interested in foreign policy, they are tempted to meddle in the bureaucracy's actions and insert themselves into interagency conflicts. When Congress is disunified, this meddling leads to bureaucratic fragmentation as members demand

Competing for Foreign Aid. Shannon P. Carcelli, Oxford University Press. © Oxford University Press (2025).
DOI: 10.1093/9780197799284.003.0009

disparate pet projects and side with diverse agencies. Rather than working as a unitary whole, then, the federal bureaucracy works against itself, limiting the policy coherence of US foreign aid.

In Chapter 3, I laid out the mechanisms of the vote-buying theory of foreign aid fragmentation. I argued that a combination of congressional interest and congressional disunity in an issue creates the conditions for a fragmented foreign aid bureaucracy. In line with previous literature on congressional vote-buying, I suggested that a thinly spread moderate section of Congress will lead to fragmentation. In Chapters 4 and 5 I carried out statistical tests considering both the congressional interest and congressional disunity aspects of the theory. The large-N evidence support both hypotheses.

The three case studies provide variation on the independent variables and consistently support the vote-buying theory of foreign aid fragmentation. The Afghan reconstruction case described in Chapter 6 highlights the role of congressional interest in bureaucratic fragmentation. Rather than allow the federal bureaucracy to make its own decisions regarding the complexities of fighting an insurgency while rebuilding a country's infrastructure, Congress became deeply involved in the process. Members of Congress took sides in interagency disputes, which in turn incentivized more interagency conflict. Although Congress attempted to direct the bureaucracy to create a centralized structure, these attempts were weak because Congress itself could not agree on a structure. This lack of a unified vision, combined with heavily interested members, led Congress to exacerbate bureaucratic fragmentation in Afghanistan.

Similarly, democracy-building in the FSU, outlined in Chapter 7, provides another case of high congressional interest and disunity. In this case, once again, most people agreed that the goals were important. However, members of Congress disagreed on how best to develop the FSU. Like the Afghanistan case, many of the pet projects in the FSU case were distributive in nature. That is, members of Congress demanded pet projects that would materially prioritize their own constituents. Moderate legislators were the most likely to successfully achieve this for their own constituents, as the theory would suggest.

Chapter 8, on the other hand, provides a negative case of bureaucratic fragmentation. The HIV/AIDS epidemic in sub-Saharan Africa is not a particularly salient issue to many Americans or their representatives. Because of this, legislators had little incentive to spend time and energy meddling in the bureaucracy's work on the issue. When the Bush administration set up PEPFAR in 2003, Congress passed the policy with little talk of pet projects. This was possible because relatively few representatives were concerned with the details of the epidemic, beyond the typical partisan issues of women's health and family planning. Parties themselves were unified enough on the issues that they were able to negotiate as party blocs rather than creating a fragmented list of pet projects. This has led to a program often hailed as one of the greatest success stories in US foreign aid.

9.2 Foreign Aid and Foreign Policy Literature

Because of its rather limited scope, this book was able to introduce new ideas about US foreign policy. As already mentioned, this book takes just one subset of foreign policy mistakes and makes a case for one of its many causes. In that sense, the goals of this book are limited. However, as one of the first pieces to seriously consider the structure of foreign aid bureaucracy, this book is ambitious. Most work on US foreign policy does not consider bureaucratic structure and does little to investigate the policy power of US foreign aid. For its part, most work on foreign aid does not dive into the domestic bargaining that creates foreign aid policy. By merging the foreign policy, foreign aid, and bureaucratic politics literatures, this book hopes to move all three areas of study forward.

The foreign policy literature would benefit from the closer consideration of Congress that this book offers. Throughout the empirical chapters, I highlighted the role of moderate legislators in seeking and receiving pet projects in foreign policy. Rather than considering Congress as a monolith, this theory is able to show the important differences between different members of Congress. Although I assume that all members have similar *motivations*, I am still able to explain differences in *outcomes* between different members. This is an important contribution of this book, and a path forward for future scholars of foreign policy.

Future work on foreign aid would also benefit from a closer look at the bargains and negotiations taking place within donor-state governments. The foreign aid literature is often broken up into work on the causes of foreign aid and work on the consequences. The literature on the *consequences* of foreign aid has increasingly begun considering heterogeneity between different aid recipients, types, and donors, showing that variation on these aspects of aid can influence effectiveness. The literature on the *causes* of aid spending, however, has rarely considered this variation, instead focusing on the question of whether or how much foreign aid a country spends. This book attempts to reconcile these differences, showing how different types of foreign aid can follow very different trends in the policymaking process.

More broadly, those with normative concerns about foreign aid's effectiveness would benefit from a consideration of the political trade-offs involved in crafting foreign aid policy. It is common and popular to criticize US foreign aid for its lack of localization, inefficiency, and red tape. However, this book suggests that such criticism might be misplaced. Previous work on bureaucratic failures has highlighted the role of policymakers (and voters themselves) in limiting the effectiveness of the bureaucracy.[1] Insofar as organizational pathologies are the result of collective action problems within the legislature, it is unclear who should actually be the targets of this type of criticism. Perhaps a more useful critique of foreign aid would consider how to address the root causes (such as the government institutions that leave politicians vulnerable to private interests), rather than vilifying aid bureaucrats, or even politicians, for forces beyond their control.

Building on this book, future work should more deeply consider the sources of heterogeneous legislator preferences. Although I give several examples of the personal, constituent, and special-interest factors driving legislators, I do not offer a systematic theory of legislator preferences. This is a shortcoming of this work and could be addressed by future research. Why do some legislators pay more attention to their constituents' demands while others follow ideological goals? Why do special interests drive some legislators while others are convinced by one-on-one meetings with outside experts? The dynamics driving legislators' heterogeneous preferences is an area for future research.

Another way to build on this book would be to create a more systematic measure of interagency conflict. The qualitative chapters provided many examples of US agencies failing to cooperate due to congressional micromanagement. However, it would be interesting to be able to test this hypothesis with data. On a larger scale, what factors increase agencies' ability and willingness to work together? Is there systematic evidence that congressional interest and involvement consistently hampers interagency

[1] Wilson (1989); Bozeman (1993)

cooperation? Why might it do so in some cases but not in others? Future work can build on this book to answer these questions.

9.2.1 Bureaucracy as a Response to Global Shocks

Although this book is about international relations, there is little discussion of the international forces driving US foreign policy and foreign aid. Throughout the time period considered in the book, a lot happened in the world. The rise and fall of the Soviet Union, the Global War on Terrorism, several pandemics and health emergencies, the Great Recession, and the creation and dissolution of global treaties and agreements all combine to create an ever-shifting global environment. The role of these global changes in shaping the foreign policy bureaucracy is all but ignored in this book. However, it is almost certain that the structure of the bureaucracy should shift in response to these global changes.

Future research, then, must seriously consider the role of domestic versus international factors in shaping the foreign policy bureaucracy. First, as the needs of US foreign policy change, the ideal bureaucratic structure almost certainly changes with it. As the world becomes more complicated, it is possible that the US bureaucracy must necessarily fracture and split along with it. On the other hand, it is possible that the solving of complex problems requires the simplest bureaucratic structure possible. The ideal bureaucracy is difficult to measure, but determining the costs and benefits of bureaucratic fragmentation is necessary for moving policy forward.

Beyond thinking about the "ideal" bureaucracy, it also worth considering how changes to the international system might empirically reshape it. For example, did the creation of the European Union decrease the need for separate US agencies with a comparative advantage in trade with different member states? Does its partial dissolution, as a result of Brexit, threaten any parts of the US bureaucracy? How might other regional agreements, especially in the Global South, impact the shape of the foreign aid bureaucracy?

Another possibility is that global shocks are a catalyst for change and adaptation in the bureaucracy. The September 11 attacks, for example, spurred the creation of the Department of Homeland Security. Work by Zegart (2005) would suggest the bureaucratic response to such global shocks might be mostly cosmetic. However, it is worth considering that the structure and function of the bureaucracy can improve with international shocks. For example, the structure of the Joint Chiefs of Staff came about partially in an attempt to mirror our allies' military bureaucracies in World War II.[2] When these global shocks create lasting changes, it is worth considering the causes and consequences. This is also an open question for future work.

9.3 Alternative Explanations

Two alternative frameworks from different areas of literature could provide competing explanations for foreign policy fragmentation. First, Congress may consciously choose to fragment foreign aid during times of divided government in hopes of constraining the executive branch. If fragmenting the bureaucracy can help tame inter-branch conflict, it could be rational for Congress to do so. Second, Congress may allow the bureaucracy to proliferate due to apathy. When Congress doesn't much care about a foreign policy tool or domain, there may be little interest in preserving it by maintaining a functional bureaucracy. Congressional inattention could then lead to bureaucratic proliferation as a product of inertia. This, for example, could explain why fragmentation is so high in foreign aid, which is rarely a salient part of campaigns or voting choices. In this section, I address these competing theories and suggest the testable predictions of each competing framework.

9.3.1 Congressional Delegation

Inter-branch conflict is a feature of American democracy. The US system of divided government provides an opportunity for Congress to check and balance the executive, including the federal bureaucracy. This is no less true in foreign policy. One way that Congress can exert power in foreign policy is to restrict the options for the executive branch.[3] What better way to accomplish this than to make sure federal bureaucracy is as fragmented and ineffective as possible?

[2] Locher (2002, p. 20)
[3] Howell and Pevehouse (2007)

The literature on inter-branch relations often considers the relationship between Congress and the bureaucracy as a form of principal-agent relationship. Scholars like Epstein and O'Halloran (1999) and Kiewiet and McCubbins (1991) developed robust theories suggesting that Congress can limit delegation to the executive branch when they disagree with what the executive is doing. According to these theories, Congress is most likely to limit executive discretion during times of divided party government—when Congress and the presidency are controlled by opposing parties. Congress's power to limit bureaucratic actions allows it to keep policy control when the president and Congress disagree.

Some of this work on delegation has considered bureaucratic structure, suggesting that divided party government should lead to greater bureaucratic fragmentation. Epstein and O'Halloran (1999) dedicate a paragraph to a consideration of the mean number of agencies Congress authorizes under divided (4.38) versus unified (3.91) government, implying that an unfriendly Congress might purposefully create conflict within the executive branch. The authors chalk this difference up to Congress's decision to "play agencies against each other more under divided government."[4] Farhang and Yaver (2016) and Ting (2003) also developed theories suggesting that bureaucratic fragmentation should increase when the two branches disagree, as Congress attempts to prevent the executive from taking an undesirable action.[5]

Previous work in delegation theory has also considered the role of congressional disunity, if only in passing. For example, Epstein and O'Halloran (1999) find that party polarization increases congressional delegation to the executive. They argue that inefficiencies in the legislative process lead legislators to rely more on the executive branch for policymaking. In essence, they consider bureaucracies and congressional committees to be *substitutes* for policymaking, predicting that "less cohesive majority parties should... be associated with greater delegation to the executive."[6] This would suggest that a strong congressional leadership provides less fragmentation.

Huber and Shipan (2002) make similar predictions but suggest a slightly different mechanism. They argue that legislative capacity should

[4] Epstein and O'Halloran (1999, p. 160)

[5] It should be noted that Farhang and Yaver (2016) focus on an element of bureaucratic rulemaking that is not particularly relevant to the study of foreign aid. They consider regulatory authority, rather than policymaking authority, which provides an easier test of the divided government theory.

[6] Epstein and O'Halloran (1999, p. 168)

increase delegation constraints, but not because of substitution. They note that specification of bill text—their measure of delegation constraints—is costly and may be more difficult for gridlocked legislatures. Therefore, weak congressional leadership should default to greater levels of bureaucratic discretion because they are not *able* to agree on delegation constraints.[7]

Although neither set of authors explicitly hypothesize on congressional disunity, the implications of these studies are clear: if disunity in Congress increases delegation, and bureaucratic fragmentation is a delegation constraint, then disunity should *decrease* fragmentation. A more unified Congress, according to this logic, is more capable of constraining (fragmenting) bureaucracy. This is the opposite of the predictions coming out of the vote-buying theory.

Along with the *disunity* hypothesis, delegation theory can also be relevant to the congressional *interest* hypothesis, although less directly. Again, drawing from the assumption by Huber and Shipan (2002) that delegation constraints are inherently difficult, it stands to reason that Congress would not bother to use them unless it was relatively motivated to do so. Therefore, like the vote-buying theory, a delegation theory of fragmentation would predict that fragmentation (a form of delegation constraint) should be *higher* when congressional interest increases.

Although this alternative framework is difficult to differentiate from the vote-buying theory's *interest* hypothesis, the expectation regarding congressional *disunity* stands in stark contrast to the vote-buying theory. The mechanisms described above also provide opportunities to trace the causal story at the legislator level. For example, this theory would suggest that bureaucratic fragmentation should be driven by the legislators most ideologically opposed to the president. This stands in contrast to the vote-buying theory, which predicts that fragmentation and new agency creation should be driven by congressional *moderates* of both parties.

The cases and statistical evidence in the preceding chapters provide little to no support for the idea that congressional delegation is a factor in the foreign aid bureaucracy. First, the case studies in Chapters 6 and 7 describe cases of both unified and divided-party government. Fragmentation was high in both cases. This suggests that interbranch divisions are not the main

[7] Bolton and Thrower (2016) more explicitly theorize the connection between legislative capacity and increased delegation constraints.

factor driving bureaucratic fragmentation. This is backed up by the quantitative chapters, neither of which provide any statistical correlation between divided-party government and fragmentation.

Further, in the case studies, there is little evidence that the legislators most opposed to the president are the ones most likely to demand the creation of new programs. As described again and again, it is *moderate* legislators, from both parties, demanding these pet projects. This provides further evidence for the vote-buying hypothesis and further detracts from the idea that inter-branch delegation is driving variation in foreign aid fragmentation.

9.3.2 Congressional Abdication

Another alternative theory comes more directly from the foreign policy literature. A long-standing literature accuses Congress of abdicating its role in foreign policy. Hinckley (1994), in response to work by scholars like Pastor (1982), notes the lack of interest in foreign affairs that Congress has appeared to show since World War II. Deering (2009) highlights the lack of major authorizing legislation coming out of foreign relations committees in Congress, and Fowler (2015) measures a decrease in congressional oversight of foreign policy. Scholars have long noticed a difference between the president's power in domestic versus foreign policy.[8] Together, these scholars make the claim that Congress has abdicated its role in foreign policy.

If this supposition is correct, then perhaps the increasingly bloated foreign policy bureaucracy is a direct result of Congress's apathy. Presumably, if Congress truly cared about foreign policy, it would do something about the inefficiencies resulting from fragmentation. The fact that it does not could simply be a reflection of shifting priorities within Congress.

There are at least two mechanisms through which congressional apathy could lead to a fragmented bureaucracy. First, entrepreneurial bureaucrats in the executive branch could be taking advantage of a power vacuum left behind by Congress when expanding their own power. This argument would suggest that bureaucratic expansion is a result of scheming bureaucrats. Second, bureaucratic apathy could lead to fragmentation

[8] Wildavsky (1966); Marshall and Pacelle Jr (2005); Canes-Wrone et al. (2008); Milner and Tingley (2015).

through a decrease in congressional expertise. This argument would suggest that bureaucrats serve as *substitutes* for congressional staffers in creating policy. These two sets of mechanisms are not mutually exclusive, but they are both worth further elucidation.

Scholars of organizational systems tend to agree that organizational inertia creates "institutional pathologies," causing organizations to expand "beyond their optimal size."[9] This perspective suggests that bureaucrats themselves can create an unwieldy bureaucracy if no one steps in to control it. Without congressional watchdogs to check them, bureaucrats may take the opportunity to gain control over policies that they do not traditionally control. This might explain, for example, the tendency of bureaucracies without traditional foreign policy agendas, like the Departments of Agriculture and Labor, to become involved in foreign policy.

Alternatively, congressional apathy could grow the bureaucracy through a decrease in legislative capacity. When Congress is short-staffed, the executive branch is empowered to carry out policy unilaterally that Congress would have done otherwise.[10] As Congress becomes increasingly understaffed and overworked, the ability of any given legislator or staffer to retain up-to-date knowledge of the federal bureaucracy becomes more and more constrained. Less salient policy areas might fall by the wayside. When legislators are poorly informed about the existing bureaucracy, they may create duplicative programs and agencies simply because they did not know that other agencies existed.[11]

Congressional apathy in foreign policy is not a constant. Congress differs in its interest in different foreign policy areas and tools.[12] In fact, foreign economic assistance is one area on which Congress may be especially active. Additionally, conventional measures may overestimate congressional apathy when Congress is simply moving its policymaking authority to non-traditional realms.[13]

[9] Büthe et al. (2012, p. 580). Also see foundational work, for example, by Baumol (1959).
[10] LaPira et al. (2020)
[11] In fact, in one interview a high-level bureaucrat from USAID recalled a Clinton aide in Congress lamenting the lack of a US agency devoted to foreign aid and suggesting that Congress should create one (Anonymous interview by author, 4/13/2016).
[12] This is the main thesis of Milner and Tingley (2015), but even the Congress skeptic Hinckley (1994) acknowledges the role of Congress in some policy areas, and many scholars have noted the relative importance of various foreign policy areas to Congress (Tama 2020). Additionally, Wang (2024) shows that Congress is more focused on foreign policy during times of divided government than unified government.
[13] Carcelli (2021)

Variation in congressional apathy in foreign policy provides an opportunity to directly test this alternative framework. Most obviously, congressional interest would go directly *against* the theoretical mechanisms of the congressional abdication theory. If apathy in Congress is creating fragmentation—either due to bureaucrats taking advantage of an opportunity or due to the ignorance of politicians—then we should expect that relationship to be relative. An increase in congressional interest should lead to an decrease in fragmentation. Of course, this is opposite to what the vote-buying theory predicts.

It goes without saying that the evidence in this book does not support the idea that congressional abdication is the driver of foreign aid fragmentation. To the contrary, areas of foreign aid that attract the most interest from Congress are the ones with the highest levels of fragmentation. Similarly, in the case studies, I find that congressional inquiries tend to *exacerbate* the problems of fragmentation by giving agencies the incentive to compete with one another. Although it could certainly be true that Congress is abdicating its role in foreign policy, the findings of this book would not suggest that the bureaucracy is growing wild as a result.

9.4 Generalizability

The issue of foreign aid fragmentation is not unique to the United States. Donor states vary in the number and spread of their foreign aid delivery tools. Not incidentally, the United States is also not the only country that relies upon distributive side payments to pass legislation. Many countries' leaders depend on vote-buying to build a legislative agenda. These side payments, of course, can take many forms. As discussed in this book, when side payments involve the diverting of funding within a bill to a particular legislator's pet project, they can lead to a fragmented budget.

Not all countries are equally likely to provide these types of side payments in an attempt to pass legislation. In previous work, I have shown that electoral institutions can play a large role in shaping the foreign aid bureaucracy.[14] Democracies with proportional representation (PR) electoral institutions provide less incentive for legislators to pursue personal or district-wide projects. This means that the process leading to foreign aid

[14] Carcelli (2023)

fragmentation is dampened in PR systems. The institutional make-up of the United States makes it especially vulnerable to bureaucratic fragmentation. Many other countries face similar vulnerabilities.

This work is also generalizable outside the realm of foreign aid. Foreign aid is not the only policy that Congress micromanages to the detriment of policy outcomes. Indeed, much of US foreign policy seems to involve a complex web of regulatory and service provision agencies. Trade is one area with an often-complex bureaucratic backdrop.[15] In his 2011 State of Union address, President Obama famously complained that "there are 12 different agencies that deal with exports... The Interior Department is in charge of salmon while they're in fresh water, but the Commerce Department handles them when they're in saltwater. I hear it gets even more complicated once they're smoked."

Trade, defense, nuclear security, intelligence, and other areas of foreign policy are controlled by multiple bureaucracies. However, the fragmentation in many of these areas can be difficult to measure. When multiple bureaucracies play a *regulatory* role over a specific commodity, such as the salmon example above, it can be unclear how the agencies divide decision-making power. Do they have a clear division, negating any concern about inter agency conflict? Does one agency have policy primacy, simply delegating smaller decisions to the other agency? There is nothing obvious about the relationship between regulatory agencies to answer this question. Therefore, future research generalizing the theory to other areas of foreign policy will face empirical challenges in measuring fragmentation.

In contrast, foreign aid policy is made almost entirely by appropriations. Rather than regulating policy, aid agencies are almost entirely tasked with spending money. Congressional and administrative regulations, such as limitations on which countries can receive aid projects, which contractors are eligible, and what types of projects can be carried out, are visible in the funding. For example, when the Trump administration impounded foreign aid projects to Ukraine—an extreme version of a regulatory constraint—the policy decision was made clear by the fact that no aid appropriations reached Ukraine. In foreign aid, government spending *is* government policy. This is not true in all areas of foreign policy.

Various areas of *domestic* policy also display many of the features that lead to foreign aid fragmentation. Some of these domestic policy areas may

[15] See Stanescu et al. (2020) for more details on trade bureaucracies.

be simpler to measure due to their similarities to foreign aid. The GAO now issues an annual "Report on Fragmentation, Overlap, and Duplication in the Federal Government."[16] In recent elections, several candidates have promised to shut down or consolidate government agencies. Politicians and the public clearly care a lot about federal bureaucracy, which often goes beyond foreign aid and foreign policy.

Some domestic policy areas are similar to foreign aid in their dependence on appropriations. Like foreign aid, social welfare legislation can be difficult for leaders to pass. And social welfare can touch upon several domestic policy debates, such as those about healthcare, mortgage and finance, agriculture, and education. This may lead to an incentive to introduce pet projects. Fragmentation among domestic social welfare issues, therefore, may be explained through the same theoretical mechanisms that this book develops.

Future work should begin to generalize this theory to explain bureaucratic fragmentation throughout the federal government. Perhaps such an effort would bring up more solutions that have been tried and succeeded in similar situations. Solving overall problems of bureaucratic fragmentation will require more creativity and work than I could consider in the limited scope of this book.

9.5 Policy Implications

Before now, the academic community has spent considerably more resources on studying the *effects* of foreign aid fragmentation than on understanding its root causes. In some ways, this is understandable. The fast pace of the policy world demands more research on the outcomes with the most proximate relevance; from this perspective, actual foreign policy outcomes are more interesting than the institutional processes that lead to them. Also, a full understanding of the problems are a necessary place to start for anyone trying to study solutions. This book would not have been possible without previous scholars learning that aid fragmentation is a problem.

However, this book's attempt to study the political causes of foreign aid fragmentation is important for at least two reasons. First, fragmentation is not randomly distributed. Certain historical periods and countries tend

[16] Dodaro (2015)

to create more fragmented policy than others. True causal inference on the effects of fragmentation requires scholars be able to control for the factors that caused fragmented policy in the first place. Second, policymakers demand solutions. The emerging policy consensus of the ill effects of fragmentation will logically lead to an increasing desire to fix the problem. Politicians in the last electoral cycle insisted that they were going to shut down agencies, or "drain the swamp" in Washington. Other solutions for bureaucratic complexity have included merging agencies or creating new coordinators. As this book suggests, however, there are no easy solutions. Bureaucratic fragmentation is deeply ingrained into electoral institutions and the necessities of lawmaking in the United States and elsewhere.

If bureaucratic fragmentation is causing inefficiencies in US foreign policy, then what is the solution? Here I highlight the importance of considering the trade-offs inherent in all policymaking. For example, if vote-buying is intended to increase the foreign aid budget, then a decrease in vote-buying may also decrease foreign aid. As the constituency in support of a policy diminishes, so will the policy. In evaluating the policy implications of this book, it is important to consider the trade-offs that it entails. Only after a clear-eyed discussion of the costs and benefits will lawmakers be able to create the best possible solution.

9.5.1 Policy Trade-Offs

Leaders, legislators, and the American public want to have it all: great policy that benefits them and does not have any unintended consequences. Unfortunately, this is just not possible, for at least two reasons. First, the more that a policy provides private benefits, the less it will benefit the public good. If every legislator wants foreign aid to support their own unique definition of "good policy," then aid will simply be a collection of pet projects. This conflicts with national-level goals of foreign aid and foreign policy.

Second, policy improvements are even more difficult within the US system. The US Constitution does not allow much space for the evidence-based institutional innovations that would improve policy as a whole, such as multi-member districts and party-controlled ballots. The outdated US institutions, which seemed state of the art in 1776, make it difficult to improve foreign and domestic policy. This is not to say that institutions themselves do not have their own trade-offs; the entire subfield of comparative politics has much to say about these global differences. However, the most realistic way to think about policy implications is to consider the trade-offs inherent in the US electoral system.

In the absence of institutional changes, what can be done on the domestic front? Once again, this requires a consideration of the costs and benefits of alternative policy options. First, policymakers should consider the substitutability of vote-buying tools. If Congress is serious about doing away with fragmentation in foreign aid budgets, one solution may be to allow greater numbers of earmarks and policy riders in bills. Earmarks have recently reached a new low in popularity, and an unintended consequence of earmark prohibitions may be an increase in other vote-buying tools, leading to even more bureaucratic fragmentation. On the other hand, allowing earmarks is not a perfect solution. It is likely that earmarks and other vote-buying tools have their own policy problems. The benefits and drawbacks of alternative means of congressional vote-buying should be the subject of further research if we are to solve these problems in foreign aid.

9.5.2 Substituting Foreign Policy

Beyond the obvious policy considerations of improving foreign aid provision, the research on foreign aid effectiveness can be important for a deeper reason. Research on substitutability in foreign policy tools suggests that foreign policy will become increasingly militarized when more peaceful policies are more difficult to implement.[17] Insofar as foreign aid can be used as a substitute for military policies, it is important that it be relatively easy to effectively deliver aid. As aid becomes more cumbersome and inefficient, other policy tools will become increasingly attractive by comparison. In extreme cases, the ineffectiveness of foreign aid may lead powerful states to rely more heavily on military solutions. The peacefulness of foreign policy depends in part upon countries' ability to effectively employ peaceful tools.

Whether the goal of foreign aid is international development, geopolitical strategy, or something else, it is in every country's best interest to use their

[17] Milner and Tingley (2015); Morgan and Palmer (2000); Most and Starr (1984)

foreign policy tools as effectively as possible. More research on solutions to policy gridlock, in domestic and foreign policy, is necessary before further progress can be made. This book is just one step in understanding the processes involved in foreign policymaking and, eventually, creating peaceful, effective tools that prevent domestic conflict from crossing the border and influencing international cooperation.

Bibliography

Arnab Acharya, Ana Teresa Fuzzo De Lima, and Mick Moore. Proliferation and fragmentation: Transactions costs and the value of aid. *The Journal of Development Studies*, 42(1):1–21, 2006.

E Scott Adler and John D Wilkerson. *Congress and the Politics of Problem Solving.* Cambridge University Press, 2013.

Iñaki Aldasoro, Peter Nunnenkamp, and Rainer Thiele. Less aid proliferation and more donor coordination? The wide gap between words and deeds. *Journal of International Development*, 22(7):920–940, 2010.

Alberto Alesina and David Dollar. Who gives foreign aid to whom and why? *Journal of Economic Growth*, 5(1):33–63, 2000.

Dan Alexander, Christopher R Berry, and William G Howell. Distributive politics and legislator ideology. *The Journal of Politics*, 78(1):214–231, 2016.

Susan Hannah Allen and Michael E Flynn. Donor government ideology and aid bypass. *Foreign Policy Analysis*, 14(4):449–468, 2018.

Graham T Allison. Conceptual models and the Cuban Missile Crisis. *American Political Science Review*, 63(03):689–718, 1969.

Kurt Annen and Stephen Kosempel. Foreign aid, donor fragmentation, and economic growth. *The BE Journal of Macroeconomics*, 9(1):33

Vincent Arel-Bundock, James Atkinson, and Rachel Augustine Potter. The limits of foreign aid diplomacy: How bureaucratic design shapes aid distribution. *International Studies Quarterly*, 59:544–556, 2015.

D Austen-Smith, and J R Wright (1994). Counteractive lobbying. *American Journal of Political Science, 38*(1):25–44.

Fabian Barthel, Eric Neumayer, Peter Nunnenkamp, and Pablo Selaya. Competition for export markets and the allocation of foreign aid: The role of spatial dependence among donor countries. *World Development*, 64:350–365, 2014.

Péter Tamás Bauer *Dissent on Development.* Harvard University Press, 1976.

Frank R Baumgartner, Virginia Gray, and David Lowery. Federal policy activity and the mobilization of state lobbying organizations. *Political Research Quarterly*, 62(3): 552–567, 2009.

Frank R Baumgartner, Heather A Larsen-Price, Beth L Leech, and Paul Rutledge. Congressional and presidential effects on the demand for lobbying. *Political Research Quarterly*, 64(1):3–16, 2011.

W J Baumol. *Business Behavior, Value and Growth.* Macmillan, 1959.

David H Bearce and Daniel C Tirone. Foreign aid effectiveness and the strategic goals of donor governments. *The Journal of Politics*, 72(3):837–851, 2010.

Michael B Berkman (2001). Legislative professionalism and the demand for groups: The institutional context of interest population density. *Legislative Studies Quarterly*, *26*(4):661–679.

Sarah Blodgett Bermeo. Foreign aid and regime change: A role for donor intent. *World Development*, 39(11):2021–2031, 2011.

Sarah Blodgett Bermeo. Aid is not oil: Donor utility, heterogeneous aid, and the aid-democratization relationship. *International Organization*, 70(1):1–32, 2016.

Sarah Blodgett Bermeo (2017). Aid allocation and targeted development in an increasingly connected world. *International Organization*, *71*(4):735–766.

Sarah Blodgett Bermeo and David Leblang. Migration and foreign aid. *International Organization*, 69(3):627–657, 2015.

Christopher R Berry, Barry C Burden, and William G Howell. The president and the distribution of federal spending. *American Political Science Review*, 104(4):783–799, 2010.

Philip A Berry. Allies at war in Afghanistan: Anglo–American friction over aerial poppy eradication, 2004–2007. *Diplomacy & Statecraft*, 29(2):274–297, 2018.

Anthony M Bertelli and Christian R Grose. Secretaries of pork? A new theory of distributive public policy. *The Journal of Politics*, 71(3):926–945, 2009.

Jean-Claude Berthélemy. Bilateral donors' interest vs. recipients' development motives in aid allocation: Do all donors behave the same? *Review of Development Economics*, 10(2):179–194, 2006.

Nancy Birdsall, Homi J Kharas, Ayah Mahgoub, and Rita Perakis, *Quality of official development assistance assessment*. Center for Global Development Washington, DC, 2010.

Dennis Blair, Ronald Neumann, and Eric Olson. Fixing fragile states. *The National Interest*, (133):11–20, 2014.

Matteo Bobba and Andrew Powell. Multilateral intermediation of foreign aid: What is the trade-off for donor countries? Technical report, Inter-American Development Bank, 2006.

Alexander Bolton and Sharece Thrower. Legislative capacity and executive unilateralism. *American Journal of Political Science*, 60(3):649–663, 2016.

Peter Boone. *The Impact of Foreign Aid on Savings and Growth*. London School of Economics and Political Science, Centre for Economic Performance, 1994.

François Bourguignon and Mark Sundberg. Aid effectiveness – opening the black box. *American Economic Review*, 97(2):316–321, 2007.

Stuart Bowen. Applying Iraq's hard lessons to the reform of stabilization and reconstruction operations. *Special Inspector General for Iraqi Reconstruction Report*, February 2010.

Lydia Boyd. *Preaching Prevention: Born-Again christianity and the Moral Politics of AIDS in Uganda*. Ohio University Press, 2015.

Barry Bozeman. A theory of government "red tape". *Journal of Public Administration Research and Theory*, 3(3):273–304, 1993.

Viktor Brech and Niklas Potrafke. Donor ideology and types of foreign aid. *Journal of Comparative Economics*, 42(1):61–75, 2014.

George W Bush. Fact sheet: The president's emergency plan for AIDS relief. https://georgewbush-whitehouse.archives.gov/news/releases/2003/01/20030129-1.html, January 2003. (Accessed on 05/04/2021).

George W Bush. *Decision Points.* Broadway Books, 2011.

T. Büthe, S. Major, and A. de Mello e Souza. The politics of private foreign aid: Humanitarian principles, economic development objectives, and organizational interests in NGO private aid allocation. *International Organization, 66*(4):571–607, 2011.

Brandice Canes-Wrone, William G Howell, and David E Lewis. Toward a broader understanding of presidential power: A reevaluation of the two presidencies thesis. *The Journal of Politics,* 70(01):1–16, 2008.

Shannon P Carcelli. Congressional polarization and limitation riders in foreign aid appropriations. *International Politics, 59,* 898–924, 2021.

Shannon P Carcelli. Special interests in foreign policy bureaucracies: Evidence from foreign aid. *The Journal of Politics,* 85(3):905–918, 2023.

Shannon P Carcelli. Bureaucratic structure and compliance with international agreements. *American Journal of Political Science,* 68(1):177–192, 2024.

Alison Carnegie, and Dolan. The effects of rejecting aid on recipients' reputations: Evidence from natural disaster responses. *The Review of International Organizations, 16*:495–519, 2020.

Daniel Carpenter. *The Forging of Bureaucratic Autonomy: Reputations, Networks, and Policy Innovation in Executive Agencies, 1862–1928,* volume 78. Princeton University Press, 2001.

Royce Carroll and Henry A Kim. Party government and the "cohesive power of public plunder". *American Journal of Political Science,* 54(1):34–44, 2010.

WR Castle. The Secretary of State to Mr. Fred l. Eberhardt. https://history.state.gov/historicaldocuments/frus1933-39/d3, March 1933. (Accessed on 08/17/2021).

Hillary Rodham Clinton. *Hard Choices.* Simon and Schuster, 2014.

Joshua D Clinton and David E Lewis. Expert opinion, agency characteristics, and agency preferences. *Political Analysis,* 16(1):3–20, 2007.

Joshua D Clinton, Anthony Bertelli, Christian R Grose, David E Lewis, and David C Nixon. Separated powers in the United States: The ideology of agencies, presidents, and Congress. *American Journal of Political Science,* 56(2):341–354, 2012.

Gary W Cox and Mathew D McCubbins. *Legislative Leviathan: Party Government in the House.* Cambridge University Press, 1993.

Gary W Cox and Mathew D McCubbins. *Setting the Agenda: Responsible Party Government in the US House of Representatives.* Cambridge University Press, 2005.

CQ-Almanac. Congress approves foreign economic aid bill. 31st ed., 1975. Retrieved from http://library...

CQ-Almanac. Bush signs Freedom Support Act, 1992a. URL https://library.cqpress.com/cqalmanac/document.php?id=cqal92-1108566. (Accessed on 03/24/2017).

CQ-Almanac. Bush signs freedom support act. 48th ed., 1992b. (http://library.cqpress.com/cqalmanac/cqal92-1108566,) Accessed on 5/9/17.

Neta C Crawford. United states budgetary costs and obligations of post-9/11 wars through FY2020: $6.4 trillion. *Costs of War,* 2019. https://watson.brown.edu/costsofwar/files/cow/imce/papers/2019/US%20Budgetary%20Costs%20of%20Wars%20November%202019.pdf

Michael H Crespin and David W Rohde. Dimensions, issues, and bills: Appropriations voting on the house floor. *The Journal of Politics*, 72(4):976–989, 2010.

Barbara Crossettes. A warning on Russian aid: Some in congress balk at Soviet aid. *New York Times*, page A1, May 1992.

James M Curry, and Frances E Lee. *The Limits of Party: Congress and Lawmaking in a Polarized Era*. University of Chicago Press, 2020.

John M De Figueiredo. The timing, intensity, and composition of interest group lobbying: An analysis of structural policy windows in the States. Technical report, National Bureau of Economic Research, 2004.

Christopher J Deering. Congress's role in foreign policymaking. Woodrow Wilson Center, 2009.

Christopher J Deering and Steven S Smith. *Committees in Congress*. Sage, 1997.

Eddie Dekel, Matthew O Jackson, and Asher Wolinsky. Vote buying: Legislatures and lobbying. *Quarterly Journal of Political Science*, 4(2):103–128, 2009.

John W Dietrich. The politics of PEPFAR: President Bush's emergency plan for AIDS relief. *Ethics & International Affairs, 21*(3):277–292, 2007.

Simone Dietrich. Donor political economies and the pursuit of aid effectiveness. *International Organization*, 70(1):65–102, 2016.

Simone Dietrich. *States, Markets, and Foreign Aid*. Cambridge University Press, 2021.

Simone Dietrich, Helen V Milner, and Jonathan B Slapin. From text to political positions on foreign aid: Analysis of aid mentions in party manifestos from 1960 to 2015. *International Studies Quarterly*, 64(4):980–990, 2020.

Simeon Djankov, Jose G Montalvo, and Marta Reynal-Querol. Aid with multiple personalities. *Journal of Comparative Economics*, 37(2):217–229, 2009.

James F Dobbins. *After the Taliban: Nation-Building in Afghanistan*. Potomac Books, Inc., 2008.

Gene L Dodaro. Opportunities to reduce potential duplication in government programs, save tax dollars, and enhance revenue. Technical report, DTIC Document, 2011.

Gene L Dodaro. Government efficiency and effectiveness: Opportunities to reduce fragmentation, overlap, and duplication and achieve other financial benefits. Technical report, Government Accountability Office, April 2015.

David Dollar and Victoria Levin. The increasing selectivity of foreign aid, 1984–2003. *World Development*, 34(12):2034–2046, 2006.

DOS (Department of State). Quadrennial diplomacy and development review. *Official website*, 2010.

DOT (Department of Transportation). Intelligent transportation systems joint program office. https://its.dot.gov/about/its_jpo.htm. (Accessed on 08/14/2021). n.d.

Axel Dreher, Anna Minasyan, and Peter Nunnenkamp. Government ideology in donor and recipient countries: Does ideological proximity matter for the effectiveness of aid? *European Economic Review*, 79:80–92, 2015.

A Cooper Drury, Richard Stuart Olson, and Douglas A Van Belle. The politics of humanitarian aid: U.S. foreign disaster assistance, 1964–1995. *The Journal of Politics*, 67(2):454–473, 2005.

EADS (United States Economic Analysis Data Services). USAID foreign aid explorer. https://explorer.usaid.gov/data-download.html, Aug 2015. (Accessed on 05/09/2018).

William Easterly. The white man's burden. *The Lancet*, 367(9528):2060, 2006.

William Easterly, & Tobias Pfutze (2008). Where does the money go? Best and worst practices in foreign aid. *Journal of Economic Perspectives*, *22*(2):29–52.

William Easterly, Ross Levine, and David Roodman. New data, new doubts: A comment on Burnside and Dollar's "aid, policies, and growth" (2003). Technical report, National Bureau of Economic Research, 2003.

Edmondson, C. How Mike Johnson got to 'yes' on aid to Ukraine., April 2024. The New York times 21 April https://www.nytimes.com/2024/04/21/us/politics/mike-johnson-turnaround.html?campaign_id=2&emc=edit_th_20240422&instance_id=121155&nl=todaysheadlines®i_id=69643266&segment_id=164429&user_id=af478df72952d8b1909da009a3c5a73b

David Epstein, and Sharyn O'Halloran. *Delegating Powers: A Transaction Cost Politics Approach to Policy Making under Separate Powers.* Cambridge University Press, 1999.

Diana Evans. *Greasing the Wheels: Using Pork Barrel Projects to Build Majority Coalitions in Congress.* Cambridge University Press, 2004.

EXIM. 1935 annual report. https://www.digitalarchives.exim.gov/digital/collection/ExImD01/id/8169/rec/2, 1935. (Accessed on 08/17/2021).

Sean Farhang and Miranda Yaver. Divided government and the fragmentation of American law. *American Journal of Political Science*, 60(2):401–417, 2016.

Christopher J Fariss. The strategic substitution of United States foreign aid. *Foreign Policy Analysis*, 6(2):107–131, 2010.

Richard F Fenno. *Congressmen in Committees.* Little, Brown, 1973.

Margaret Jacobson, Mariam Jalalzada, and Paul Fishstein. Interview of Ken Yamashita, December 2015

Paul Fishstein, Margaret Jalalzada, and Mariam Jalalzada. Interview of Micheal Flynn. *SIGAR Lessons Learned Interviews*, 2015.

Paul Fishstein, Margaret Jalalzada, and Mariam Jalalzada. Interview of state department employee. *SIGAR Lessons Learned Interviews*, 2016a.

Paul Fishstein, Margaret Jalalzada, and Mariam Jalalzada. Interview of USAID employee. *SIGAR Lessons Learned Interviews*, 2016b.

Paul Fishstein, Margaret Jalalzada, and Mariam Jalalzada. Interview of USAID employee. *SIGAR Lessons Learned Interviews*, 2016c.

Paul Fishstein, Margaret Jalalzada, and Mariam Jalalzada. Interview of USAID employee. *SIGAR Lessons Learned Interviews*, 2016d.

Paul Fishstein, Margaret Jalalzada, and Mariam Jalalzada. Interview of congressional staffer. *SIGAR Lessons Learned Interviews*, 2016e.

Paul Fishstein, Margaret Jalalzada, and Mariam Jalalzada. Interview of British Liaison. *SIGAR Lessons Learned Interviews*, 2016f.

Paul Fishstein. *Despair or hope: Rural livelihoods and opium poppy dynamics in Afghanistan.* Afghanistan Research and Evaluation Unit Kabul, 2014.

Robert K Fleck and Christopher Kilby. Foreign aid and domestic politics: Voting in Congress and the allocation of USAID contracts across congressional districts. *Southern Economic Journal*, 67:598–617, 2001.

Robert K Fleck, and Christopher Kilby. How do political changes influence US bilateral aid allocations? Evidence from panel data. *Review of Development Economics*, 10(2):210–223, 2006.

Jess T Ford. Foreign assistance: Enhanced coordination and better methods to assess the results of U.S. international basic education efforts are needed (GAO-07-523). *Government Accountability Office*, March 2007.

Pat Forgey. How a "bridge to nowhere" became a road from nowhere to nowhere. https://www.adn.com/alaska-news/article/how-bridge-nowhere-became-road-nowhere/2015/11/17/, November 2015. (Accessed on 04/19/2024).

Linda L Fowler. *Watchdogs on the Hill: The Decline of Congressional Oversight of U.S. Foreign Relations*. Princeton University Press, 2015.

Andreas Fuchs, Peter Nunnenkamp, and Hannes Öhler. Why donors of foreign aid do not coordinate: The role of competition for export markets and political support. *The World Economy*, 38(2):255–285, 2015.

R Gates. Striking the right balance. *Joint Force Quarterly*, 52:2–7, 2009.

Robert M Gates. *Duty: Memoirs of a Secretary at War*. Vintage, 2014.

Douglas M Gibler and Steven V Miller. Comparing the foreign aid policies of presidents Bush and Obama. *Social Science Quarterly*, 93(5):1202–1217, 2012.

Desha M Girod. Effective foreign aid following civil war: The nonstrategic-desperation hypothesis. *American Journal of Political Science*, 56(1):188–201, 2012.

Virginia Gray and David Lowery. *The Population Ecology of Interest Representation: Lobbying Communities in the American States*. University of Michigan Press, 1996.

Virginia Gray and David Lowery. The density of state interest-communities: Do regional variables matter? *Publius: The Journal of Federalism*, 28(2):61–79, 1998.

Zachary D Greene, and Amanda A Licht. Domestic politics and changes in foreign aid allocation: The role of party preferences. *Political Research Quarterly*, 71(2):284–301, 2018.

Tim Groseclose and James M Snyder. Buying supermajorities. *American Political Science Review*, 90(02):303–315, 1996.

George J Hall, & Thomas J Sargent (2019). Complications for the United States from international credits: 1913–1940. In (Era Dabla-Norris, ed.), *Debt and Entanglements Between the Wars* (pp. 1–58).

Henrik Hansen and Finn Tarp. Aid effectiveness disputed. *Foreign Aid and Development: Lessons Learnt and Directions for the Future*, pages 103–128, 2000.

Tobias Heinrich. When is foreign aid selfish, when is it selfless? *The Journal of Politics*, 75(2):422–435, 2013.

Barbara Hinckley. *Less Than Meets the Eye: Foreign Policy Making and the Myth of the Assertive Congress*. University of Chicago Press, 1994.

Michael J Hiscox. Class versus industry cleavages: Inter-industry factor mobility and the politics of trade. *International Organization*, 55(1):1–46, 2001.

Marek Hlavac. Extreme Bounds: Extreme bounds analysis in R. *Journal of Statistical Software*, 72, 2016.

Marie Hojnacki, and David C Kimball. Organized interests and the decision of whom to lobby in Congress. *American Political Science Review*, pages 775–790, 1998.

Marie Hojnacki, David C Kimball, Frank R Baumgartner, Jeffrey M Berry, and Beth L Leech. Studying organizational advocacy and influence: Reexamining interest group research. *Annual Review of Political Science*, 15:379–399, 2012.

Richard D Hooker Jr. and Joseph J Collins. *Lessons Encountered: Learning from the Long War*. 2015.

William G Howell and Jon C Pevehouse. *While Dangers Gather: Congressional Checks on Presidential War Powers*. Princeton University Press, 2007.

William G Howell, Saul P Jackman, and Jon C Rogowski. *The Wartime President: Executive Influence and the Nationalizing Politics of Threat*. University of Chicago Press, 2013.

John D Huber and Charles R Shipan. *Deliberate Discretion? The Institutional Foundations of Bureaucratic Autonomy*. Cambridge University Press, 2002.

John Hudak. *Presidential Pork: White House Influence over the Distribution of Federal Grants*. Brookings Institution Press, 2014.

Julia F Irwin. The origins of US foreign disaster assistance. *The American Historian*, 15:43, 2018.

Jeffery A Jenkins and Nathan W Monroe. Buying negative agenda control in the US House. *American Journal of Political Science*, 56(4):897–912, 2012.

Gyung-Ho Jeong. Troops in "harm's way," the president, and congressional war-funding decisions. *Presidential Studies Quarterly*, 50(3):568–591, 2020.

Gyung-Ho Jeong and Paul J Quirk. Division at the water's edge: The polarization of foreign policy. *American Politics Research*, 47(1):58–87, 2019.

Harold J Johnson. GAO/NSIAD-95-10 coordinating U.S. programs for the FSU. *Government Accountability Office*, February 1995a.

Harold J Johnson. GAO/NSIAD-96-16 former Soviet Union. *Government Accountability Office*, December 1995b.

Tyler Jost. *Bureaucracies at War: The Institutional Origins of Miscalculation*, volume 167. Cambridge University Press, 2024.

Frederick M Kaiser. Gao: Government accountability office and general accounting office. Congressional Research Service, 2007.

Saori N Katada. Two aid hegemons: Japanese-US interaction and aid allocation to Latin America and the Caribbean. *World Development*, 25(6):931–945, 1997.

Conor Keane. The impact of bureaucratic conflict on US counternarcotics efforts in Afghanistan. *Foreign Policy Analysis*, 12(3):295–314, 2016a.

Conor Keane. *US Nation Building in Afghanistan*. Taylor & Francis, 2016b.

Robert F Kelley. Memorandum by the chief of the division of eastern european affairs. https://history.state.gov/historicaldocuments/frus1933-39/d17, October 1933. (Accessed on 08/17/2021).

D Roderick Kiewiet and Mathew D McCubbins. *The Logic of Delegation*. University of Chicago Press, 1991.

In Song Kim. Lobby View: Firm-level lobbying & congressional bills database. Working Paper available from http://web.mit.edu/insong/www/pdf/lobbyview.pdf, 2018.

Stephen Knack and Aminur Rahman. Donor fragmentation and bureaucratic quality in aid recipients. *Journal of Development Economics*, 83(1):176–197, 2007.

Stephen D Krasner. *Defending the National Interest: Raw Materials Investments and US Foreign Policy*. Princeton University Press, 1978.

Douglas L Kriner and Andrew Reeves. *The Particularistic President: Executive Branch Politics and Political Inequality*. Cambridge University Press, 2015.

Douglas L Kriner, and Eric Schickler. *Investigating the President: Congressional Checks on Presidential Power*. Princeton University Press, 2016.

Brian Lai. Examining the goals of US foreign assistance in the post-Cold War period, 1991–96. *Journal of Peace Research*, 40(1):103–128, 2003.

John S Lapinski. *The Substance of Representation*. Princeton University Press, 2013.

Timothy M LaPira, and Herschel F Thomas. *Revolving Door Lobbying: Public Service, Private Influence, and the Unequal Representation of Interests*. University Press of Kansas, 2017.

Timothy M LaPira, Lee Drutman, and Kevin R Kosar. *Congress Overwhelmed: The Decline in Congressional Capacity and Prospects for Reform*. University of Chicago Press, 2020.

Matthew J Lebo, Adam J McGlynn, and Gregory Koger. Strategic party government: Party influence in Congress, 1789–2000. *American Journal of Political Science*, 51(3):464–481, 2007.

James H Lebovic and Erik Voeten. The cost of shame: International organizations and foreign aid in the punishing of human rights violators. *Journal of Peace Research*, 46(1):79–97, 2009.

Melissa M Lee and Melina Platas Izama. Aid externalities: Evidence from PEPFAR in Africa. *World Development*, 67:281–294, 2015.

Beth L Leech, Frank R Baumgartner, Timothy La Pira, and Nicholas A Semanko. Drawing lobbyists to Washington: Government activity and interest-group mobilization. *Political Research Quarterly*, 58(1):19–30, 2005.

Victor Levy. Aid and growth in sub-Saharan Africa: The recent experience. *European Economic Review*, 32(9):1777–1795, 1988.

David E Lewis. *Presidents and the Politics of Agency Design: Political Insulation in the United States Government Bureaucracy, 1946–1997*. Stanford University Press, 2003.

James R Locher. *Victory on the Potomac: The Goldwater-Nichols Act Unifies the Pentagon*, 79. Texas A&M University Press, 2002.

Samuel Loewenberg. Coburn puts hold on HIV/AIDS bill. *Politico*, 6 2008. (Accessed on 05/13/2021).

Geoffrey Miles Lorenz. Prioritized interests: Diverse lobbying coalitions and congressional committee agenda setting. *The Journal of Politics*, 82(1):225–240, 2020.

Mona M Lyne, Daniel L Nielson, and Michael J Tierney. Who delegates? Alternative models of principals in development aid. *Delegation and agency in international organizations*, 44, 2006.

Jason A Macdonald. The US Congress and the institutional design of agencies. *Legislative Studies Quarterly*, 32(3):395–420, 2007.

Mark Tauber. *Interview of Patrick Fine: Foreign affairs oral history project*. The Association for Diplomatic Studies and Training, 2018, 80.

Bryan W Marshall and Richard L Pacelle Jr. Revisiting the two presidencies: The strategic use of executive orders. *American Politics Research*, 33(1):81–105, 2005.

Emma Mawdsley. National interests and the paradox of foreign aid under austerity: Conservative governments and the domestic politics of international development since 2010. *The Geographical Journal*, 183(3):223–232, 2017.

David R Mayhew. *Congress: The Electoral Connection*. Yale University Press, 1974.

David R Mayhew. *Divided We Govern*. Yale University Press, 1991.

Nolan M McCarty. Presidential pork: Executive veto power and distributive politics. *American Political Science Review*, 94(1):117–129, 2000.

Megan McCloskey, Tobin Asher, Lena Groeger, and Sisi Wei. We blew 17 billion in Afghanistan. How would you have spent it? https://projects.propublica.org/graphics/afghan, December 2015. (Accessed on 08/04/2021).

Mathew D McCubbins, Roger G Noll, and Barry R Weingast. Administrative procedures as instruments of political control. *Journal of Law, Economics, & Organization*, 3(2):243–277, 1987.

JG McIlroy. The military attaché in Japan (Mcilroy) to the assistant chief of staff (Smith). https://history.state.gov/historicaldocuments/frus1933-39/d2, February 1933. (Accessed on 08/17/2021).

Kathleen J McInnis. Overview: The Department of Defense and COVID-19. *Congressional Research Service Reports*, March 2020.

Robert McMahon. Transforming U.S. foreign aid | council on foreign relations. https://www.cfr.org/backgrounder/transforming-us-foreign-aid, May 2007. (Accessed on 05/09/2018).

James Meernik, Eric L Krueger, and Steven C Poe. Testing models of US foreign policy: Foreign aid during and after the cold war. *The Journal of Politics*, 60(1):63–85, 1998.

Mark Memmott. Jobs, The Future And Salmon: Key Words From State Of The Union: The Two-Way. *National Public Radio*. January 26, 2011. https://www.npr.org/sections/thetwo-way/2011/01/26/133234249/jobs-the-future-and-salmon-key-words-from-state-of-the-union.

Gary J Miller and Andrew B Whitford. *Above Politics: Bureaucratic Discretion and Credible Commitment*. Cambridge University Press, 2016.

Helen V Milner, and Keiko Kubota. Why the move to free trade? Democracy and trade policy in the developing countries. *International organization*, 59(1):107–143, 2005.

Helen V Milner, and Dustin Tingley. The choice for multilateralism: Foreign aid and American foreign policy. *The Review of International Organizations*, 8(3):313–341, 2013.

Helen V Milner and Dustin Tingley. *Sailing the Water's Edge: The Domestic Politics of American Foreign Policy*. Princeton University Press, 2015.

Helen V Milner and Dustin H Tingley. The political economy of US foreign aid: American legislators and the domestic politics of aid. *Economics & Politics*, 22(2):200–232, 2010.

Helen V Milner, and Dustin H Tingley. Who supports global economic engagement? The sources of preferences in American foreign economic policy. *International Organization*, 65(1):37–68, 2011.

William Minozzi, and Craig Volden. Who heeds the call of the party in Congress? *The Journal of Politics*, 75(3):787–802, 2013.

Terry M Moe. The new economics of organization. *American Journal of Political Science*, 28(4):739–777, 1984.

Terry M Moe. The politics of bureaucratic structure. *Can the government govern*, 267:271, 1989.

Andrew Moravcsik. The origins of human rights regimes: Democratic delegation in postwar Europe. *International organization*, 54(2):217–252, 2000.

T Clifton Morgan, and Glenn Palmer. A model of foreign policy substitutability: Selecting the right tools for the job(s). *Journal of Conflict Resolution*, 44(1):11–32, 2000.

Kellie Moss. PEPFAR reauthorization: Key policy debates and changes to US international HIV/AIDS, tuberculosis, and malaria programs and funding. January 2009.

Benjamin A Most and Harvey Starr. International relations theory, foreign policy substitutability, and "nice" laws. *World Politics*, 36(3):383–406, 1984.

Andrew Natsios. *The Clash of the Counter-bureaucracy and Development*. Center for Global Development, 2011.

Ronald E Neumann. *The Other War: Winning and Losing in Afghanistan*. Potomac Books, Inc., 2009.

Alain Noël, and Jean-Philippe Thérien. From domestic to international justice: The welfare state and foreign aid. *International Organization*, 49(3):523–553, 1995.

Nathan Nunn, and Nancy Qian. US food aid and civil conflict. *American Economic Review*, 104(6):1630–66, 2014.

OECD. Whole of government approaches to fragile states. 2006. URL https://www.oecd.org/dac/conflict-fragility-resilience/docs/37826256.pdf.

OECD. How fragmented is aid? 10, 2009. doi: http://dx.doi.org/10.1787/dcr-2009-7-en. URL /content/chapter/dcr-2009-7-en.

Jinhwan Oh and Yunjeong Kim. Proliferation and fragmentation: Uphill struggle of aid effectiveness. *Journal of Development Effectiveness*, (ahead-of-print):1–18, 2014.

Michele Orza, Kimberly Scott, Helen Smits, William Holzemer, James Curran, Charles Carpenter, Jaime Sepúlveda, et al. *PEPFAR Implementation: Progress and Promise*. National Academies Press, 2007.

EL Packer. The assistant chief of the division of Eastern European affairs (Packer) to the special assistant to the secretary of state (Bullitt). https://history.state.gov/historicaldocuments/frus1933-39/d5, August 1933. (Accessed on 08/17/2021).

Adam Pain. Narcotics and counter-narcotics: Responding to an irrepressible market? *Afghanistan's Security Sector Governance Challenges*, page 159, 2011.

Gustav F Papanek. Aid, foreign private investment, savings, and growth in less developed countries. *Journal of Political Economy*, 81(1):120–130, 1973.

Robert A Pastor. *Congress and the Politics of US Foreign Economic Policy, 1929–1976*, volume 5. Univ of California Press, 1982.

Carol Peasley. Interview of Andrew Natsios. *Foreign Affairs Oral History Project*, 2019.

Heidi M Peters. Defense primer: U.S. defense industrial base. *Congressional Research Service Reports*, January 2021.

John Pielemeier. Interview of Robert M. Clay. *Foreign Affairs Oral History Project*, 2018.

Keith T Poole and Howard Rosenthal. Patterns of congressional voting. *American Journal of Political Science*, 35(1):228–78, 1991.

Rachel Augustine Potter. *Bending the Rules: Procedural Politicking in the Bureaucracy.* University of Chicago Press, 2019.

Ryan M Powers, David A Leblang, and Michael J Tierney. Overseas economic aid or domestic electoral assistance: The political economy of foreign aid voting in the US Congress. In *APSA 2010 Annual Meeting Paper*, 2010.

Lauren Prather. Values at the water's edge: Social welfare values and foreign aid. 2014.

Lauren Prather. Transnational ties and support for foreign aid. *International Studies Quarterly*, 64(1):133–147, 2020.

Tahir Qadiry. Afghanistan, the drug addiction capital. *BBC News*, April 2013. (Accessed on 03/01/2021).

Steve Radelet, Michael Clemens, and Rikhil Bhavnani. Aid and growth: The current debate and some new evidence. *Center for Global Development*, 2004.

Raghuram G Rajan, and Arvind Subramanian. Aid and growth: What does the cross-country evidence really show? *The Review of Economics and Statistics*, 90(4):643–665, 2008.

Dan Reiter and Allan C Stam. Democracy, war initiation, and victory. *American Political Science Review*, 92(2):377–389, 1998.

Condoleezza Rice. *No Higher Honor: A Memoir of My Years in Washington.* Crown, 2011.

Melinda N Ritchie. Back-channel representation: A study of the strategic communication of senators with the US Department of Labor. *The Journal of Politics*, 80(1):240–253, 2018.

David W Rohde. Reflections on the practice of theorizing: Conditional party government in the twenty-first century. *The Journal of Politics*, 75(4):849–864, 2013.

Franklin D Roosevelt. Executive order 6581: Creating the export-import bank of Washington. www.presidency.ucsb.edu/documents/executive-order-6581-creating-the-export-import-bank-washingtonaxzz1pBsWshWq, February 1934. (Accessed on 08/17/2021).

Clinton Rossiter. *Constitutional Dictatorship.* Transaction Publishers, 1948.

Beth Ford Roth. Helicopter crash in Afghanistan injures 3 Americans, kills 1 NATO soldier. https://www.kpbs.org/news/2014/may/29/helicopter-crash-afghanistan-americans-killed/, May 2014. (Accessed on 07/31/2021).

Donald Rumsfeld. *Known and Unknown: A Memoir.* Penguin, 2011.

Jeremiah McLain Rusk. *Annual Reports, Together with Selected Correspondence Relating to the Export Trade of the United States in the Live Stock and Meat Products, of Jeremiah M. Rusk, Secretary of Agriculture. 1889–1892.* US Government Printing Office, 1893.

Vernon W Ruttan. *United States Development Assistance Policy: The Domestic Politics of Foreign Economic Aid.* Johns Hopkins University Press, 1996.

Jeffrey Sachs, John W McArthur, Guido Schmidt-Traub, Margaret Kruk, Chandrika Bahadur, Michael Faye, and Gordon McCord. Ending Africa's poverty trap. *Brookings Papers on Economic Activity*, 2004(1):117–240, 2004.

Jeffrey D Sachs. *The End of Poverty: Economic Possibilities for Our Time.* Penguin, 2006.

Adva Saldinger. US Congress approves long-sought foreign aid transparency and accountability act. https://www.devex.com/news/us-congress-approves-long-sought-foreign-aid-transparency-and-accountability-act-88392, July 2016. (Accessed on 05/09/2018).

Elizabeth Nathan Saunders. *Leaders at War: How Presidents Shape Military Interventions.* Cornell University Press, 2011.

Arthur Meier Schlesinger. *The Imperial Presidency.* Houghton Mifflin Harcourt, 1973.

Andres B Schwarzenberg. Tracking China's global economic activities: Data challenges and issues for Congress. *Congressional Research Service Reports*, July 2020.

US Senate. Joint hearing on aid to the former Soviet Union. S. Hrg. 102–84, 1992.

Nina Serafino. Peacekeeping/stabilization and conflict transitions: Background and congressional action on the civilian response/reserve corps and other civilian stabilization and reconstruction capabilities. *Congressional Research Service Report for Congress*, October 2012.

Robert Siegel. Origins of Bridge to Nowhere explained. https://www.npr.org/2008/09/10/94481285/origins-of-bridge-to-nowhere-explained, September 2008. (Accessed on 04/19/2024).

James M Snyder. On buying legislatures. *Economics & Politics*, 3(2):93–109, 1991.

John Sopko. Counternarcotics: Lessons from the U.S. experience in Afghanistan. *Special Inspector General for Afghanistan Reconstruction Lessons Learned Report*, June 2018.

Niels C Sorrells. House passes Bush anti-AIDS plan; Democrats challenge GOP changes. *CQ Weekly*, pages 1056–57, May 2003a.

Niels C Sorrells. Political expediency takes over as Senate passes AIDS relief bill. *CQ Weekly*, pages 1210–11, May 2003b.

Niels C Sorrells. International AIDS programs authorized for 15 billion as lawmakers search for funding. *CQ Weekly*, page 1280, May 2003c.

Diana M Stanescu et al. The bureaucratic politics of foreign economic policymaking. https://dataspace-princeton-edu.proxy-um.researchport.umd.edu/handle/88435/dsp01d217qs572, 2020.

Martin C Steinwand. Compete or coordinate? Aid fragmentation and lead donorship. *International Organization*, 69(2):443–472, 2015.

James Stephenson. *Losing the Golden Hour: An Insider's View of Iraq's Reconstruction.* Potomac Books, Inc., 2007.

Randall W Stone. *Lending Credibility: The International Monetary Fund and the Post-Communist Transition.* Princeton University Press, 2002.

Mao Suzuki. Profits before patients? Analyzing donors' economic motives for foreign aid in the health sector. *World Development*, 132:104966, 2020.

Haley J Swedlund. *The Development Dance*. Cornell University Press, 2017.

Jordan Tama. Forcing the president's hand: How the US Congress shapes foreign policy through sanctions legislation. *Foreign Policy Analysis*, 16(3):397–416, 2020.

Jordan Tama. *Bipartisanship and US Foreign Policy: Cooperation in a Polarized Age*. Oxford University Press, 2024.

Curt Tarnoff. The former Soviet Union and US foreign assistance in 1992: The role of Congress. May 2004.

Jean-Philippe Thérien and Alain Noël. Political parties and foreign aid. *American Political Science Review*, 94(1):151–162, 2000.

Michael J Tierney, Daniel L Nielson, Darren G Hawkins, J Timmons Roberts, Michael G Findley, Ryan M Powers, Bradley Parks, Sven E Wilson, and Robert L Hicks. More dollars than sense: Refining our knowledge of development finance using AidData. *World Development*, 39(11):1891–1906, 2011.

Michael M Ting. A strategic theory of bureaucratic redundancy. *American Journal of Political Science*, 47(2):274–292, 2003.

Dustin Tingley. Donors and domestic politics: Political influences on foreign aid effort. *The Quarterly Review of Economics and Finance*, 50(1):40–49, 2010.

Peter Tomsen. *The Wars of Afghanistan: Messianic Terrorism, Tribal Conflicts, and the Failures of Great Powers*. PublicAffairs, 2013.

Rick Travis. Problems, politics, and policy streams: A reconsideration US foreign aid behavior toward Africa. *International Studies Quarterly*, 54(3):797–821, 2010.

Chicago Tribune. Holding the Soviet aid bill hostage. *Chicago Tribune*, page D16, May 1992.

United States Department of State Inspector General USIG. Review of the office of the U.S. global AIDS coordinator. Technical report, February 2008.

Rochelle P Walensky and Daniel R Kuritzkes. The impact of the president's emergency plan for AIDS relief (PEPFAR) beyond HIV and why it remains essential. *Clinical Infectious Diseases*, 50(2):272–275, 2010.

Guan Wang. *Divided We Stand: Partisan Control and U.S. Foreign Policy*. 2024.

Craig Whitlock. The Afghanistan papers: A secret history of the war: Built to fail. https://www.washingtonpost.com/graphics/2019/investigations/afghanistan-papers/, December 2019. (Accessed on 08/04/2021).

Aaron Wildavsky. The two presidencies. *Society*, 35(2):23–31, 1966.

JQ Wilson. Bureaucracy: What government agencies do and why they do it. 1989.

Alan E Wiseman. Tests of vote-buyer theories of coalition formation in legislatures. *Political Research Quarterly*, 57(3):441–450, 2004.

B Dan Wood and John Bohte. Political transaction costs and the politics of administrative design. *Journal of Politics*, 66(1):176–202, 2004.

Amy B Zegart. September 11 and the adaptation failure of US intelligence agencies. *International Security*, 29(4):78–111, 2005.

Amy B Zegart. *Spying Blind: The CIA, the FBI, and the Origins of 9/11*. Princeton University Press, 2009.

Amanda Ziadeh. USAID revamping data repository. https://gcn.com/articles/2016/09/29/usaid-data-repository.aspx, September 2016. (Accessed on 05/09/2018).

Index